Essays in honour of Michael Allen

Last before America
Irish and American Writing

edited by
Fran Brearton and Eamonn Hughes

THE
BLACKSTAFF
PRESS
BELFAST

First published in 2001 by
The Blackstaff Press Limited
Wildflower Way, Apollo Road
Belfast BT12 6TA, Northern Ireland
with the assistance of
the Arts Council of Northern Ireland

ARTS
COUNCIL
of Northern Ireland

Typeset by Techniset Typesetters, Newton-le-Willows, Merseyside

Printed in Ireland by ColourBooks Limited

A CIP catalogue record for this book
is available from the British Library

ISBN 0-85640-701-1

www.blackstaffpress.com

Contents

Acknowledgements

The editors gratefully acknowledge the financial support of the Arts Council of Northern Ireland, and the Queen's University of Belfast Publications Fund.

A number of people have also offered help and advice throughout this project, and we are much indebted to them. They include: Kerry Adamson, Ian Adamson, Maureen Alden, Douglas Carson, Marie Carson, Ellen Douglas-Cowie, Peter Devlin, Edith Devlin, Colin Graham, David Lodge, Edna Longley, Michael Longley, Nicholas Roe, and Elaine Stockman. Anne Tannahill's support and enthusiasm for the project helped to make it happen. We would like to thank the staff at Blackstaff Press, and in particular Patricia Horton, for all their work on the book. The contributors to this volume all made our job easier, from their initial enthusiastic responses through to their willingness and patience in answering our various demands and queries. Lastly, a word of thanks to all those who have managed, in the gossipy world of Belfast and academia, to keep this project a secret for so long.

Grateful acknowledgment is made for permission to reprint the following copyright material:

SEAMUS HEANEY: extracts from *Death of a Naturalist* (1966), *Wintering Out* (1972), *Station Island* (1984), and *Seeing Things* (1991), reprinted by permission of Faber and Faber Ltd.

MICHAEL LONGLEY: extracts from *Poems 1963–1983* (Secker & Warburg,1985); *Gorse Fires* (Secker & Warburg, 1990); and *The Ghost Orchid* (Jonathan Cape, 1995), reprinted by permission of The Random House Group Ltd.

MEDBH McGUCKIAN: extracts from *The Flower Master and other Poems* (1993), reprinted by permission of The Gallery Press.

LOUIS MacNEICE: extracts from *Collected Poems* (1966), reprinted by permission of David Higham Associates Ltd.

DEREK MAHON: extracts from *The Yellow Book* (1997), reprinted by permission of The Gallery Press.

PAUL MULDOON: extracts from *Madoc: A Mystery* (1990), and *Meeting the British* (1987), reprinted by permission of Faber and Faber Ltd.

FRAN BREARTON AND EAMONN HUGHES

Introduction

Both myth and seismic history have been long suppressed
Which made and unmade Hy Brasil – now an image
For those who despise charts but find their dream's endorsement
In certain long low islets snouting towards the west
Like cubs that have lost their mother.

LOUIS MACNEICE, 'Last before America'

MacNeice's 'Last before America' recognises the poignancy of desire; it also questions the nature of that desire. America may be an illusion, 'a land of a better because an impossible promise', but the search for a 'dream's endorsement' is part of an inescapable human condition. Perhaps there is no end of the rainbow; it is the quest itself that matters. The search for imaginative compensation for 'seismic history' is not escapist – the poem never finds Hy Brasil – but in another sense it too is driven by an 'impossible promise', an aspiration underpinning poetry which is never attainable, but which makes it worth the writing.

MacNeice's themes here, expressed with a combination of critical intelligence and a compassionate, imaginative music, make the poem and the poet paradigmatic of the figure who stands as inspiration for this collection of essays and poems. Michael Allen shares with MacNeice a critical acuity, allied with a belief in poetry and an enviable understanding of, and sensitivity to, its form. 'Musicalisation pluralises meanings', as Julia Kristeva writes, in a phrase which stands as key to Allen's own critical practice. Crucially, he is also one of the few critics who grasps the nature of Irish and American intersections by drawing on an informed knowledge of literary culture on both sides of the Atlantic. That knowledge and understanding, shared and disseminated among students, critics and writers, has, over the years, helped to engender new dimensions in an Irish-American cultural relationship.

Michael Allen joined the English department at Queen's University Belfast in 1965 (after holding fellowships at Birmingham then Yale) as an American literature specialist, and as part of the expansion of American Studies in the universities. He retires from that department in 2001 as an American and an Irish literature specialist, one whose influence on Irish writing has been as profound as it has been unassuming. The dedicatee of many poems and poetry collections from Ireland, he remains, as he has been over the last thirty-five years, a significant presence in the cultural life of Ireland, particularly Northern Ireland.

Michael Allen was a member of the original Belfast 'Group' in the mid-1960s; he has been, at various times, 'the reader over my shoulder' for the generation of Seamus Heaney, Michael Longley and Derek Mahon; he taught Paul Muldoon, Medbh McGuckian, and Ciaran Carson. McGuckian describes him as 'the first person in my life who could really explain what a poem was. I still recall clearly his beautiful intonation of "I wake to sleep and take my waking slow" with his swaying hand beating out the time. He possesses that rare thing, a real ear for a true line, or for poetic truth.' Michael Allen also worked as a visiting lecturer in the States in the late 1960s, and helped to establish links – and friendships – between Irish and American writers; and he has been instrumental in the development of many of the critics included in this book in ways that only they can properly quantify. He has been, in other words, in the context of Northern Ireland, a constant critical presence. Equally importantly, he maintained that presence at times, notably through the 1970s, when the North was not an easy or popular place to be – certainly before Irish Studies took on some of the seductiveness it now seems to have in abundance. The self-effacement which characterises Michael Allen's approach, the concern to open up avenues for others rather than to seize the pot of gold at the end of the rainbow for himself, is indicative of an extraordinary critical generosity of spirit and a delight in literature for its own sake. Such generosity is, in the current climate, and in universities that are subject to new pressures, increasingly rare and immeasurably valuable, both in itself and as an example. As one of our contributors, Adrienne Janus, put it, Michael Allen's 'exemplary habits of thought and grace of presence will be a motivating inspiration for many more years to come'.

Michael Allen's critical career began with work on Poe, Ellison, and Dickinson. His work on provincialism in Dickinson (discussed by Peter Stoneley in his essay for this collection) is also part of a broader, cross-Atlantic exploration of 'theories of regional and national literature'. In recent years, his focus has increasingly been on contemporary Irish poetry. Allen's analyses of rhythm, revisions, and rhyme in Longley's, Mahon's and Muldoon's poetry respectively, challenge less formally alert readers, while his Macmillan Casebook on Heaney in its introduction and selection negotiates its way through the complex and contentious critical debates surrounding Heaney's poetry with an admirable clear-sightedness. Allen is also exceptional in bringing to his work on Irish writing an illuminating sense of its moments of indebtedness to the American tradition, and without any trace of the uncritical sentimentality sometimes invested in the Irish-American hyphen. (How far he himself, in teaching American literature at Queen's, may be the cause as well as the literary critic of some of those Irish/American poetic connections is open to speculation.) His important essay, 'The Parish and the Dream: Heaney and America' (1995), brings together the two sides of his research in an alert and sensitive charting of transatlantic poetic waters. In Ireland, America may be projected as the ideal, the aspiration, or as the elsewhere that validates a sometimes metaphysical sense of place – it offers a way of leaving, but also, significantly, a way of bringing it all back home. Allen's concern is to pluralise meaning, to illuminate musicality, to open up the work to multi-layered complexities frequently unrecognised, and, in a way, to explain poetry and criticism (and poets and critics) to themselves.

The essays in this book highlight Michael Allen's various spheres of influence as a critic of both Irish and American literature, and in many cases pick up on, or develop out of, the themes in his criticism. More unusually, the poems and prose extracts included here bear witness to the extraordinary circumstance whereby a critic has proved to have an influence on creative writing that at least equals his influence on literary criticism. Heaney's version of Robert Henryson's fable 'The Two Mice' mischievously revisits the themes of 'The Parish and the Dream' in a reworking and reconsideration of the parochial and the cosmopolitan. For Muldoon, Michael Allen's sophisticated formalism and background in American Studies bear obvious poetic fruit, as they have also made Allen one of the foremost critics of Muldoon's work. That mutual influence, which has also engendered the placing of creative and critical writing side by side in this collection, refutes the often artificial separation of the two activities.

The contributors to this volume – many of whom have been connected with Queen's University – would all acknowledge an indebtedness to Michael Allen in his various roles as colleague, tutor, and critic, but also as friend and inspiration. This is, evidently, the originating link for the diverse body of work collected here. But this book also finds its own, perhaps Muldoonian narrative, in Atlantean links and leaps from something else to something else again, links that bring its journey full circle. The contributions implicitly retrace, from its present moment to its beginnings, some of the steps of the critical journey that for Michael Allen began in nineteenth-century America and found its way to twenty-first-century Ireland, but that also, in another sense, found its way to two places at the one time.

The principal places under consideration here are Ireland and America; the essays implicitly, and in some cases explicitly, explore and open up connections and/or disjunctions between the two. True to the critical spirit that recognises no one story is ever the only story, this volume may be seen as a series of conversations – not least between poets and critics – returning to certain issues and themes but never in the same way twice. Many of the writers here are concerned with journeys, actual and metaphorical: analytically in the work of Richard Kirkland (who registers the collision of American criticism and Irish poetry), and Colin Graham (who sees America as only ever glimpsed from Ireland); creatively in the narrative poems by Seamus Heaney, Ciaran Carson, and in William Wiser's account of the move from America to Ireland. Ireland and America each figure in at least two ways. As in MacNeice's 'Last before America', with its sense of multivalence, and its projection of America as both actual place and aspiration, America can be the actual setting of the conference from which Adrienne Janus takes her lead, the actual context for Emily Dickinson in Peter Stoneley's essay, the site of aspiration in Nicholas Roe's essay, the possible embodiment of aspiration in Graham's work.

Ireland, not least by being brought into conjunction with America, is also rendered here in multiple ways. It is the specific location in which voices, poetic and otherwise, are formed, deformed and, too often, silenced, as the work of Edna Longley, Nicholas Allen and Elmer Kennedy-Andrews demonstrates. Each of these critics is concerned in different ways with different aspects of Ireland, spatially and temporally. Ireland is also a site of crossings, a complex mid-point between Britain and America. For Patricia Horton and Nicholas Roe, who examine links between Ireland, Romanticism and America, it works in precisely this way. Identity and tradition, defined as the location of poetic and other voices, form the subject of their work (though each approaches from a different direction), while Nicholas Allen and Edna Longley write about the ways in which the expression of identity is allowed and disallowed in different traditions. For Elmer Kennedy-Andrews, the fracturing of identity lies at the heart of contemporary Irish fiction, and, in another sense, at the heart of the late twentieth-century condition.

That fracturing may be negative; but it also allows for conversations, dialogue, shifting perspectives. Poetry too is considered here in such a fashion. In Peter Stoneley's essay, Dickinson's poetry takes the material as its subject, both linking it to the specifics of nineteenth-century America, and showing how it resonates with a wider world. Poetry can be the living, breathing voice which embodies memory, analysed by Janus, or a materiality of a different kind in the work of Watkin and Kirkland where it compensates for the dead or displaces death. These essays not only speak to Medbh McGuckian's poems here, they also reverberate in an understanding of elegiac practice in Northern Irish poetry more generally. If these pieces are about impossible but desired conversations, between the living and the dead, they are also, as are many of our contributors, concerned with urgent and necessary conversations: between poetry and criticism, as in Peter McDonald's commentary on the services and disservices done to the poetry of Heaney and Longley by its criticism; and, more overarchingly, between culture and politics, as in Edna Longley and Nicholas Allen's work.

As a critic, Michael Allen is both an avowed formalist and also a sophisticated reader of theory: the outcome of this rare combination is a self-awareness about the practice of criticism which is in turn a keynote of this volume. To put that another way, the volume challenges the too-neat separation of critical and creative writing in the way that both criticism and creativity are here seen as proper objects of analysis. We begin this critical journey with Michael Allen's own recent preoccupations in focussing on the work of contemporary Irish poetry. McDonald's study of Heaney and Longley in mid-career, pitched between new poems by Longley and Heaney themselves, offers an assessment not only of the careers to date of the two poets, but also an assessment of the kinds of critical attention and inattention which have served and failed to serve their work. Such an accounting inevitably sets aside much that has been written about them: if McDonald is in no doubt that the poetry will survive, he also has little doubt that much criticism will eventually fade. His celebration of 'acting younger and thinking older' thus reverberates in criticism as well as poetry. That argument both explicitly validates Allen's own critical practice and implicitly sets a standard for what follows in the remainder of this volume.

The prologue poem to this collection, Michael Longley's 'Level Pegging', not only marks a long and deep friendship, it also tells a history which places Michael Allen's critical acuity and political intelligence at the heart of Irish literary life. It is fitting, therefore, that Longley's poetic tribute should open this book. It is equally fitting that Bernard MacLaverty's acknowledgment of Michael Allen as someone who still makes you 'see things', should close it by bringing us back to the point where we began, since the roles of teacher, reader and critic merge in what is, these days, an increasingly rare combination. Throughout the essays and poems in this book, there is a preoccupation with exile and return, presence and absence, loss and compensation. *Last before America* marks Michael Allen's retirement from Queen's; in doing so it acknowledges within the university itself a gap that cannot be filled and the end of an era. But there are beginnings as well as endings here: this volume also stands as tribute to a critical presence, to an on-going influence, and to the opening up of possible futures.

BELFAST, APRIL 2001

MICHAEL LONGLEY

Level Pegging

for Michael Allen

I

After a whole day shore fishing off Allaran Point
And Tonakeera you brought back one mackerel
Which I cooked with reverence and mustard sauce.
At the stepping stones near the burial mound
I tickled a somnolent salmon to death for you.
We nabbed nothing at all with the butterfly net.

Hunters, gatherers, would-be retiarii
We succeeded at least in entangling ourselves.
When the red Canadian kite became invisible
In Donegal, we fastened the line to a bollard
And sat for hours and looked at people on the pier
Looking up at our sky-dot, fishing in the sky.

II

You were driving my Escort in the Mournes when –
Brake-failure – Robert Lowell and you careered
Downhill: 'Longley's car is a bundle of wounds.'
When his last big poem had done for Hugh MacDiarmid
And he collapsed, we wrapped his dentures in a hanky
And carried them like a relic to the hospital.

We looked after poets after a fashion. And you
Who over the decades in the Crown, the Eglantine,
The Bot, the Wellie, the Chelsea have washed down
Poetry and pottage without splashing a page
And scanned for life-threatening affectation
My latest 'wee poem' – you have looked after me.

III

I was a booby-trapped corpse in the squaddies' sights.
The arsehole of nowhere. Dawn in a mountainy bog.
From the backseat alcohol fumed as I slumbered
Surrounded by Paras, then – all innocence – you
Turned up with explanations and a petrol can.
They lowered their rifles when I opened my eyes.

Our Stingers-and-Harvey-Wallbangers period
With its plaintive anthem 'The Long and Winding Road'
Was a time of assassinations, tit-for-tat
Terror. You were Ulster's only floating voter, your
Political intelligence a wonky hedge-hopping
Bi-plane that looped the loop above the killing fields.

IV

Rubbed out by winds Anaximines imagined,
The burial mound at Templedoomore has gone.
Locals have driven their tractors along the strand
And tugged apart the wooden wreck for gateposts.
There are fewer exits than you'd think, fewer spars
For us to build our ship of death and sail away.

Remember playing cards to the crash of breakers,
Snipe drumming from the estuary, smoky gossip
In Carrigskeewaun about marriages and making wills?
I'll cut if you deal – a last game of cribbage, burnt
Matches our representatives, stick men who race
Slowly round the board with peg legs stuck in the hole.

PETER McDONALD

Faiths and Fidelities

Heaney and Longley in Mid–Career

Some are both more upfront and more wide-ranging in their operations than others, but there is one area where no poet can easily avoid acting as a literary critic: selecting, and indeed collecting, his own poetry presents any writer with a critical job which will not exactly do itself, and which may be done more and less well. There are famous modern instances of the latter, with both W.B. Yeats and W.H. Auden the obviously prominent names from the past; and in the present too, it is easy to foresee the hours of work and acres of argument for future scholars in the comings and goings of Derek Mahon's poems through successive Collecteds and Selecteds (is Mahon the only contemporary poet whose *Discarded Poems* might rival his own *Collected* in both quality and overall coherence?). Putting together his *Collected Poems 1925–1948* (in the wake of previous selected editions, an American quasi-collected, and some years in advance of yet another Selected), Louis MacNeice allowed himself a whole poem in which to reflect on the process, a middle-aged man reading the younger man who was 'Acting younger than I am and thinking older'. It was, of course, a dizzying perspective, and a self-estranging one:

> For having lived, and too much, in the present,
> Askance at the coming gods, estranged from those older
> Who had created my fathers in their image,

> I stand here now dumbfounded by the volume
> Of angry sound which pours from every turning
> Of those who only so lately knew the answers.[1]

Perhaps the poem becomes stranger still once it serves as the dedicatory pages to a volume MacNeice did not live to see commissioned or in print, the *Collected Poems* edited by his friend E.R. Dodds, in which the previous *Collected* is supplemented by the addition of the individual volumes which the poet published after 1949. The poem taking an overview, in other words, is written long before the end of the story.

Of course, the full picture of the situation facing poets as they assemble and reassemble their work on different occasions is one which requires a great deal of information about the specific market judgements that publishers make in a given case. There are, too, other factors at work in the assembly process which might be classed as contextual: notably, there is the matter of *other* poets making their decisions about collection and selection at the same time, and how far this affects the poet in question. In MacNeice's case, the obviously relevant point of comparison – one involving the same publishing house – is the publication history of W.H. Auden (who also, by a nice irony, was to make a posthumous selection of MacNeice). Often, the publication of a new edition of this kind means an opportunity for widespread critical assessment, and sometimes even reassessment – this latter a phenomenon much announced but, in truth, little realised in much modern critical effort. Certainly, the attempt to draw critical attention, and at the same time to help direct it, is part of the process of publishing and arranging collected editions, on the parts both of poets and their publishers.

The publication in the same year – 1998 – of Seamus Heaney's *Opened Ground: Poems 1966–1996* and Michael Longley's *Selected Poems* marks a useful coincidence, as well as an interesting contrast: two poets from the same place and generation, each of whom seems indispensable to contemporary poetry, and two books of differing lengths (Heaney's is 478 pages, as against Longley's 130) but overlapping bearings and concerns; such a conjunction makes large-scale critical comparisons almost unavoidable.[2] And yet, the two books have more and better things to do than line their authors up in some head-to-head play-off for the title of Top Poet, since they provide an opportunity to see both Heaney and Longley in the act of seeing themselves whole, presenting their own work in ways that might in some respects question or correct the terms of their contemporary reception.

For Heaney, *Opened Ground* is 'somewhere between the two categories' of a Collected and a Selected Poems, while Longley has taken his *Selected* (the successor to an earlier American-published *Selected*, and to the much more complete selection contained in his *Poems 1963–1983*) to be just that, and has attempted to slim down an already slimline oeuvre. In both cases, however, the new publications have fresh perspectives to offer on important bodies of work; and both cases have been – despite appearances – in need of new lines of critical evaluation for some time. Neither book, as readers may be presumed to know, offers a final perspective on the body of work; each offers its poet (however discreetly) as both participant in and observer of the process of its decades-long formation.

Seamus Heaney's situation, over most of the last twenty years, has been one subject to an excessive (but in crucial respects myopic) critical scrutiny. There is certainly a sense in which we have now *too much* published criticism of Heaney for our (and just possibly the poet's) own good. If this seems an enviable situation for a writer, it cannot seem so for long; the critical agenda by which Heaney has been accommodated has proved remarkably limited, and its demands have been, from time to time, limiting in themselves for the poet's creativity. Perhaps Longley has therefore been the luckier of the two poets, in that he has for the most part escaped the kinds of attention lavished on his more celebrated contemporary, and has had the advantage of a comparative privacy in which to write. It is fair to say that, on balance, Longley has tended to be undervalued by critics, and Heaney to be overpraised, or praised by them for the wrong reasons; but it is also right to add that both poets have passed the test of keeping faith with their own best strengths and instincts over these years: Heaney's originality, as much as Longley's, has survived it all. In their different ways and circumstances, the careers of both poets offer object lessons in fortitude.

Northern Ireland, and its history during the last three decades, has been allowed to set the terms for almost all critical writing on poetry by Northern Irish poets. Inevitable as this must appear, there are senses in which it needs, and has long needed, to be resisted. It would be refreshing, and genuinely heartening, to see the critical and academic industries beginning to shift gear with regard to this: to see the publication of work, and the completion of theses within academe, on poets like Heaney and Longley in the properly broad poetic contexts where they actually belong, and to encounter the resistance to now-hackneyed imperatives of time and place (and academic fashion) which all good criticism ought to contain. It should be said that one place in which such resistance has had its steady, intelligent, and responsible voice consistently over the years of Heaney's increasing international renown is in Northern Ireland itself: the reasoned and perceptive praise accorded to Heaney and Longley by Michael Allen, along with the far-reaching and sure-footed meditations on Heaney's poetry and the other writing of its time and place given by Edna Longley, are in themselves trustworthy signs of the worth and enduring quality of the writing. In the scheme of things, praise from Belfast means more, and reveals much more, than celebration from American academe, or inclusion in the latest optimistic pitch for punters of another new MA course in modern poetry. But the signs of resistance to this too easy assimilation into a critical or cultural narrative are there to be read in Heaney's poetry as well as in Michael Longley's, not to mention in the work of other poets of their generation and later, who have written or lived in Northern Ireland. For the critical orthodoxy outside Northern Ireland, even so, such signs are largely illegible. In the process, of course, the actualities of Northern Ireland tend to evaporate, leaving behind only a residue in which an abstracted artistic conscience struggles against the demands of some under-defined political commitment: though the place in question looks like Ireland, it could be anywhere, and in a way this is the whole point. Helen Vendler's recent book on Heaney, for example, renders him almost contextless, like a Made-in-Ireland Grecian Urn; taking for granted poetry's ability to transcend its circumstances, such an attitude forgets how real poetry also answers to its circumstances. But this is an answerability which Seamus Heaney, like Michael Longley, knows a great deal about.

The circumstances most important to both poets' earlier work are not those into which their later writing has found itself propelled, and it is useful to think of Heaney, until the watershed of *North* in 1975, as a predominantly pastoral poet, just as much of Michael Longley's work has continued to inhabit pastoral modes. To say this is not to equate pastoral with some kind of literary state of innocence; on the contrary, pastoral needs to be recognised as, at least in part, a perspective of principled retirement, as much a vantage-point on urbanity as a retreat from it. Longley's first collection, *No Continuing City* (1969), was precociously accomplished in terms of its technique, but the book's sights were fixed on what 'Leaving Inishmore' calls the 'perfect standstill' of a 'point of no return', where poetic sophistication can be tempered.[3] The programmatic 'A Personal Statement' ends:

> Lest I with fears and hopes capsize,
>   By your own lights
> Sail, Body, cargoless towards surprise.
> And come, Mind, raise your sights –
>   Believe my eyes.[4]

This conclusion (in a poem dedicated to Seamus Heaney) sets the terms for what was to be indeed Longley's point of growth, and its instructions to the Mind from the Body (which have about them a distinct whiff of the seventeenth century) are ones which much of his later poetry was to follow. As Longley's work in the 1970s progressed, it took on board more and more of the senses' evidence, and developed a habit of observation of the natural environment in which significance had to take second place to surprise. In terms of technique, also, this work sets about removing the kinds of formality the early poems had so brilliantly put on, which might become obstacles in the way of an immediacy or naturalness of voice.

'Letter to Seamus Heaney' in *An Exploded View* (1973) leaves 'Mind open like a half-door / To the speckled hill, the plovers' shore', and speaks with full awareness of the contextual situation both poets by then are facing:

> So let it be the lapwing's cry
> That lodges in the throat as I
> Raise its alarum from the mud,
> Seeking for your sake to conclude
> Ulster Poet our Union Title
> And prolong this sad recital
> By leaving careful footprints round
> A wind-encircled burial mound.[5]

The alarums and excursions which gave rise to labels like 'Ulster Poet' are being modulated here into a voice which can avoid the too easily rhetorical or urbane in favour of 'the lapwing's cry'. At the same time, Longley knows that poems, like creatures, are not weightless, and they cannot proceed without leaving some trace of themselves; so these 'footprints' on the dense and compacted matter of Northern Ireland in the 1970s are of necessity 'careful' ones. The extraordinary nature-poetry which Longley was to produce in that decade makes good the promises of this poem; if, on the one hand, it is hard to read such poetry entirely without some awareness of its sombre historical surroundings, it remains true, on the other hand, that the poetry's worth depends ultimately on just such a falling-away of specific circumstance. The injunction to 'Believe my eyes' served as Longley's artistic watchword in this respect, and the poetry of *Man Lying on a Wall* (1976) and *The Echo Gate* (1979) reveals a poet who, rather than accept the 'Union Title' of 'Ulster Poet', with all it might imply about a perceived 'relevance' or historical awareness in observation, chooses perspectives which are devoted to the minuteness of a different kind of truth; thus, the dominant modes are nature poetry and love poetry.

It is perhaps no longer all that daring to claim Longley as one of the best poets in these modes which the century has produced; it will be more controversial, however, to maintain that these modes are, in themselves, more ambitious than some of the aims behind Heaney's larger-scale projects of the 1970s and 1980s. Longley's goals in poetry, after all, have seldom been formulated or made the subjects of his writing. And yet, artistic ambitions too readily (or frequently) expressed may not be all that ambitious in the end. Almost from the beginning, Heaney has been in this sense a more literary poet than Longley, and his early 'Personal Helicon' (dedicated to Longley) not only overhears itself, but eavesdrops on itself being heard elsewhere:

> Now, to pry into roots, to finger slime,
> To stare, big-eyed Narcissus, into some spring
> Is beneath all adult dignity. I rhyme
> To see myself, to set the darkness echoing.[6]

The young Longley's armour of formal expression brings with it a degree of irony at moments of programmatic announcement; Heaney here is (winningly) straight by comparison. But the ambition comes through unmediated, and it wears its stylistic directness as though it could be a badge of poetic authenticity. *Death of a Naturalist* (1966), and some of *Door into the Dark* (1969), operate on the assumption that certain turns of style (in part, imitated and adapted skilfully from figures like Hopkins or the early Ted Hughes) are authentic and unmediated; and certainly, the terms of Heaney's early success made that assumption a justifiable one.

Nevertheless, pastoral is a sophisticated, and not a naïve, genre of poetry. Even the early Heaney is written in a dialect that is as much indebted to English and American verse as it is to County Derry; the poet's most important achievement in the 1970s was to understand this, and to put it to original use in the volumes *Wintering Out* (1972) and, especially, *North* (1975). This is poetry of an extreme, and in some respects an academic, self-consciousness about language; the books mark a formal breakthrough for Heaney, since he finds there the way in which to expose language by cadence (and, in part, by visual arrangement) to interrogative attention rather than potentially inattentive and passive recognition. 'The backward look', in *Wintering Out*, begins with the snipe:

> A stagger in air
> as if a language
> failed, a sleight
> of wing.
>
> A snipe's bleat is fleeing
> its nesting-ground
> into dialect,
> into variants[7]

The materiality of language for Heaney is put to proof here, in ways that his earlier writing did little more than gesture towards, and in the process the poetry achieves an arresting originality. Language itself becomes Heaney's focus, and the object of his most attentive observation. The snipe 'corkscrews away / into the vaults / that we live off',

> his flight
> through the sniper's eyrie,
> over twilit earthworks
> and wallsteads
>
> disappearing among
> gleanings and leavings
> in the combs
> of a fieldworker's archive.

What is so unsettling about this poetry is its essential brevity, or the apparent slenderness of the means it employs in achieving so much. Like the snipe, the poem's acuteness of attention seems to be gone almost as soon as it has been noticed. Heaney's discovery of his own form – as something in which he could find something other than just himself, in the terms of 'Personal Helicon', is of a piece with his discovery of subject-matter. The snipe, after all, leads to 'the sniper's eyrie', and Heaney's pastoral perspectives include the connotations of this in their own evolving 'archive'.

North has always attracted controversy, in part because the book is pastoral which breaks its cover, so to speak, and addresses its own situation in clear terms. For all the critical talk of Heaney's uses for the oblique angle of approach in this volume, *North* is memorable mainly for its directness. But the book embodies directness of more than one kind: the 'bog-poems' have the unpredictable and surprising directness of an observing imagination on edge, absolutely at one with the form of its own expression; some other poems, especially those in the book's second section, attempt directness of a less original cast, when Heaney speaks autobiographically about his own relation to the matter of Northern Ireland. With regard to these pieces, the critical scepticism from some Irish readers has been matched (and maybe overpowered) by a more widespread international interest in Heaney's self-portraiture. However, poems like 'Singing School' and 'Whatever You Say Say Nothing' remain disappointing by comparison with Heaney's best work, and they read like a series of low-impact commentaries on the kinds of risk and originality brought off so well elsewhere in *North*. In fact, one of the things which helped to make the volume a turning-point for Heaney was this very weakness, since self-observation was to become one of his principal modes in the following collections. Originality, like pastoral, was from now on no longer always enough for a self-scrutinising and self-evaluating writer.

The comparisons with Longley's 1970s work are obvious, but they should not be over-schematised or simplified. Heaney's writing is not 'political' in any very clear sense of that term, though the poet's inclination to congratulate himself on this has not always been completely avoided; and Longley's work has not been deaf to the 'political' resonances which its reports from the front lines of nature or love poetry might generate. For both poets, too, the obligation to absorb imaginatively events in Northern Ireland has been understood, and honoured. The real difference lies at the level of ambition, where Heaney has worked expansively, and Longley intensively, over the last twenty years. In their publication histories, the two writers diverged markedly during the 1980s, with Heaney following *Field Work* of 1979 (still, perhaps, his best individual collection) with large projects such as *Station Island* (1984), and prose books and translations, while Longley spent much of the decade, at least as far as new publications were concerned, in a silence to be broken only with the appearance of *Gorse Fires* (1991). For Heaney, there were no formal breakthroughs on the scale of that of the mid-1970s, although poems of extraordinary accomplishment and vividness continued to flow; for Longley, the poems of *Gorse Fires* brought his work to a formal consummation whose lyric momentum has continued in *The Ghost Orchid* (1995) and *The Weather in Japan* (2000). Both bodies of work supply the context for the ambitions from which they take their bearings, but in this respect Heaney's programme is by far the more accessible of the two, while Longley's sense of purpose remains, however strong, at the same time genuinely oblique and mysterious in its expression.

Discussion of Heaney's artistic ambitions has tended to be confused with discussion of his artistic situation, but the two things are not the same; indeed, it might well be argued that a central ambition for Heaney is to write beyond the possible restrictions of his work's historical context. Like Longley, Heaney understands this ambition in terms of an ultimately religious conception of poetry; unlike Longley, his religious sensibility is a Catholic one, and this has implications for the ways in which his poetry sees itself. The long poem 'Station Island', which occupies more or less the centre of *Opened Ground*, is Heaney's artistic confession of faith, though in effect it conveys more powerfully the poet's faith in confession, as he meets ghost after ghost on his artistic visit to a place of religious penance. As well as their specific identities, these ghosts are also importantly the ghosts of a faith which the poet can no longer actually share; a young priest's spirit, for example, accused by the poet of being like 'some sort of holy mascot' to the local community, who 'gave too much relief' to them, gives back as good as he gets:

> 'And you,' he faltered, 'what are you doing here
> but the same thing? What possessed you?
> I at least was young and unaware
>
> that what I thought was chosen was convention.
> But all this you were clear of you walked into
> over again. And the god has, as they say, withdrawn.
>
> What are you doing, going through these motions?
> Unless ... Unless ...' Again he was short of breath
> and his whole fevered body yellowed and shook.
>
> 'Unless you are here taking the last look.'[8]

11

Once the god has withdrawn, only the reflexes, instincts, and habits of the communal act remain, and 'Station Island' situates itself within a community all of whom, the living and the dead, are 'going through these motions' without much confidence or hope, and apparently principally for Heaney's benefit, as though they were somehow investing in his artistic future.

The poetry in which Heaney has tried to register a kind of secular faith is not always his strongest, and some of the more programmatic pieces in *The Haw Lantern* (1987) are dull affairs by comparison with the luminous sonnets of the 'Clearances' sequence in that volume, or with the long series of poems grouped as 'Squarings' in *Seeing Things* (1991) – a series which is unfortunately cut down in length for *Opened Ground* (unlike 'Station Island', included in its entirety). It may well be that Heaney as self-editor is doing himself few favours here. More and more, it comes to seem that Heaney's most startling successes require quantities of largely programmatic, or sometimes slightly obvious poetry as back-up material, or limbering-up exercises; wonderful poems in *The Spirit Level*, like 'Mint' or 'Postscript', stand dramatically apart from a good deal of their surrounding material. It is in the most successful of his poems, though, that Heaney reaps the benefits of the religious sensibility which his more routine work registers more dutifully: the lyric medium at these points can seize as its own moments of visionary brilliance, or make such moments out of the given material in life, without need for validating theory or any voiced ambition. In 'The Skylight', in *Seeing Things*, a loft conversion triggers an unlofty, but utterly convincing conclusion:

> But when the slates came off, extravagant
> Sky entered and held surprise wide open.
> For days I felt like an inhabitant
> Of that house where the man sick of the palsy
> Was lowered through the roof, had his sins forgiven,
> Was healed, took up his bed and walked away.[9]

Poetry like this is completely sufficient to itself, and is not a promise of something else to come hereafter; its authority as poetry (to use for a moment a concept of which Heaney has been perhaps too fond over the years) comes from its ease with the authority of its biblical source-text, and its satisfaction with that text as something shared with others, and held in common rather than believed in exclusively.

Longley's poetry is not capable of this kind of comfort, partly because it draws so much of its strength not from the shared and communal, but from the unique and the unrepeatable. On the face of it, this seems odd in a poet of Longley's evident humane feeling, imaginative compassion, and openness of interest. But the ambition which Longley's poetry has made good, especially since *Gorse Fires*, is one for precision and fidelity rather than an ambition for some achieved and verifiable authority: authority, in these terms, is not the poet's business, and can be of no productive interest to his poetry. Put in this way, this tells only half the story, for the formal medium of the writing is crucially important, and Longley has perfected a voice which combines an instinct for natural expression with an extraordinary elegance, economy, and suppleness in its range. Furthermore, Longley's insistence on the individuality of perception and perspective does not drive his poetry towards a position of human or social isolation; on the contrary, an insistence on a broadly conceived civility and human openness has become more and more explicit in his writing in recent years. In terms of religion, Longley accepts the situation faced more bluntly by Heaney, that 'The god has, as they say, withdrawn', and his poetry, again like Heaney's, comes to terms with the human spaces left by this *deus absconditus*. However, where Heaney tries, in effect, to do this by strengthening what Yeats called 'the infallible Church of poetic tradition', Longley allows his poetry to take more direct, spontaneous, and apparently improvisatory routes, in which the issue of the poet's function, powers, or responsibilities is never the poems' central concern.

The artistic effort, for Longley, remains essentially that of making the mind believe the eyes; and that belief, in its way, demands artistic work analogous to religious faith in its realisation. Here, the poetry's identity as pastoral is still relevant, and has continued to deepen and complicate for Longley in ways that Heaney's pastoral modes have not really kept pace with: Heaney's remembered County Derry remains in thrall to one (comparatively narrow) mode of writing, whereas Longley's west of Ireland has become more strange as it has accrued more detail, and it continues to challenge, rather than confirm, the poet's sense of his own place in things. The same could be said for the two poets' literariness, for Longley's absorption of Homer and Ovid has galvanised his poetry, and taken it to new places, where Heaney's use of Virgil, Greek tragedy, or even perhaps Dante, has been more in the nature of grafting on supporting evidence for his own achievements.

Longley's attraction to the miniature, to short poems and poems that work in short units of expression, might give a misleading impression of a poet who works on a small scale. In fact Longley's writing, especially since *Gorse Fires*, has established large, albeit unfixed, structures of association and reference, in which shifting patterns of recapitulation and development give his volumes their own kind of resonance and intensity. In this way, the Longley of the 1990s has achieved what the Heaney of the 1980s failed to do, creating a poetry of high ambitions in which those ambitions can remain implicit. A poem like 'The Ghost Orchid' brings such issues close to the surface, but at the same time it knows all about keeping them in their place:

> Added to its few remaining sites will be the stanza
> I compose about leaves like flakes of skin, a colour
> Dithering between pink and yellow, and then the root
> That grows like coral among shadows and leaf-litter.
> Just touching the petals bruises them into darkness.[10]

To call poetry like this programmatic, or to identify it as a kind of manifesto, would be to ruin the poem itself, or kill it in critical translation. Of course, that is the point; but the poem's success, like its delicacy, is also a pointed business. The perception, acuteness, and restraint of this poetry are those of a voice which can face loss, love, public and private murder, and a century's history with the same absolute attention to the individual detail; its faith lies in fidelities like these.

Already, both Heaney and Longley have proved themselves central to any reading of contemporary poetry, and they will go on being centrally significant not only to the satisfaction and challenge, but to the critical arguments and artistic provocations that good poetry ought to generate. By comparing Heaney and Longley, one is in fact taking account of different kinds of success. The very limited nature of much criticism of poetry means that Longley tends to be seen as a failed Heaney (or, indeed, Heaney to be read as a failed Longley); neither poet is well served by such attention, nor by the tendency to see their poetry in over-defined relation to the 'context' of Northern Ireland. Nevertheless, both *Opened Ground* and Longley's *Selected Poems* contain poetry which is stronger and more resourceful than the critical attention it has often received, and which can outlast the more modish varieties of contemporary celebration. And both books, remarkably, seem to prepare the ground for what is still in store – this is the rarest of feats for poets in mid-career, and one which needs to be welcomed. Heaney ends his book, not with 'Postscript' and its Yeatsian swans, but with his Nobel lecture on 'Crediting Poetry', and its Yeatsian anxieties: this feels like the last word on a topic Heaney knows must now be dropped. In Longley's *Selected Poems* too, the momentum of fresh achievement in the last pages seems unstoppable. Perhaps both poets, in selecting their poems and reading themselves, acting younger than they are and thinking older, are properly prepared for the poetry that is still to come.

PATRICIA HORTON

'A Truly Uninvited Shade'

Romantic Legacies in the Work of Seamus Heaney
and Paul Muldoon

The literatures of the past, if left to themselves, confront us as despotic structures: what Sartre calls totalities ... It's not a question ... of calling up the past and making it speak. The past is with us all the time and it never stops speaking. Without an aggressive re-enactment of the past, it re-enacts us.[1]

As these opening remarks make clear, the question of how to define 'the Romantic' and the challenge of dealing with the legacies of the Romantic period continue to be a source of controversy and debate in contemporary criticism and writing. At least part of the dilemma stems from what some critics have seen as an insistent overlapping between the Romantic period and the contemporary one. As Cynthia Chase argues:

Romanticism resists being defined as a period or a set of qualities that can be comfortably ascribed to others and assigned to a historical past. There are several reasons why this is so. One is that major historical changes of the Romantic period still determine basic conditions of our lives: the invention of democracy, the invention of revolution, and the emergence of a reading public.[2]

While that overlap may make itself felt in historical and political terms, it is equally applicable to literary history. As Raymond Williams has noted, the Romantic period is the locus for a whole new set of ideas about the role of the poet and the function of poetry, legacies with which contemporary writers continue to engage and struggle.[3] To this extent Romanticism can be read as a set of responses for dealing with profound intellectual, social and political shifts in society. Since such shifts, as Chase argues, 'still determine basic conditions of our lives' it is not surprising that many of these responses and strategies should be replicated across historical time, albeit mediated and inflected by specific historical and cultural formations.

These issues are at the heart of my discussion of Romantic legacies, a discussion which focuses on how two contemporary poets, Seamus Heaney and Paul Muldoon, self-consciously draw on particular elements of and debates about Romanticism and find literary models among English Romantic writers. They do so as a way of defining their own aesthetic/political stances and also as a way of locating themselves within contemporary literary and political debates. By examining how Heaney and Muldoon construct Romanticism, by being alert to elements of kinship with as well as to moments of critical distance between them and their Romantic precursors, we can trace a number of intersections between contemporary concerns and those of the Romantic period. The Romantic intersections with which I am concerned make clear a complex set of strategies which centre on questions of tradition and inheritance and, more broadly, alert us to shared assumptions and agendas. The continuities between our own period and the Romantic one enable Northern Irish writers to draw on specific English Romantic writers as literary models which they can use and modify in a contemporary context. Equally, these Romantic intersections bring the Romantic period face to face with the contemporary moment and its challenges and, in doing so, may also help us to redefine and revise our understanding of 'the Romantic'.

Seamus Heaney's sense of kinship with William Wordsworth is evident in a number of poems and prose writings, and spans his literary career. His earliest sustained discussion of Wordsworth appears in 1978 with 'The Makings of a Music: Reflections on Wordsworth and Yeats'. Here Heaney uses Wordsworth to limit the influence of Yeats and so establish his own authority within the Irish poetic canon. Wordsworth's poetry, he argues, is 'feminine', a poetry that makes us want to 'surrender' to it and be 'carried by its initial rhythmic suggestiveness, to become somnambulist after its invitations'. Its 'music' is 'hypnotic, swimming with the current of its form rather than against it'. Yeats's poetry, by contrast, is described as masculine, characterised by 'discipline ... seeking to master rather than to mesmerise the ear, swimming strongly against the current of its form'.[4] Rational, conscious, and forceful, Yeats's poetry is an act of will. Heaney's separation of Wordsworth and Yeats on a gender basis allows him to limit, absorb and transcend the influence of both, while also leaving the potential to effect some kind of reconciliation in the idea of a sexual union or marriage to be achieved in his own writing.

As Heaney's other prose writings make clear, the gender constructions used to describe Wordsworth and Yeats depend on Heaney's sense of his own identity and are open to negotiation and manipulation as that identity shifts and develops. In his early writings Heaney clearly aligns himself with the feminine principle and with a Wordsworthian tradition from which Yeats and his 'masculine' tradition have been eliminated. Thus, in 'The Sense of Place' (1977), Heaney constructs 'Wordsworth' in his own image. He focuses on the 'pedestrian' Wordsworth who walked the land and whose childhood was lulled by the sounds of the river Derwent.[5] He is, for Heaney, an example of the 'poet as ploughman' bringing together agriculture and culture in 'verse', a word which, as Heaney points out, comes 'from the Latin *versus* which could mean a line of poetry but could also mean the turn that a ploughman made at the head of a field as he finished one furrow and faced back into another'.[6] The significance of this Wordsworthian model is clear when we turn to Heaney's discussions of his own identity. In his 1972 essay, 'Belfast', Heaney grounds his poetic creativity and essential identity in his rural Derry childhood, identifying this in turn with the feminine presence, and finally with the 'matter of Ireland' itself.[7] Heaney's feminisation of Wordsworth, his emphasis on Wordsworth's commitment to the local and to communal affiliations, and his location of Wordsworth as mediator between nature and culture, clearly corresponds to Heaney's sense of his own obligations and responsibilities as a rural Catholic poet writing in Northern Ireland in the 1970s.

Yet if Heaney's sense of communal obligation, felt as the need to articulate some kind of 'national consciousness', leads him, particularly in his early work, to identify with an oppressed Ireland which is gendered feminine, this in turn provokes problems for assertions of individuality and constructions of masculinity. Increasingly in his work there is an attempt to construct 'an individuated masculine self'.[8] Again Wordsworth and Yeats play a part in

Heaney's manoeuvres. In 'The Fully Exposed Poem' (1983) we find Heaney taking Romantic poetry to task:

> In spite of a period of castigation about the necessity for 'intelligence' and 'irony', poetry in English has not moved all that far from the shelter of the Romantic tradition. Even our self-mocking dandies pirouette to a narcotic music. The dream's the thing, not the diagnosis. Inwardness, yearnings and mergings of the self towards nature, cadences that drink at spots of time – in general the hopes of poets and readers still realize themselves within contexts like these. We still expect the poetic imagination to be sympathetic rather than analytic. 'Intellect' still tends to summon its rhyme from Wordsworth's pejorative 'dissect'.[9]

Romanticism is equated here with a kind of poetic immaturity and irresponsibility, even femininity – though the description is strangely reminiscent of some key elements in Heaney's own poetry. One clue as to what is behind this may lie in a comment from a letter Heaney sent to Fintan O'Toole – 'There are some lines in poetry which are like wool in texture and some that are like bare wires. I was devoted to a Keatsian woolly line, textured stuff, but now I would like to be able to write like a bare wire.'[10] There is here a desire to be disruptive and transgressive, a point reinforced in 'Sounding Auden'. The poetry written by the early Auden, he claims, 'did not sail with the current, it tangled and hassled', whereas the later poetry was 'doctrinaire in its domesticity, wanting to comfort like a thread of wool rather than shock like a bare wire'.[11] That woolly thread is associated with the domestic, with assuagement and finally with Wordsworth, whose music, as Heaney pointed out previously, is 'hypnotic, swimming with the current of its form rather than against it'.

For Heaney to make that transition from poetic immaturity to a state of independence and masculine gendered identity, and yet continue to claim kinship with Wordsworth, he is obliged to re-cast his precursor. By 1984, therefore, he creates a new 'Wordsworth' who is more in tune with Heaney's own struggles and conflicts at that time. Rather than the rooted, domestic poet of the earlier prose, Wordsworth is now the displaced and divided poet, a victim of political and imaginative crisis. Heaney is particularly interested in the threat posed to Wordsworth's radical, republican politics by the bloody events in France, and in how he preserved his creative energies amidst such political disillusionment. Thus in *Place and Displacement: Recent Poetry of Northern Ireland* (1984) Heaney focuses on that moment in *The Prelude* when Wordsworth describes how he felt when England declared war on France, and goes on to give this gloss:

> The good place where Wordsworth's nurture happened and to which his habitual feelings are most naturally attuned has become, for the revolutionary poet, the wrong place. Life, where he is situated, is not as he wants it to be. He is displaced from his own affections by a vision of the good that is located elsewhere. His political, utopian aspirations deracinate him from the beloved actuality of his surroundings so that his instinctive being and his appetitive intelligence are knocked out of alignment. He feels like a traitor among those he knows and loves. To be true to one part of himself, he must betray another part. The inner state of man is thus shaken and the shock waves in the consciousness reflect the upheavals in the surrounding world.[12]

In keeping with his literal displacement from his roots in Derry (Heaney has by this point moved to Dublin), and in tandem with a desire to liberate himself from communal pressures and obligations, Heaney recasts Wordsworth as a poet who was equally aware of tensions in and conflicts with his own place and community. In this re-casting, Wordsworth leaves behind the immaturity of the domestic and the feminine, and enters, like Heaney, into the public, masculine world of politics, transgression and independence.

This shift in Heaney's construction of Wordsworth is accompanied by an attempt to feminise Yeats, a manoeuvre that bridges the gap not only between Wordsworth and Yeats, but also between himself and Yeats. Thus, in 'The Place of Writing: W.B. Yeats and Thoor Ballylee' (1990), Heaney details two attitudes to place in Yeats's poetry. The young Yeats has a 'filial relationship' with Sligo; the older Yeats has developed 'a domineering rather than a grateful relation to place, one whose poems have created a country of the mind rather than the other way round, (and the more usual way) where the country has created the mind which in turn creates the poems'.[13] In terms of the distinctions that Heaney set up earlier we are being offered a comparison between an early 'feminine' poetry and a more mature 'masculine' poetry. The feminine has been absorbed and transcended, and the poet is now possessed by a fully masculine vision which dominates the material at its disposal. Heaney constructs Yeats's career to mirror and validate the plotting of his own. In doing so maturity becomes synonymous with the severing of communal ties, a rupture which is both an assertion of masculinity and a coming of age in which Heaney can rightfully take up his place in a Yeatsian tradition.

However, Heaney's Yeatsian tradition is now uncannily similar to his Wordsworthian tradition and, by 1991, in the introduction to *The Essential Wordsworth*, a collection of Wordsworth's poetry edited and introduced by Heaney, Wordsworth becomes the originator of a fully masculine tradition in which Yeats plays a secondary role:

> Wordsworth's power over us stems from the manifest strength of his efforts to integrate several strenuous and potentially contradictory efforts. More than a century before Yeats imposed upon himself the order to hammer his thoughts into unity, Wordsworth was fulfilling it with resolute intent. Indeed, it is not until Yeats that we encounter another poet in whom emotional susceptibility, intellectual force, psychological acuteness, political awareness, artistic self-knowledge, and bardic representativeness are so truly and responsibly combined.[14]

The introduction to *The Essential Wordsworth* goes on to mark out those key areas that Heaney wants to privilege in Wordsworth. First, childhood, where Wordsworth found 'not only the source of his emotional being, but the clue to his fulfilled identity'. Second, and linked to this, is Wordsworth's supreme confidence in the 'self-as-subject' and the ability of that conscious self to order, dominate and subdue the external world. In spite of his privileging of 'nature' and 'imagination' Wordsworth is, Heaney argues, a profoundly social poet who is 'extended and animated by the capacities and expectations of his friends'.[15] Thus he reads Wordsworth's 'Resolution and Independence' as:

> Democratic, even republican, in its characteristic eye-level encounter with the outcast, and in its curiosity about his economic survival. Visionary in its presentation of the old man transfigured by the moment of epiphany. Philosophic in its retrieval of the stance of wisdom out of experience of wonder. Cathartic in the forthrightness of its self-analysis. Masterful in its handling of the Spenserian stanza, a mastery not come by without many previous efforts in the form. Salutary – not just picturesque – in its evocation of landscape and weather, inciting us to perceive connections between the leech-gatherer's ascetic majesty and the austere setting of moorland, cloud, and pool. In a word, Wordsworthian.[16]

There is here, as elsewhere, a sense of elision in Heaney's reading of

Wordsworth, for 'Resolution and Independence', like many of Wordsworth's poems, is profoundly self-obsessed. That 'democratic, even republican' ideal is far from present in the poem since the leech–gatherer is reduced to little more than an object through which Wordsworth can explore his own subjectivity. Heaney's own autobiographical tendency directs and distorts his interpretation of Wordsworth, and leads him to plot Wordsworth's career in terms of his own poetic development. The early Wordsworth is 'wide awake, entering the thicket of himself like a readied hunter, as capable of deeply receptive stillness as of silent, almost erotic foragings, forward and inward'. He then has an experience of crisis from which he is rescued by the 'enabling light' of memory, and the 'spontaneous, trustful energies unconsciously available in the world of childhood'. However, this means that Wordsworth, 'somewhat prematurely on the chronological scale, but with perfect timing on the psychological one ... [has] to undertake the Dantesque, midlife journey in memory, back through the dark wood'. All of which leads to the great theme of Wordsworth's poetry:

> the contradictory allegiances which his work displays to the numinous and to the matter–of–fact, his conflicting awareness of a necessity to attend to 'the calm that nature breathes' and a responsibility to confront the grievous facts of 'what man has made of man', his double bind between politics and transcendence, morality and mysticism, suffering and song.[17]

The parallels with Heaney's own career are obvious here: his sense of his own childhood as an 'omphalos' or 'a completely trustworthy centre';[18] his experience of political crisis in *North* (1975); his subsequent recovery through a return to childhood terrain in *Field Work* (1979); the 'Dantesque mid–life journey' of *Station Island* (1984); and his own bind between 'suffering and song' explored most extensively in *The Government of the Tongue* (1988). Heaney's refusal to acknowledge the deep–seated anxiety apparent in so much of Wordsworth's poetry seems here to be part of a desire to disguise those same anxieties in his own work. He does acknowledge the Wordsworth who, in later life, 'became more an institution than an individual', but this he consigns to the sphere of the 'inessential Wordsworth'. 'The essential poet', in contrast, 'remains the one struggling to become a whole person, to reconcile a sense of incoherence and disappointment forced upon him by the external circumstances of life with those intimations of harmonious communion promised by his childhood visions, and seemingly ratified by his glimpse of a society trembling at the moment of revolution'.[19]

Heaney constructs Wordsworth as a self-legitimising model and uses him to validate his own artistic practices and manoeuvres. 'Wordsworth' is a shape-changer in Heaney's prose, prone to metamorphosis depending on Heaney's priorities, agendas and anxieties. He is a 'rooted' Wordsworth in 'The Makings of a Music', a 'displaced' Wordsworth in *Place and Displacement*, and finally a 'whole' Wordsworth in *The Essential Wordsworth*. But beneath these variations remains a fundamental conservatism in reading Wordsworth, indicative of Heaney's own rather conservative poetics. In the final analysis, Heaney uses Wordsworth to privilege the idea of the poet as transcendent genius, and while he does give some sense of the politics of the period, this is ultimately only to uphold the view that such a world is antithetical and hostile to the psychic equilibrium of the poet.

Heaney's sense of kinship with Wordsworth stimulates Paul Muldoon to turn to the figure of Byron. In Byron, Muldoon finds an aesthetic precursor whose relationship and responses to Coleridge, Southey and Wordsworth mirror his own to Seamus Heaney. The grounds for this identification with Byron are made clear in Muldoon's introduction to *The Essential Byron* where his focus is the parodic, self-mocking quality in Byron's writing, his talent for 'remind[ing] us again and again that poetry can be serious without being solemn, that it might even be fun'.[20] An example of the 'poet as maverick',[21] Byron is, in Muldoon's formulation, individualistic and independent, a trickster figure, whose parodic strategies, particularly in relation to first-generation Romantics, act as a model for Muldoon's own generational clashes. The significance and importance of Byron's influence is most evident in Muldoon's *Madoc: A Mystery*, a poem which charts Coleridge's and Southey's attempts to set up a Pantisocratic community on the banks of the Susquehanna river, and the degeneration of that lofty scheme into egotism, greed, despotism and drug addiction. Both title and subject matter alert us to Muldoon's Byronic pose. Like Byron's *Vision of Judgement*, Muldoon's *Madoc* rewrites a poem which was originally penned by Southey, and like Byron's poem, it does so in order to undermine the ideals and moral standpoint taken by Southey in the original text. This intersection between Byron and Muldoon initiates what is to be a continuous and sustained process of doubling in the poem, for at least one of Muldoon's ploys is to relocate or re-contextualise the political conflict and literary debates of Northern Ireland in a late-eighteenth-century Romantic setting. 'Ulster' becomes one of the colonies on the banks of the Susquehanna, and if Muldoon casts himself as a Byronic figure, Southey clearly operates within the text as a Heaneyesque figure. The poem works, therefore, by driving the Romantic and the contemporary moment into creative dialogue with one another.

As suggested, Muldoon's sense of artistic sympathy with Byron rests not simply on their shared parodic strategies but also on their similarly antagonistic attitudes towards their respective first-generation precursors. Broadly speaking, Byron's hostility was based on the first-generation Romantics's renunciation of their republican principles and their pandering to monarchy and government. Scathing of Southey's poetic pride and egotism and of the self-absorption of all of 'the Lakers', Byron saw their seclusion and self-communings as sexual sublimation. His own poetry, by contrast, sought to deflate the holy task of the poet and freely embraced sexuality and hedonism. Byron's attempt to deflate the epic quest, and its concomitant moral and religious ideals, can be seen, to some extent, as a response to Southey's own epic poems. The protagonists in Southey's *Madoc* and *Thalaba the Destroyer* share a sense of election, of being chosen by Fate to fulfil some pre-ordained mission.[22] In *Thalaba the Destroyer*, for example, the hero rejects magic for Faith, rejects pleasure in all its forms, espouses self-denial, and renounces revenge in favour of forgiveness. On one level the poem is a denial of the darker emotions of the human psyche, an endorsement of Christian morality and theology over the magic and voluptuousness of the paganistic, the magical, and the pleasure-seeking. Southey's *Madoc* works on the same principle, with its tale of a Welsh conquest of the Aztecs followed not by vengeful slaughter but by a reforming zeal.[23] Byron was quite right to be suspicious of such epic tales for, as Marilyn Butler has pointed out, Southey's *Madoc* set out 'to popularize the case for "missionizing", which was also a case for imposing Western culture and goals of material progress on Eastern populations'.[24] The poem stands as 'a frank, very urgent justification of colonialism as a move entirely for the native's own good'.[25] The supposed republican and egalitarian ideals of Southey's apparent Pantisocracy are in fact an endorsement and justification of the British government's imperialist and expansionist policy.

The links between Byron's attitude to Southey and Muldoon's toward Heaney are made clear in Muldoon's review of Heaney's *Station Island*. Muldoon, for example, focuses on Heaney's treatment of sex which is, he argues:

by turns coldly clinical ('She is twig-boned, saddle-sexed'), adolescently furtive ('my nightly shadow feasts, / Haunting the granaries of words like *breasts*', 'Who would have thought it? At the White Gates / She let them do whatever they liked'), or the customary heady brew of voyeurism and Catholicism.[26]

His remaining complaints are encompassed in a short section of the review in which Muldoon gives Heaney some advice on being a better poet:

> In the unlikely event of a truly uninvited shade being summoned up in some reworking of the 'Station Island' sequence, I suspect that its advice to Seamus Heaney would be along the following lines. 1. That he should, indeed, take the advice he gave himself as long ago as 1975 – 'Keep your eye clear as the bleb of an icicle' – but take it quietly rather than rehearse it again and again. 2. General Absolution is too much even for a Catholic confessional poet to hope for. 3. That he should resist more firmly the idea that he must be the best Irish poet since Yeats, which arose from rather casual remarks by the power-crazed Robert Lowell and the craze-powered Clive James, who seem to have forgotten both MacNeice and Kavanagh.[27]

Muldoon is here attacking Heaney's tendency to rehearse the same material and arguments; the constant sense of guilt, not least of all sexual, that haunts his writing; his tendency to allow his work to become skewed by a particular ideological viewpoint; and finally his exaggerated sense of himself first as a poet and second as Ireland's national poet. These traits are ones Muldoon incorporates into his portrayal of Southey in *Madoc*. Thus:

> We see him reach
> into his pantaloons for a small, sea-green vial,
> then be overwhelmed by another pang of guilt.[28]

That sense of guilt is here associated with masturbation, a guilt that manifests itself in Heaney's early poetry.[29] So too, in spite of being committed to the philosophy of Epictetus, with its emphasis on self-renunciation and brother-hood, Southey is, as stressed throughout *Madoc*, profoundly self-obsessed, suffering literary insecurity and jealousy: 'Cinammond frowns / in disbelief, then squawks and squalls / as Southey rams the sheaf of goose-quills / into his eyes' (*Madoc*, 55). Indeed the literary rivalry between Coleridge and Southey is pivotal in the poem, a point made clear in Coleridge's letter to Cottle – '*I am fearful that Southey will begin to rely too much on story & event in his poems to the*

neglect of those lofty imaginings *that are peculiar to, & definitive of, the* POET'
(*Madoc*, 195). Throughout the text we see continual instances of jealousy and
doubling between Coleridge, Southey, and the figure of Byron who, while
he is never actually present on the expedition, functions as a shadowy textual
presence. Running through the poem is the name of the 'Satanic school', first
applied to Byron and others by Southey. In the poem, however, this is
manipulated so that, in actual fact, it refers to Coleridge and Southey and the
Pantisocratic enterprise. One of the ways in which Muldoon achieves this is
by turning Southey's and Coleridge's own work against them using a poem
which they co-wrote – 'The Devil's Thoughts'.[30] References to this are
scattered throughout *Madoc*, and provide another instance of the parodic
doubling which is a hallmark of this collection. The original poem was
written in 1799, at a time when Southey's and Coleridge's principles were
still largely republican, and when they were still hostile to the British
Government. The poem, amongst other things, targets Church and
government, attacks the appalling conditions in prisons and the affluence of
the rich, and condemns the 'English Establishment as Devil's agents':[31]

> From his brimstone bed at break of day
> a-walking the Devil is gone
> to look at his snug little farm the Earth
> and see how his stock went on . . .
>
> (*Madoc*, 56)

As Richard Holmes points out the Devil is 'a representative of moral and
political hypocrisy, who takes from the poor to give to the rich, and
supports all those who trade on the weak and vulnerable and sick'.[32] The
inclusion of such material in *Madoc* ironically underlines both Southey and
Coleridge's degeneration from radicals to supporters of the very establishment they once sought to undermine. With this strategic re-contextualising
of excerpts from the poem, Southey and Coleridge condemn themselves as
the Devil's agents.

It is through strategies such as these that Muldoon reveals the real roots of
the Pantisocracy scheme. As becomes clear, Southey is not driven by
egalitarian impulses but by the desire to cast himself as epic hero, conquering
evil, civilising the Indians, and building Southeyopolis, the new Jerusalem in
which he will be king – '*I could rhapsodise most delightfully upon this subject, plan
out my city, the palaces and hovels of Southeyopolis*' (*Madoc*, 158). Southeyopolis, an
ideal community founded on seemingly republican philosophies is, in effect, a

dictatorship. Equally spurious is Southey's desire to create a national canon, a literature *'distinguished by its moral purity, the effect, and in turn the cause, of an improvement in national manners'* (*Madoc*, 245). As we have seen, Southey's 'moral purity' and republican principles disguise an imperialist agenda premised on the recovery of a mythic, original identity and achieved through violence and brutality. Southey's words, taken from his Preface to *A Vision of Judgement*, are placed by Muldoon at the end of *Madoc* and serve as an ironic counterpoint to Southey's mounting egotism and brutal behaviour. The poems ends, fittingly, with Southey's execution by the Indians.

Edna Longley has pointed out that 'Southeyopolis' functions within the text not just as a failed political structure but also as 'a failed *literary* construction with Seamus Heaney (and perhaps Field Day) especially implicated'.[33] The point is an apt one. Heaney, after all, in 'The Toome Road', describes Ireland's identity in transcendent, essentialist and openly phallic terms as 'the vibrant untoppled omphalos'.[34] He excludes city experience and industrialisation from his poetry and returns nostalgically to a timeless rural landscape, grounding his own identity, like that of Ireland, in the ahistorical world of pastoral. Ultimately, such representations conceal an agenda of romantic nationalism and produce an exclusive and marginalising construction of Irish identity.

As a poetic construction, Bucephalus, Southey's trusty horse, complete with the 'star on the forehead' (*Madoc*, 50), represents this transcendent imagination, a version of Pegasus or poetic inspiration who guarantees Southey's status as a poet who travels 'on the winged steed' – 'If Southey is to Bucephalus / as a flame is to a wick / then Southey is a flame' (*Madoc*, 29). Throughout the book, he acts as a mentor to Southey, assuring him of his status as a member of the elect and of the fitness of his mission. He repeatedly reminds Southey that Pantisocracy represents '"the greatest, greatest good"' (*Madoc*, 161). That Bucephalus should fall victim to syphilis, described as 'these blenny-blebs and blets /... storming my Bastille', is no accident (*Madoc*, 167). In this way Muldoon is able to undermine both the Pantisocratic scheme and Southey's poetry as phallic constructions (another version of the 'vibrant untoppled omphalos') premised on the rational humanist assumption of an essential self-contained identity. The state of Bucephalus's penis reflects both the degeneration of the Pantisocratic scheme and the Enlightenment humanism on which it is based, and of Southey's poetic ideals. His death is described in apocalyptic terms – 'Blood-alphabets. Blood-ems. / A babble of blood out of the broken fount' – as the destruction of some sacred place, source, or origin (*Madoc*, 182). It represents the rupture and destruction of the ego, of the 'eye', and also the blood and violence at the heart of this whole poetic, Pantisocratic (Heaneyesque) enterprise.

While Muldoon's attitude to Southey is clearly one of direct condemnation, Coleridge, though subjected to ironic pressure, is treated much more positively. Muldoon is sympathetic to Coleridge's interest in magic and the unconscious, his visionary capability, and his desire for transcendence through this visionary process. As Tim Kendall argues, Coleridge's gradual initiation 'into the mysteries of Indian culture' allows him to become a visionary and shape-changer.[35] Given Muldoon's own interest in shamanism and trickster figures it is hardly surprising that there should be a significant degree of sympathy between the two.[36]

Muldoon's true allegiances, however, lie with Byron. Like him, Muldoon is a transgressor and an 'ex-centric',[37] a disruptive and disordering presence, who considers himself very much one of the devil's party. Both Byron and Muldoon are suspicious of the imperative to create a national literature and, in the same vein, refuse the notion of the self-contained, autonomous ego.[38] *Madoc*, a tour de force of parodic intent, asserts this refusal. Its re-contextualisations work both as a process of 'doubling' and 'differentiation', often producing alternative readings which undermine and radically alter the intended meaning of Romantic texts.[39] While Muldoon's purpose in rewriting *Madoc* is to deflate Southey's *Madoc* and to assert a critical distance, on another level Muldoon's parodic strategies only work because there are points of intersection and continuity between the Romantic period and the contemporary one. Ultimately Muldoon's writing shows that those inter-sections are negative as well as positive: imperialist agendas, constructions of identity which are dependent on the categories of self and other, oppression wrapped up as idealism and utopianism, totalising narratives; all of these act as points of continuity. However, in his identification with Coleridge, and more importantly with Byron, Muldoon's work also shows that Romanticism continues to offer us models of resistance and subversion and utopian possibilities which might yet have some credence.

SEAMUS HEANEY

The Two Mice

A Fable by Robert Henryson
translated from the fifteenth-century Scots

Aesop tells a tale – Aesop, my author –
Of two mice who were sisters fair and fond.
The elder had a town-house in a borough.
The younger dwelt up country, near at hand
And by herself, at times on whinny ground,
At times in corn crops, living hand to mouth
Beyond the pale and off the land, by stealth.

This country mouse, when winter came, endured
Cold and hunger and extreme distress.
The other mouse, in town, sat on a board
With guild members, an independent burgess,
Exempt from tax, from port and market cess,
Free to go roaming wherever she liked best
Among the cheese and meal, in bin and chest.

One time, well-fed and lightsome on her feet,
She thought about her sister on the land
And wondered how she fared, what kind of state

She lived in, in the greenwood out beyond.
So, barefoot and alone, with staff in hand,
Like a poor pilgrim she set out from the town
To seek her sister, over dale and down.

Through many wild and lonesome ways she goes,
By moss and moor, by bank and bush and briar,
Calling across the fallow land and furrows,
'Come out to me, my own sweet sister dear!
Just give one cheep.' With that the mouse could hear
And knew the voice, since it's in our nature
To recognize our own, and came to meet her.

If you had seen, Lord God! the high excitement
That overcame the sisters when they met,
The way the sighs passed back and forth between them,
The way they laughed and then for gladness wept.
They sweetly kissed, they held each other tight
And kept this up until they both grew calm,
Then went indoors together, arm in arm.

It was, as I have heard, a simple hut
Made expertly of foggage and of fern
On stone supports sunk into earth upright,
The jambs set close, the lintel near the ground,
And into it they went and there remained.
No fire burned for them nor candle bright
For shady rooms best suit the fly-by-night.

When they were lodged and settled, these poor mice,
The younger sister to the pantry hurries
And brings out nuts and peas instead of spice.
Without being there, who'll say how good it was?
The burgess then gets haughty and pretentious,
And asks her sister, 'Is this how you eat?'
'Why,' she replies, 'is there something wrong with it?'

'No, by my soul, it's just so ordinary!'
'Madam,' she said, 'you are the more to blame.
When we were born I heard my mother say
The womb we both came out of was the same.
I'm true to her example and good name
And to my father's, to their frugal ways.
We own no lands or grounds or properties.'

'Please,' the reply came, 'let me be excused.
My tastes and this rough diet are at odds.
I live a lady's life now and am used
To tender meat; it's what my system needs.
These withered peas and nuts and shells and pods
Will break my teeth and hurt me in the stomach
Now that I know what standards to expect.'

'Well, well, my sister,' says the country mouse,
'If you would like, and seeing that you're here,
You're welcome to the free run of the house
And food and drink. Stay on for the year!
It'll warm my heart to keep you and to share.
Our friendship matters more than middling food.
Who sniffs at cooking when the company's good?

Delicacies pall, and fancy dishes,
When they are served up by a scowling face.
A sweetness in the giver's more delicious.
Fine sauces don't make up for lack of grace.
A modicum suffices, we do with less
When the carver carves from the goodness of his heart.
A sour-faced host can blink the best cook's art.'

In spite of all this well-disposed advice
The burgess was in no mood to be humoured.
She knit her brows above two glowering eyes

No matter what choice pickings she was offered
Until, at last, she half-sighed and half-sneered,
'Sister, for a country mouse, this stuff
You've laid on makes a spread and is good enough.

Give over this place, be my visitor:
Come where I live, and learn when you're my guest
How my Good Friday's better than your Easter,
My dish-lickings more luscious than your feast.
My quarters are among the very safest.
Of cat or trap or trip I have no dread.'
'All right,' says sister, and they take the road.

Under cover, through clumps of corn and weed,
Keeping themselves hidden, on they creep.
The elder acts as guide and stays ahead.
The younger follows close and minds her step.
By night they make a run, by day they sleep,
Until one morning, when the lark was singing,
They reached the town and thankfully went in.

To a residence not far along the way
The town mouse led on and they made their entry
With none to greet or give them time of day.
Next thing they stood inside a well-stocked pantry
With cheese and butter stacked on shelves, great plenty
Of red meat and hung game, fish fresh and salt,
Sacks full of groats, milled corn and meal and malt.

Later, when they felt the urge to dine,
They washed their hands and sat, but said no grace.
There was every course a cook's art could design,
Roast beef and mutton relished slice by slice,
A meal fit for a lord. But they were mice
And showed it when they drank not wine but water,
Yet could hardly have enjoyed their banquet better.

Taunting and cajoling all at once,
The elder mouse enquired of her guest
Whether she thought there was real difference
Between that chamber and her sorry nest.
'Yes ma'am,' said she, 'but how long will this last?'
'Forever, I expect, and even longer.'
'In that case, it's a safe house,' said the younger.

The town mouse, for their pleasure, produced more:
Groats on a plate and meal piled in a pan,
And didn't stay her hand, you can be sure,
When she doled the oatcakes out and served a scone
Of best white baker's bread instead of brawn,
Then stole a tall white candle from a chest
As a final touch, to give the meal more taste.

And so they revelled on and raised a cry
And shouted 'Hail, Yule, hail!' and made merry.
Yet often care comes on the heels of joy
And trouble after great prosperity.
Thus, as they sat in all their jollity,
The steward comes along swinging his keys,
Opens the door and finds them at their ease.

They didn't wait to wash, as I imagine,
But rushed and raced and sped off desperately;
The burgess had a hole and in she ran,
Her sister no such place of sanctuary.
To see that mouse in panic was great pity,
In dread, bewildered, cornered and astray
So that she swooned and nearly passed away.

But God had willed and worked a happy outcome:
The hard-pressed steward could not afford to bide.
He hadn't time to harry or to hunt them

But hurried on, and left the room-door wide.
The burgess watched him make his way outside,
Then scooted from her hole and cried on high,
'How are you, sister? Where? Just cheep for me!'

Sure she was doomed, and terrified to die,
This country mouse lay on the ground prostrate.
Her heart beat fast, she was like somebody
Shaken by fever, trembling hand and foot,
And when her sister found her in this state
For very pity she broke down in tears,
Then spoke these words, sweet honey to her ears:

'Why do you cower like this, dear sister? Rise!
Return to table. Come. The danger's past.'
The other answered in a stricken voice,
'I cannot eat, I am so sore aghast.
I'd rather do Lent's forty days of fast
On cabbage water, gnawing peas and beans,
Than feast with you here in such dread conditions.'

Still, being soothed so sweetly, she got up
And went to table where again they sat,
But hardly had they time to drink one cup
When in comes Hunter Gib, our jolly cat,
And bids good day. The burgess ups with that
And speedy as the spark from flint makes off.
His nibs then takes the other by the scruff.

From foot to foot he chased her to and fro,
Whiles up, whiles down, as quick as any kid,
Whiles letting her go free beneath the straw,
Whiles playing blind man's buff with her, shut-eyed.
And thus he kept that poor mouse in great dread
Until by lucky chance, at the last call,
She slipped between the hangings and the wall.

Then up in haste behind the tapestry
She climbed so high that Gilbert couldn't get her
And hung by the claws there very expertly
Till he was gone; and when her mood was better
And she could move with no cat to upset her,
Down she came on the town mouse, shouting out,
'Sister, farewell. Your feast I set at nought.

Your spread is spoiled, your cream in curds from worry.
Your goose is good, your sauce as sour as gall,
Your second helpings sure to make you sorry,
Mishaps still sure to haunt you and befall.
I thank that curtain and partition-wall
For guarding me against yon cruel beast.
Save me, Almighty God, from such a feast.

If I were back on home ground, I would stay,
Never, for weal or woe, come forth again.'
With that she took her leave and went her way,
Now through the corn, now on the open plain,
Glad to be on the loose and given rein
To gambol and be giddy on the moor.
What then became of her I can't be sure,

Though I've heard tell she made it to her nest
That was as warm as wool, if small and strait,
Packed snugly from back wall to chimney-breast
With peas and nuts and beans and rye and wheat.
When she inclined, she had enough to eat
In peace and quiet there, amidst her store,
But to her sister's house she went no more.

WILLIAM WATKIN

Poppypetal

Thanatropism, Pathos and Pathology in Contemporary Elegy Theory

This bitter thing did I learn as I mused upon thee one day;
For a poppy-petal I smote as it lay on my forearm smooth,
And the love-in-absence made no smear but withered away.

Ah grievous love, why hast thou clung to me
Leech-like, until of all my life I'm bled![1]

SILANUS: To console, lady, is not to do away with sorrow, but to teach one
how to overcome it.[2]

To define the essence of elegy conceptually one need go no further than Theocritus' paradox of the poppypetal. Love-in-absence contains the heady mix of presence and absence, affirmation and negation, that establishes the parameters of the genre. The traditional role of elegy is to set in a structure of presence – poem, monument, epitaph, name – a radical and irreversible absence: the lost beloved. However, there is also a second paradox to elegy to which Maeterlinck alerts us. Elegy is treatment for a psychic wound from which one might 'bleed' to death through heartache. It is about overcoming sorrow, meaning simultaneously to master, and to pass over it, depriving it of its self-possession. Sorrow's 'self', which suffering purports to possess and which elegy cures, is the self *in absentia*, a subject that lives through death. And yet to conquer this self, the figure of the lost beloved, means to negate it while affirming it. One wants to testify to the nature of the lost, but one also wants to get over the loss by destroying it.

Elegy's paradox, I am tempted to say elegy *is* paradox, is that it has to affirm negation, speak of what is no longer with us, and also to negate affirmation, console by stressing that what is gone *is* really gone. It *is* a very painful process, and it *is* a process. The elegist must lose twice over, must lose the lost beloved, and then lose this loss. When the elegy is complete, absence is negated and effectively the dead have been 'killed' twice, once in their own life, and once in ours. This paradoxical mix of absence and presence is what I want to investigate through traditional theories of elegy as a genre and the means by which it seeks to trope death.

Elegy can be dangerous; it will always be elusive for it sometimes uses absence to deconstruct presence, sometimes imposes presence to negate absence, but it is never an entirely successful advocate for either force. It is, in effect, the precondition for our existence as beings in language. From the first linguistic utterance, our lives in language are marked by the smear/nonsmear of the poppypetal's impossible logic: if there is a mark, there must also be all around it the terrible emptiness of the nonmark. Yet our lives have been enriched by the obverse truth, that within every absence the potentially consoling mark of presence is imminent.

The history of elegiac theory is that of the establishment of what I call thanatropism; the figures of death. In as much as death can never be a referent for language, all talk of death is tropic. To speak of loss is to speak figuratively with no hope of communicating the truth of it; thanatropism is arguably a mature acceptance of language's inability to render the presence of the real thing. The simplest result of absence is that it allows us to relax around the lack of presence in our words and in our world, providing us with a zone, which theorists identify as pastoral, where the radical incommensurable forces beneath rational certainties – death, silence, absence, loss, nonsense, endless repetition – can be viewed safely.[3]

Associative and contiguous tropes both have difficulty with radical absence. Association has, built into it, a false gap between the signifier and the signified, which it then overleaps spectacularly. But like all magic, it's a trick. It carries its gap up its sleeve to produce it theatrically at the point when it knows it can erase it. The poppypetal, for example, uses the gap between expectation and actuality to produce an impossible symbol of presence in absence. The smear of the petal is retained on the mind, but the bare outstretched arm of the poem's pastoral reality conveys an alternative logic. We can easily make this leap. Contiguous tropes, such as metonymy and allegory, have a much more localised relation to the gap. For them the gap is small, but equally foundational. Without the gap there can be no concatenation, and their ability to convey meaning through physical or causal proximity is removed. They also jump the gap, but they do not attempt to erase it or fill it in. Contiguities love their locality, while association yearns upwards for something metaphysical.

Again the poppypetal's logic is instructive. The arm is a symbol of metonymy, the act of touching and in doing so effecting your desires, and here the angry lover seeks to make a metonymic link between his fury and the delicate beauty of the petal. Yet when he strikes the red patch to actuate the contiguous narrative of his desires, he discovers a causal disjuncture: striking does not produce smearing, and this becomes the *real* cause of his musing. The petal as metaphor, the association of its physical qualities with those of love, becomes the petal as metonym. It is the actual physicality of the petal which defeats association. Unlike love it leaves no smear. However the petal as metonym – he strikes the petal to bring about the smear – allows for the petal's overall associative power in the passage. The nonsmear is a cause of musing with the result that he associates this quality with that of love. Desire becomes a heuristic pursuit of loss, a loss which chases after love.

It should be apparent immediately that death's gap – really a chasm – cannot be bridged by either association or contiguity. One cannot associate with death, actual and radical absence, and the leap that this requires the mind to make is a suicidal one. Similarly, radical absence is not proximate to life, and there can be no causality with it. It puts causality to death. So the first point to be made is that the gaps of tropism are not radical, and while they suggest in both cases an intimacy with absence at the heart of meaning, hence the need for a figure, such an absence is *not* the same as radical absence. Which is why the sign 'death' is the most mature of all signs, it revels in its excessive arbitrariness, always suggesting that, while there is more to be said about death than it can ever express, at the same time it cannot even say one good thing about it. If the sign 'death' is already self consciously a figuration of absence, tropes involved with such an absence become meta-tropic, tropes laid down on top of tropes. This is the essence of the thanatropic concerns of elegy, making it doubly distant from that to which the idea of distanciation makes no sense. There can be no distance from absence because that suggests some idea of association or proximity. Absence is never just over there, absence just *is not*.

In the work of the major generic theorists of elegy I want to consider, Peter Sacks, Ellen Zetzel Lambert, and Eric Smith, as well as supplemental work by Renato Poggioli, Jahan Ramazani and W. David Shaw, we find suggestions about the irresolvability between absence and presence that is endemic to elegy. Sacks, Lambert, and Smith form a thanatropic triumvirate in their respective theories of elegy as trope, topos, and the consolation conundrum. I want to pursue two alternative strands of opinion as regards the paradox of the poppypetal. These traditional critics seem to follow a path of enquiry into thanatropism which I would call the pathology of pathos. Sacks especially makes it clear, as I have done, that there is a crucial difference between lack in language and actual loss.[4] I would go further and stipulate that there is a central difference, in terms of critical theory, between lack and loss, as much as there is between absence and radical absence. In reference to this differentiation Sacks notes that elegy is ideal for an examination of 'the connections between language and the pathos of human consciousness', because 'elegy ... is characterized by an unusually powerful intertwining of emotion and rhetoric, of loss and figuration ... both an event and a structure'.[5] Pathos is the process of exciting pity or sadness in another, but its root sense also connotes a sense of disease, forming the basis of the idea of pathology. It seems immanent, therefore, that one *could* speak of the pathology of pathos, of the way pity makes one sick enough to design a complex generic history of figuration to help with the healing process. The history of the theory of elegy is that it is not about the lost beloved but about that which is left alive, but feeling deadened and lonely. Elegy intertwines radical absence with forms of generic presence, such as figuration and structure, so as to steal the radical from absence and produce instead loss and its figures. To rebut this I want to posit the pathos of pathology, or the inability to cure, as a source of elegiac pity. The radical terror and pity of the unknowable is not something that should be swept under a carpet of false tropes and imposed structures. It ought to be confronted as it is, as an actual loss one can do nothing about.

Sacks' theory of the trope comes from a sophisticated yet flawed sense of how thanatropism occurs, and it suffers from a belief in the pathology of pathos. Tracing elegy through its accepted origins in pastoral to the more complex and ancient realm of vegetation rites, he realises that above and beyond the traditional strategies of mourning in such rites there is a greater pain:

> More painful and more crucial, however, is the elegist's reluctant submission to language itself. One of the least well observed elements of the genre is this enforced accommodation between the mourning self on the one hand and the very words of grief and fictions of consolation on the other.[6]

Discussing Ovid's myth of Apollo and Daphne, Sacks reads the process of the transformation of Daphne into a tree from which Apollo makes a wreath to stand in for her and to compensate for his loss of sexual consummation of his desire, as an allegory for this differentiation between actual loss and its representations. He rightly notes that the wreath is a typical act of elegiac troping which contains a necessary mix of positive and negative elements. The subject loses the beloved and yet this opens up the preconditions of desire. The beloved is turned into a sign to stand in for the loss, which both gives presence to absence and yet indicates the absence at the heart of expressions of presence. The sign is metonymic as the wreath substitute is now part of Daphne's body since her metamorphosis into a tree. Thus it both affirms her, as metonym is causal, and also mutilates her. Apollo turns from her to her sign, losing her but gaining a mutilated language. He must perform the act of troping to console himself and stave off the pathos of pathology, but this naming or giving a sign for one's loss is subject to the pathology of pathos. His troping is a self-indulgence dressed up as love, a pitiable stand-in for the real experience of losing, containing nothing except its second order linguistic materiality. The trope content is irrelevant, rather it is its physicality, its shape and positioning which matter. The thanatrope is a placebo self-prescribed to deal with the heartache of losing something, oftentimes reducible to saying the lost beloved's name over and over as Sacks points out. Pre-empting Derrida's work on mourning,[7] Sacks realises that in speaking the name of the lost beloved, one is substituting signs for a lost actuality: the name is the simplest and most poignant of thanatropes.

Like all pathologies, the pathology of pathos is infectious as indeed is the affective power of pathos. Daphne is lost and the wreath becomes her permanent presence. The actual loss, loss as cognitive event, is also lost, and language's figurative structures come into play. The result is health actuating a final paradoxical mix of positive and negative forces: the pleasure of being well again is mixed with guilt over the loss of loss. As Sacks establishes, what is lost in thanatropic substitution is any *real* sense of absence. The half-truths of self-pity infect the truth of absence. Elegy tries to treat death with the same medicine as it treats life: the result is poetry.

Sacks' mix of psychoanalysis, literary theory, and anthropology is the basis of the idea of thanatropic substitutions typical of the pathology of pathos. The mourning subject feels sorry for itself, not for the lost beloved, feels bad about feeling bad, indicating that loss in the work of elegy is effectively sensed four times over. *The loss as event*: semi-mythical and yet present in most modern theories of loss and absence is that loss is an irreducible event, but when we try to express it we immediately find ourselves using signs as substitutes for it. *The loss as sign, Thanatropism*: all signs of loss are tropic or gap-fillers, as poststructuralism argues all signs are. Loss, radical loss as an event, however, throws this into relief by accepting that one cannot concatenate with what is not there, and so other material is brought in to allow either for associative leaps less frightening than the leap into nothingness, or causal links that establish a myth of continuance even after the end. *The loss of loss*: Thanatropism loses loss, or, better, loss loses out to other forms of dealing with absence within our structures of presence. The pity we feel for the illness of not having what we once had and still want motivates us to create processes with specific rules, into which we introduce over-significant counters. Elegy seems little more than an elaborate and grown up version of Freud's *fort/da*. *The retroactive infection of the event by the figure*: the pathology of pathos itself is a kind of dis-ease, a discomfort with the violent challenge of an absence that has no relation to presence. And so we create retroactive tropes to argue back into the original loss as event, recreating it as a pathetic situation from the start. This is the role of the thanatrope and perhaps its ultimate paradox: death comes before life as a startling precondition which in some ways is comforting. If we can deal with the event of loss, what can't we deal with? Yet death also dies here, usurped from its all-conquering position by a shoddy, sentimental, tropic second cousin.

Of these four modes of losing which form a basic thanatropic narratology, the first three are accorded positive as well as negative aspects. The loss as event confirms reality, the loss as sign yields the gift of language, and the loss of loss results in good mental health. But the final infection can only be good news to those actively involved in deconstructive attacks on metaphysics, because it proves that structures of subjective presence are predicated on absence to such a threatening degree that presence is forced to retrace its history of losing and erase absence under second-order substitutions. Relating the myth of Daphne and Apollo to Freud's conception of the healthy work of mourning Sacks concludes: 'Of course only the object *as lost*, and not the object itself, enters into the substitutive sign, and the latter is accepted only by a turning away from the actual identity of what was lost. Consolation thus depends on a trope that remains at an essential remove from what it replaces.'[8] Somewhat tautological – the trope *must* by definition be at a remove from what it replaces – Sacks' point is still well made and he presents us with a radical process of troping death out of our lives through his reconsideration of the ritual/pastoral origins of elegy. But what is it exactly about the pastoral realm that facilitates this thanatropic working out of the pathology of pathos?

Ellen Zetzel Lambert, like Sacks, comes at elegy from the perspective of the ancient genre of pastoral poetry through what she calls 'pastoral elegy'. A generic hybrid, it raises questions about the significant history of the genre, described in Smith and Shaw, which covers several thousand years from vegetation rites, through pastoral poetry, to pastoral poetry about loss, eventually ending up in the modern, post-Christian elegy. However, while Sacks makes a great deal out of the vegetative logic of the thanatropic lexicon that allows such an easy shift from pastoral to elegiac conventions, Lambert is much more 'syntactic': 'The pastoral elegy, I would suggest, proposes not one *solution* to the questions raised by death but rather a *setting* in which those questions may be posed, or better, "placed". It offers us a landscape.'[9] Elegy's 'solutions' to loss are those tropic substitutions already adumbrated through Sacks' work. The radical, uncrossable expanse of actual loss is contracted to allow for a consoling myth of association or causality, so that the trope substitutes less for the lost object as for the space that loss leaves. Thanatropism is, therefore, not a process of Freudian substitution as Sacks argues, so much as occupation, and here Lambert's placement theory is extremely valuable. Like the elegiac trope, one should not dismiss the pastoral setting as a naïvely unreal zone wherein one can escape the challenges of daily life. Rather, as Lambert argues, the pastoral is like the trope in having a mature attitude towards loss: 'This poetic world to which the pastoral elegist "escapes" ... is not ... *less* substantial than the world he actually inhabits. On the contrary, it is in important ways made to seem *more* substantial ... than the "real" world ... The pastoral landscape pleases us not ... because it *excludes* pain, but because of the way it includes it. Pastoral offers us a vision of life stripped not of pain but of complexity.'[10]

Freud notes that mourning and melancholic subjects are identical in dealing with loss through reality testing, up to the zero point of withdrawal of attachment from the absent love object. Then the normal, healthy work of the mourner goes back over this systematically vacated ground, replanting love along the way. The melancholic, however, lingers, keeps on testing reality. The melancholic is a sceptic who would rather occupy the petrified realm of pathology than succumb to the occupation of their grief by saccharine and maudlin tropes of love and loss. The pastoral world is, paradoxically, the world of the real: an unreal world wherein the reality of loss as event can be, if not encountered, at least not infected with pathos. Renato Poggioli reinforces this in *The Oaten Flute*: 'Man may linger in the pastoral dreamworld a short while or a whole lifetime. Pastoral poetry makes more poignant and real the dream it wishes to convey when the retreat is not a lasting but a passing experience, acting as a pause in the process of living, as a breathing spell from the fever and anguish of being.'[11] Poggioli's pathetic perspective suggests that lingering is somehow less normal, less healthy than living, and that while the pastoral does make loss more real, it is only a dream of reality. These arguments aside, one can conclude that the pastoral's relation to loss *is* that of syntax to the lexicon, favouring contiguous tropes and reserving associative substitutions for elegy proper. Elegy is primarily associative, pastoral causal or contiguous.

These may seem like dry distinctions, but the difference in the thanatropic base of pastoral and elegy indicates that Lambert's conception of 'pastoral elegy' must be reappraised as tropically, and thus logically, impossible. Following Freud's classic distinction between mourning and melancholia, it is clear that elegy is ultimately the realm of mourning, of the healthy work of substitution and occupation of the space left in the world, in fact left in the subject, by the evacuation of the love object. In contradistinction, the pastoral realm is pathological, for, as the critics universally note, the pastoral realm is where the subject meets with the actuality of loss. The pastoral, generically, occurs before the elegy, the pastoral being pagan and elegy Christian, but psychologically they are parallel or alternative options. The subject can choose to get well through association thus losing their loss, or remain ill through contiguity but retain the reality of losing.

Lambert assumes that the pain of pastoral is simple, robbed of complexity. It is a problematic point and leads us towards a second significance as to the thanatropic dissimilarities between pastoral and elegy. What is a complex pain? Pain, like pleasure or *jouissance*, is irreducible and non-divisible. It is sublime. The pleasure/pain dichotomy of Freudian psychoanalysis is shadowed aesthetically by Kantian conceptions of the sublime. So while the implications of pain, or loss, are apparently complex, pain itself cannot be. The pastoral allows a setting for this, forces the subject to try to touch its pain and feel it as cause of its being effected through the radical power of the affect.

Poggioli argues for the pastoral as a world apart from pain, Lambert as the world where pain can be confronted as such. Who is correct? We seem to be dealing with a different mode of addressing pain within the pastoral which, in contrast to the pathology of pathos – a sense that pain and pity, love of the lost, while laudable, is ultimately a dangerous sickness – could be termed the pathos of pathology. This is how contiguity works thanatropically. The pathos of pathology is the pity one gets from one's sickness, viewing one's sickness as all one has of the lost beloved, perhaps all one has of worth in the world. One loves one's lack of the beloved, almost as much as one loved the beloved. We believe that we should pity the sick, but perhaps that pity is tinged with envy. Clearly these issues bisect with those of the scapegoat;[12] the pastoral is a world apart from the real cares of daily life in the city state, and it is this which allows both Lambert's and Poggioli's apparently contradictory assumptions to be read as correct. There are two types of loss, two types of pain. That which we experience in the so-called real world, an impetus to trope absence out of its radical existence through the traditional activities of elegy, and that which we experience as unexperienceable and yet occurring. We reach out to connect with it, we do not shy away from sickness or view the affect as something transitory, but we desire the pain of loss. Unreachable, untenable, without apparent cause, it is the very essence of the real. This cannot occur in the city state, all sickness must be quarantined and expelled; the pastoral world is wrapped in the pathos of exile. Lambert thus concludes: 'Now in the pastoral elegy, when we invite nature to turn her order upside-down or to weep with us, what we are asking for is not a display of anger, or a promise of revenge, or even (primarily) a display of grief. We are asking for a demonstration of love.'[13] Poggioli, perhaps unwittingly, implicitly agrees when he suggests: 'the task of the pastoral imagination is to overcome the conflict between passion and remorse, to reconcile innocence and happiness, to exalt the pleasure principle at the expense of the reality principle'.[14] Both critics argue in favour of the pastoral realm as that of the pathos of pathology: pathos is love and love is pleasure. It is the reality principle that demands we get over loss, that we associate with a new object. The pleasure principle doesn't want to lose its love object because it still has a use for it: this object still affords it pleasure and, after all, what else is love for?

However, both Lambert and Poggioli are *terminologically* incorrect. There is no such thing as pastoral elegy. Pastoral demands we stay within the environs of the petrified landscape of allegorical nature famously described by Walter Benjamin.[15] Elegy insists we get over our illness by occupying this dead topos with a new trope. Further, there is no pastoral 'imagination' as Poggioli suggests: the pastoral world is all too real in the way that only allegory can be. Allegory, as both Benjamin and de Man show,[16] reveals to us the unreality of our tropes of reality, while simultaneously disallowing this insight to itself take the place of, or mask, the radical event of the real thing. In the pastoral world we are forced to touch absence to find out that we cannot, but no more can we withdraw from it. In the elegiac world we fill the topography of absence with tropes, and thus evacuate absence from its place. Absence is absented and the presence of absence as a figure of itself is affirmed. Such is the paradox of mourning: the more positive we are about negativity, the more we negate it. It makes terrible, logical sense.

Sacks notes that 'the pipe or flute is appropriate to mourning, for it joins a sighing breath to hollowness',[17] suggesting that the mythical/ritual origins of the modern elegy place at its base a double thanatropic procedure: the laurel wreath stands in for the lost beloved, and the pipe implies a basic causality between the asymbolia of sighs of pure grief, and its expression through music and poetry. Sacks does not make this distinction but one can note that while the 'wreath' and the 'pipe' – within elegy the monument and the elegy proper – in our culture symbolise mourning, they are not associative but metonymic. The wreath *comes* from the tree, the pipe is in *contact* with the breath. Tennyson's *In Memoriam*, a work of melancholy disguised as healthy mourning, seems to support Sacks' claim that elegy's origin is in these vegetable myths:

> I sing to him that rests below,
>> And, since the grasses round me wave,
>> I take the grasses of the grave,
> And make them pipes whereon to blow.

The traveler hears me now and then,
    And sometimes harshly will he speak:
    'This fellow would make weakness weak,
And melt the waxen hearts of men.'

Another answers: 'Let him be,
    He loves to make parade of pain,
    That with his piping he may gain
The praise that comes to constancy.' ...

Tonight ungathered let us leave
    This laurel, let this holly stand:
    We live within the stranger's land,
And strangely falls our Christmas eve.[18]

The grass grows from the dead body Tennyson is mourning, and combines the wreath and the song in one. Ostensibly, all that modern elegy has done is to remove a crucial articulating gap between two metonyms, one for loss and one for reactions to that loss, and in fusing them create a mockery, a masque of death. Note the second 'traveler's' [sic.] response. Tennyson is accused of loving not his lost beloved, but the modes of his apparent mourning. When he exchanges his melancholia for proper mourning, he opts not to gather the substitutive wreath, and the pastoral cycle of Christmas, a repetitive rhythm throughout the poem, becomes estranged to him.[19] He then adds, 'No more shall wayward grief abuse / The genial hour with mask and mime'.[20] He is right to note that grief strays from normality, but incorrect to assume that the negation of the pastoral playing at mourning is necessarily a negation of trope in favour of the actual. Elegy does not negate thanatropism, it contracts the contiguous thanatropic powers of the pastoral and allegorical realm into more familiar associative tropes. Our reaction to loss, in elegy, becomes our loss. The poem is both a substitute for the lost beloved and a process of commenting on this. It becomes self-devouring and in many ways this apparently healthy way of mourning is more threatening to subjectivity than pastoral melancholia.

I want now to consider modern, Christian elegy not as part of a generic continuum but actually as a violent imposition and abbreviation of the double thanatrope of the pathos of pathology. The singular, organic trope of the elegiac monument typified by Tennyson's *In Memoriam* embodies this violent imposition fully. Eric Smith begins a debate on the ethical nature of expressions of loss through his 'consolation conundrum'. Sacks taught us to consider the ancient origins of tropic substitutions in our cultures, while Lambert and Poggioli alerted us to the topographical significance of the pastoral realm. Smith, inadvertently, calls our attention to that which is lost. Tropes of contiguity and vegetable syntaxes retain a physical and causal relation to the lost beloved. They try to connect with loss, even though this is impossible. Within elegy, the poem is supposed to stand as a form of consolation, it forgets about the lost love object and is designed to heal. This aggressive self re-making has the virtue of a cruel honesty: what do the dead matter compared to the living? However, because elegy either openly or implicitly flouts respect for the other, both the lost beloved as other and death as the ultimate in otherness, it tends to force our attention onto the other. So Smith describes how if the poem acts as a form of consolation one loses one's loss and one's love, and this is bad. However, consolation is what we seek, so the elegy has our best interests at heart. Its medicine may be sour, but it works.

Note then the conundrum of occupation which elegy presents us with. The poem is simultaneously a substitute for the absent thing, a laurel wreath, and a substitute for the hysterical, repetitious utterance of real sorrow, the pipe. It is both beyond and before the actual absent thing. The pipe becomes the laurel, the song is all the monument we need. In gaining this organic and economic mode of consolation, one loses any pretence of connection with the other. Trope and topos, wreath and pipe, lost object and losing subject, are fused into one significant act. So, when Tennyson rejects the wreath and mocks his self-indulgent piping, rather than rejecting the generic conventions of elegy, he is modernising the oaten expression of the pastoral into a self-sufficient associative/symbolic mode of mourning.[21] The causal tropes of the pastoral tradition, suggestive of a degree of attention to the actuality of loss, are displaced by new, personal tropes of loss, things the mourning subject associates with the lost beloved that are personal to the subject. There is no longer any physical reason why the elegy can stand in for what is missing, instead it is all psychic association. Elegy does not come from the pastoral/ vegetable world, it attacks it. The assumed, quasi-organic continuum from the pastoral to the elegy is false. Elegy's generic relation to the pastoral is not genetic but parasitic and critical: the pastoral reaches out its hand to otherness and elegy jumps on it.

Considering the thanatropic base of elegy reveals that this establishes the pathology of pathos as the normative category of modern, European mourning at the expense of the pathos of pathology, now called depression. Smith makes it clear that the modern, Christian world is devoid of sympathy and pity:

> When, by way of consolation, the apotheosis of the beloved, or the prospect of jumping the hateful boundary between life and death so as to make renewed contact, is the final triumphant impression, human life is liable to be diminished. The passing of sorrow obstinately seems to be the death of love.[22]

To love one must diminish oneself anyway, this is a law of desire, so the death of the beloved should set the mourning subject free. As Tennyson argues, mourning is something the subject does to show off; death gives the subject a brief, unified sense of itself. The subject can make a show of love, but because that love cannot be returned the subject is liberated from the economy of desire that diminishes its sense of itself through scission and difference. In a sense Smith is right about consolation, but is this a conundrum? To jump the gap and follow the lost beloved up the ascending vortex of apotheosis (we are dealing with Christian elegy), *would* seem to require a diminishment of human life, but it is arguable as to whether elegy is a humanist discourse at all, despite Shaw's overriding argument. Smith talks of the jump as melancholia and also as pastoral,[23] but he is using the wrong metaphor. Melancholics do not jump the gap into the world of death, rather they linger in the world of death a little longer. This is a major difference in the perception of elegy in the modern world and the generic history of elegy which contravenes Shaw's argument that the best theory of elegy is elegy itself. The pastoral is all about staying put. Modern elegy is aggressive and proactive, either making mad leaps into the unknown world, arrogantly demanding proof of the lost beloved's continuing existence with God, or trying its best to get over the lost beloved by killing it again. If, as Derrida notes, after death the other exists in us, effectively splitting us so that it finally comes to rest between us in the chasm it has torn in the textured fabric of our false being, one must evacuate it to move on. This is what the modern elegy does.

Smith notes that there are two 'patterns' of elegiac consolation, the apotheosis and the memorial. Both seem directed towards the other, but in fact both aim at protecting the subject. Apotheosis is a means of packaging death and of packing the dead off into a realm which, due to its nature as radically other and literally life threatening, is off limits to the living subject.

The memorial is the method of commenting on this:

> Thus the elegy which arrives at a consolation does not leave us with consolation and say that the problem is solved. It presents us with the quest, inseparable from its ending in the work of art. The building of the tomb ... and the decking with flowers ... represent the producing of the expressive monument in words.[24]

Theorists of elegy note that elegy is a heuristic method of enquiry,[25] and for Smith this is the conundrum at its heart. The mourner wants to get well, but doesn't want to lose their loss. Traditionally, and Smith's analysis is very traditional, this puts the subject in a favourable light by suggesting they are truly committed to their love. The monument fills in the gap which the subject would be unwise to leap over. The tomb goes up and flowers are placed on it so that the subject does not have to ascend into the metaphysical realm of Christian apotheosis, literally die, nor make of itself a melancholic pastoral allegorist, a living death. In this instance the flowers are not contiguous tropes, not pastoral at all, but as the cynical traveller suggests in *In Memoriam*, they are just for show.

Smith correctly identifies elegy as anti-pastoral and anti-melancholic in its associative fusing of the tropes of loss and expression into one unified and reified monument. He goes on to describe the pastoral realm as a kind of Benjaminian asymbolic nightmare of nature, an endless and accelerating system which may retain the other, but directly at the expense of the subject's sense of unity and presence:

> The dissolution of the body brings to the forefront that side of man which is in the grip of the elemental forces whose purposes, compared with those which a conscious man may set himself, are so obscure ... The one thing which appears to be exempt from rebirth is conscious being. Thus the conservation of Nature's store in endless cycles is not calculated to inspire confidence in the immortality, the eternal significance, of the individual ... In Western poetry ... the possibility of a series of rebirths moving towards no end is a possibility of endless separation from the beloved, an eternity without the finality of perfection to make it acceptable. This prospect appears to be of an unearthly game of tag.[26]

While Smith denies the very process of dejecta, letting the physical fall so the spiritual can ascend which Kristeva sees at the heart of melancholia,[27] he also rejects the much less controversial act of mourning. The rhythm of birth and death, or of an endless series of rebirths suggesting an endless separation from the beloved, is actually Freud's healthy work of mourning. It is good to lose for then one can gain anew, and this economy is desire. There is no finality or perfection in desire, it is the *fort/da* logic. Love is an endless game of emotionally demanding tag.

Ultimately Smith can only think of elegy through vegetable logic. He conceives of the relation between the beloved and the subject as causal and contiguous so that after the beloved's death, one either keeps hold of the cadaver and destroys oneself – Derrida's being-between-us – or one casts off the dead and loses that love for good – Kristeva's sense of the dejecta or abject; that which we put aside in order that we may live.[28] However, his consolation conundrum raises important questions for elegy. Elegy is a process of conflation through association not combination through contiguity, which is the pastoral way. Elegy replaces loss with the subject's monumentally expressed loss. It doesn't take death back into the city but re-places death in the distant countryside, and dis-places the lost beloved with a short-hand form. Death and love become one in the subject's thoughts; proximity to either is mocked and parodied. Elegy's maturity is that it has nothing good to say about either force. It is less a genre, more a critical comment on a genre.

The process of thanatropism is a negotiation between positive and negative forces in language, and the enunciation of subjectivity through this negotiation between presence and absence. While the two sides, metonymic and metaphoric, seem to fall neatly into a temporal continuum from the pagan, through the classical, to Christian and finally atheistic expressions of grief, this history is false. The history is not one of faith but of the problems of responsibility to another human being, and to oneself when confronted with radical loss. Sacks deals directly with this in a move which is brave within elegy theory as it pitches mourning rituals simultaneously at the lost beloved and the losing subject:

> If the mourned *subject* of elegy is made to yield a pipe, a reborn flower, or even a stellar influence, the elegist's *own* transaction of loss and gain must, as we have seen, also work toward a trope of sexual power. Hence a remarkable convergence upon the originally sexual figure of consolation, and all its allegorical variants. It is the locus, so to speak, of this figure that the elegist erects or inherits his legacy from the dead. Indeed the figure *is* his legacy.[29]

The emphasis here is different from Smith's sense of the monument: the figures of elegy while seeming to be a typical appropriation of radical absence by the structures of presence, could be seen instead as a kind of a gift. Typically, for Sacks, the 'figure' is made to play a number of roles. In terms of a metonymic phallic figuration it begins the traditional dynamic of desire, yet it is also Smith's elegiac monument simultaneously testifying to immortality and to lack. Further, as Sacks makes clear, the subject inherits the process of figuration from loss: the figure is language itself. Mourning is, in Sacks' final analysis, the right of inheritance: giving the dead nothing, it takes from them the figure of their power. It mortifies the already dead by stealing the dead's one spark of continuing existence, that of a kind of immortality. While rebirth is supposedly actuated in the elegiac monument, it is in fact here that the poet robs the loss of its last vestiges of life. No wonder, then, that the successful mourner is consoled. They inherit their consolation and their consolation is the act of figurative supplement. They are consoled by the very idea of what consolation is. They inherit a part of loss.

Yet inheritance suggests a legal bind between two subjects, so the legacy of the figure is what the lacked other presents to the subject. The subject takes life from the other, but the other just as freely gives it up. Derrida in *The Gift of Death* talks of an unreturnable gift as the essence of the ethical position, as it places the other beyond our possessively troping grasp. Instead of our reaching out to touch loss, loss touches us, and in place of a monument constructed to leap over the gap of death, we have a gift sent over from the other side. This gift, the art of losing in language, ought to be the future role of a postmodern, ethical elegy. Shaw and Ramazani both take such an approach to the problem of modern elegy. Ramazani's phrase 'melancholic mourning'[30] conveys the ethical reluctance we have in all three eras of thanatropism: the trope as metonymic substitute, the pastoral realm as a location for encountering real loss, and the consolatory paradox of the monument. He describes modern elegies as notable 'in their fierce resistance to solace, their intense criticism and self-criticism ... unlike their literary forbears or the "normal mourner" of psychoanalysis, they attack the dead and themselves, their own work and traditions ... Scorning recovery and transcendence, modern elegists neither abandon the dead nor heal the living.'[31] Ramazani's position is half-way towards the other *as* other, and is brought about by the radical generic disjuncture between the thanatropes of the pastoral and those of elegy. In a sense modern elegy takes up the pastoral again to counteract the critical sorties elegy has made on the pastoral since Romantic elegy.

Shaw tries another approach through what he calls alternately 'wit' or 'pragmatic criticism'. He updates Todorov's classic structuralist account of genre as something which theorises itself as it goes along, leaving us as critics merely to observe and describe:

> Any study of elegy is a study of genre; and generic criticism is a traditional enemy of the literary text. To correct the tendency of a generic critic to search for axioms and norms, the rhetorical critic shows how elegies are as distinctive as a tremor of grief, or a shock wave of pain, and are never wholly explicable in general terms alone.[32]

Again this is a quasi-ethical position. In relation to 'wit criticism', Shaw proposes, by way of an experiment, that we do not read elegies in terms of how they fit into theoretical genre-markers, but instead ask what happens to these poems when read in this way: by implication, what fractures do they reveal in genre theory and to what degree, therefore, do the specific poems in elegy truly constitute the generic theory of elegy? It is a process of asking not so much what our theory of elegy can do for elegies, but what elegies themselves can do for us as theorists of elegy.

So, do we have a new thanatrope on the horizon, and if so, as elegy utilises both sides of the tropic set, metonymy and metaphor, what is its nature? We know that it accepts no substitutes for death and that it cannot easily occupy the pastoral topos, or the elegiac monumental world; in fact it sets the pastoral, contiguous world of absence against the elegiac, associative world of presence. The subjects who mourn are subject to the pathos of their pathology; they love their loss because they love what absence has done to them, made them less whole and so more wholly themselves. And while they replace the other, artificially keep them alive, or trope them out of existence with monumental metaphors, the other *still* loves them. If theory is what elegy gives to genre theory on elegy, and the figure is the unreturnable legacy the other gives, then surely the next thanatrope is elegy theory itself.

A thanatrope is a gift given to us, something which stands in for death in some way, and theory seems to be the postmodern way. Returning to our original paradox, the poppypetal, we can reconceive elegy. Who is the subject and what the object in Theocritus' poem: who is 'thee'? The anaphoric replacement of the lost beloved, Amaryllis, with the pronoun 'thee' begins with the first line of the poem, and by the time the lover gets to the poppypetal, the 'thee' of his musing becomes the heuristic 'thee' of the Romantic elegist: a self seeking a greater truth about itself by seeming to quest after another. This construction is emphasised by the object of the elegist's musing, the smear of a petal against his arm. The poet seems to be thinking about the other and interacting with the world of objects wherein the other resides. Yet his response is linguistically and physically a violent rejection, eliding the name of his lover from the first line, and destroying the possible substitutive trope of the petal. For the poet the petal stands in for his loss, his love-in-absence. It does not fill up his loss with a substitutive trope: the petal has no physical contiguity to Amaryllis, and there is no apparent psychic association between his lost love and a poppy. It is not a monument to what is lost, but an ephemeral mark of loss itself. Further, its mark is self-erasing, that is to say there never was a mark. The petal can never be made to yield up any of its pigmented essence. It remains radically unknown by the subject.

A ritual mourner would have considered the withering of the petal as a symbol of how we are all part of nature's cycle. A pastoral melancholic, how this contiguity of the lover to love-in-absence keeps love alive in death. A traditional elegist would see the self-wounding strike as a threat to the self, and elevate the battered petal as a symbol of apotheosis. In each case the subject's 'thee' upon which it muses is effectively its own mortal being. However, what does the poppypetal give? Nothing of itself, it leaves no smear. When one strikes it one ends up striking oneself. The lover's 'thee' upon which he muses is the nonmark made on him by his absented love. I would propose this as the new thanatrope that elegy can give us, a trope of non-troping, a trope for the other given to us by the other in such a way that we cannot return it. When it withers away we are left with no substitutive mark of the absent, no presence of absence, only the uncanny feeling of the three-part logic of a true elegy of otherness: one that does not seek to name the other and thus reduce them, one that cannot touch on the other and so try to link up to them, and one that leaves no consolatory smear, only the non-mark of love-in-absence. Love is encountered as the still-absent, always there in its not being there, never to be recovered.

ADRIENNE JANUS

Mnemosyne and the Mislaid Pen

The Poetics of Memory in Heaney, Longley and McGuckian

There is little so striking for someone involved in the study and appreciation of literature as the moment when two equally vibrant, equally compelling worldviews confront each other over the proper treatment of their shared territory. During a conference called 'A Day of Irish Poetry', held at Stanford University on 4 May 2000, two worlds collided over what one should do with, to, or for, Irish poetry. Representing the first world, the academic world, were three of the most esteemed critics of Irish poetry. As they read their papers, papers tracing with finesse the literary-historical context of the Irish poets in question, or examining with immeasurable insight, tact and humour the cultural politics surrounding Irish poetry, members of the audience scribbled furiously as they attempted to transcribe or remember accurately the speakers' main ideas. The talks ended amidst loud applause, but before questions could be voiced, a representative of what might be called the second world, the world of practicing poets, stood up, and the two worlds were set upon their collision course. The poet began to speak, first quietly, in the measured autobiographic tones of a venerable elder. Then the tempo of his speech increased, his gestures became more expansive, the tone of his voice moving between serious, almost melodramatic concern, and a slightly mocking anger. The audience laughed frequently at his particularly comic turns of phrase, nodded and murmured their assent or disagreement, clapped or whooped appreciatively when the poet paused for breath after a particularly astounding piece of rhetoric. The poet spoke for over ten minutes, and to all appearances, it was an impromptu performance – an entirely memorable, yet unrepeatable occasion. The meaning of his argument was nevertheless simple: to understand poetry properly, he seemed to say, academics should pay less attention to the complexities of cultural or literary history and instead study the particular habits of the poets themselves, what they were eating, drinking, listening to when they composed their poems, whom they loved and whom they despised. The audience waited in expectant silence for the academics to respond. But the academics, like the audience, were virtually silent. They didn't necessarily disagree with the poet, but neither could they agree. The two discourses belonged to two different, seemingly irreconcilable worlds.

The tension between these two discourses – the space of silence between the two worlds signaling the difficulty or indeed the impossibility of resolving such tension – might best in this context be described as the tension between the first world that understands poetry, and poetic memory, as something having to do with written literary or cultural history; and the second world that treats poetry, and the poetics of memory, as rituals of performance and habit. The attribution of the former type of discourse to the first world, one in which literature and memory have to do with semantics and cognition, is not arbitrary. It has dominated Western thought throughout most of history: from Plato and his description in the 'Theaetatus' of memory as a wax tablet, upon which images and ideas are coded and recalled, externalised and translated into another form for interpretation; to Freud's mystic writing pad, a figure for the way in which perception inscribes memory traces upon consciousness as an endless process of writing and rewriting; to Hegel's privileging of memory as 'gedächtnis', a memory narrative that sublates itself into the highest form of universal spirit as the philosophy of history.[1] In a general sense, memory of this sort seems to be conceived as a kind of filing log upon which memory traces are inscribed hierarchically, an arrangement which in itself involves an intellectual operation dependent upon the power of judgement. Accurate memory retrieval then would seem to entail an act of interpretation which must free the memory trace, so that it may be properly reflected upon, from its imbeddedness in the affective bedrock that allowed its initial incorporation into a lower, less conscious, level of memory. Memory freed from the economy of form and affect and constituted in terms of semantics thus transforms itself easily into history – first as collective historical memory and then as an (apparently) objectivised universal history. Indeed, these two types of memory-history might easily describe the general tendencies of literary criticism in, respectively, Ireland and America. For if in Ireland poetry for the most part tends to be interpreted with regard to a particular cultural and socio-political encoded memory, moving endlessly between canonisation and revisionism; in America, particularly with the new criticism which still retains firm footing amongst those who specialise in poetry, whether Irish poetry or otherwise, literature tends to be read as encoding a universalisable history, the history of human truths which the tools of critical dialectics assemble around the scaffolding of the poetic paradox and the intentional fallacy. Although Yeats may be a canonical figure for both sides, the material of preference for the first side would seem to consist of poems such as 'Easter 1916' and 'Meditations in Time of Civil War', while for the second, later poems such as 'Among School Children' and 'The Statues' stand as the poetic matter of choice.

What literary critics on both sides of the Atlantic generally tend to overlook, or to relegate to a lower order of concern, is that if poetry and memory have a particularly unique relationship, one different from that of standard prose, or other narrative genres, it is a relationship that unfolds under the aegis of that figure of the second world, Mnemosyne, the goddess of memory and the mother of the muses. Unlike the first, semantically conceived type of memory, this second type of memory seems closer to perception and performance: it demands – or even provokes in the passive subject – synthetic acts of incorporation and recollection in which affect, the impossibility of separating mind from body, meaning from its material form, dominates. Although this type of memory has received more critical attention on the continent than in the Anglophone world, its privileged place remains more the field of poetics than theory. While the involuntary memory of Proust comes immediately to mind as one of the most famous modern instantiations of Mnemosyne (the famous episode of the 'petite madeleine' stylistically more prose poem than prose), theoretical accounts of this type of memory inevitably designate it to the lowest levels of thought and socialisation. Bergson's conception of habitual memory as varied repetition and automatic action, for example, although acknowledging the role of perception in human memory, stands in tension with what he terms 'true memory' (mémoire pure), memory as representation and narrative.[2] Sartre more explicitly associates memory with poetry when he writes: 'memory presents to us the being which we were, accompanied by a plenitude of being which confers on it a sort of poetry.'[3] But for Sartre this appears to be a negative association: poetry's synthesis of affectively charged idea and material form somehow correspond to the illusory and dangerous incorporation of the transcendent 'pour-soi', the being-for-itself which is free in its intellectual capacity to negate the present and project itself into the future, into the essential facticity of the 'en-soi', the existent dominated by the necessity of an already determined past.

With these few examples, the tension between Mnemosyne's offspring and what I have called first-world memory, between memory as perception and performance and memory as conception and representation, is evident. Yet the precise nature of the relationship between memory and poetry has not yet been fully explored in its particularity: for the most part, even in theoretical texts, it remains couched in poetic figures that testify silently to its enduring importance. In order to explore the relationship between poetry and memory in greater detail, and to bring the tension between the two types of memory into sharper relief, this paper formulates a typology of memory with reference to the poetry of Seamus Heaney, Michael Longley and Medbh McGuckian. Not only do many poems in their oeuvre provide rich material for a study of memory, they also exemplify the ways in which poetry may negotiate with an environment in which the tensions between types of memory, and between contending versions of memory and history, are particularly evident.

The most basic level of memory would seem to be that instigated by, and potentially remaining within the confines of, immediate sense perception: namely, the passive, or unconsciously registered, reception of visual and auditory sequences. Pattern retention of this sort, which, in the terminology of cognitive science has been called, respectively, iconic and echoic memory, would seem to function even below the level of what has been called 'short-term memory'. Indeed, studies in cognitive science have shown that visual or auditory sequences may be retained as iconic or echoic memory only within a lapse of five seconds from the sequences' initial reception; whereas a sequence of non-equivalent images or sounds perceived within the five-second lapse of time serves effectively to disrupt the recall function, repetition at some interim moment within the five seconds of the same visual or aural pattern greatly increases the chance of the pattern being retained in short-term memory.[4] Regardless of whether such empirical studies are exact or not, the general description of iconic and echoic memory serves to isolate what might be the most basic memory function in poetry. Echoic memory in poetry could be described as the reception, unconscious retention and anticipation, of tonal and rhythmical patterns within a line; iconic memory as the reception, unconscious retention and anticipation, of visual image patterns within a line. The line break would then function as a figurative 'five-second delay', with the visual and auditory patterns of the next lines serving to reinforce or disrupt the initial pattern set up by the first line. Whether reinforced or disrupted, the patterns that serve iconic and echoic memory can be said to have an affective impact that functions to heighten sense perception and emotional response, whether or not the patterns are conciously perceived or understood as constituting meaning.

In Longley's 'Remembering Carrigskeewaun', the reinforcement of iconic and echoic memory between the first and second lines indicate affectively a certain type of perceptive memory that will be embodied later in the poem by exemplary figures representative of this type of memory:

> A wintry night, the hearth inhales
> And the chimney becomes a windpipe
> Fluffy with soot and thistledown,
> A voice-box recalling animals:
> The leveret come of age, snipe
> At an angle, then the porpoises'
> Demonstration of meaningless smiles.
> Home is a hollow between the waves,
> A clump of nettles, feathery winds,
> And memory no longer than a day
> When the animals come back to me
> From the townland of Carrickskeewaun,
> From a page lit by the Milky Way.[5]

The opening line sets up a sequence of auditory and visual patterns which the next line effectively reinforces. On the level of echoic memory, the rhythmical pattern is an iambic quadrametre, a pattern whose short foot-length and heavy second beat carries the first line quickly over the break to the second line. This second line, with a dominating anapestic rhythmical pattern of two unstressed beats followed by one long stressed beat would seem to quicken, but not to disrupt the overall pattern of the first line. Echoic memory in regards to tonal patterns works similarly between the first and second lines. The short 'in' in w**in**try/**in**hales and the aspirate 'h' of

hearth/in**ha**les build up to the second line which repeats, in a slightly variant form, the pattern of the first line, as 'in' re-emerges in ch**imn**ey/w**in**dpipe. In 'windpipe', furthermore, iconic and echoic levels merge. Not only does the aspirate 'h' pattern of the first line reappear, softened into the voiced semi-vowel [w] of 'windpipe'; but the visual patterns given by the first line – the opposition of cold and hot associated with wintry/hearth, the breathing image of 'inhales' – recur as the funneling of hot/cold/breath in the sequence chimney/wind/pipe. The confluence of iconic and echoic levels between these two lines would seem to give rise to an immediate sense perception, a perception of a moment seemingly out of all time except that which is marked by the rhythm of the line. At this point in the poem, Carrigskeewaun is remembered not as an image from the past, but as a currently felt presence, a presence that emerges and passes on the level of pure sense perception.

In the next lines of the poem, the patterns set up by the first lines appear translated into what seems to be a metaphor, but might as well be a functional description: the funelling image of hot/cold/breath of the chimney's windpipe in the first two lines reappears as 'A voice-box recalling animals'. In the recollection of animals that follows – 'The leveret come of age, snipe / At an angle, then the porpoises' / Demonstration of meaningless smiles' – the leveret, snipe and porpoises here seem to be embodied carriers of the poet's desire: for them, home is not a concept, but a sensually recognised physical environment: 'Home is a hollow between the waves, / A clump of nettles, feathery winds, / And memory no longer than a day'. As we see from this last line, memory, too, for these animals, whether of home or otherwise, is reduced to immediate sense recollection, lacking the extension of time into a distant past. The animals – especially the porpoises, with their 'Demonstration of meaningless smiles', smiles that may have a sensual or emotional impact but communicate nothing – might well be the poetic compatriots of Nietzsche's animals who, he writes, 'do not know what yesterday and today are but leap about, eat, rest, digest and leap again; [they are] enthralled by the moment'. These animals, in their happy absorption in their immediate sensual needs and desires, are, according to Nietzsche, objects of fascination and wonder for man:

> Man may well ask the animal: why do you not speak to me of your happiness but only look at me? The animal does want to answer and say: because I always immediately forget what I wanted to say – but then it already forgot this answer and remained silent: so that man could only

wonder. But he also wondered about himself, that he cannot learn to forget but always remains attached to the past.[6]

One feels that this is what the poet wonders too, a question implicitly driving the poem's composition and the poet's identification with the animals. The power of this identification, and of man's desire to detach himself from the past to live in the immediacy of the moment, is belied only by the title of the poem: 'Remembering Carrigskeewaun'. Remembering here locates Carrigskeewaun in an inaccessible past, and indicates both the poet's will, and his failure, to relive through poetry this past as though it were still present, to take revenge, as Nietzsche says, against 'time and time's "it was"'.[7]

Although what we have termed iconic and echoic memory may be said to rely in a certain fashion upon pattern repetition, the scope of these is restricted to the sphere of particular, individual (or socially unmediated), and highly transitory moments. A more durable, more encompassing, type of pattern repetition may be occasioned when perception is mediated by continued interaction with relatively stable objects in the environment, objects which at this level of non-semantically constituted interaction may be said to include people in the social environment. Pattern repetition in this case would consist of habits of speech and visual recognition, habits of movement (such as gesture or coordinated action), and affective dispositions, such as reactions of pleasure or disgust.[8] These are carried out under normal conditions on a pre-reflective level and may be said to serve an integrative function between individuals and their environments, although disturbances to the individual or in the environment may facilitate post-facto recognition on a conscious level.

Memory in this case, as repetition and action, may be said in poetry to consist in several aspects. The most basic would be the repetition of tonal and rhythmical patterns within the stanza or poem as a whole, patterns which may be either sustained or disturbed by those informing iconic and echoic memory. These larger tonal and rhythmical patterns in turn may be recognised as coordinate with verse patterns that make up an institutionally sanctioned literary-cultural tradition (the sonnet or ballad form, for example), with the general habits of style of a smaller, immanently constructed socio-cultural community of artists, or simply with the particular habits of style repeated throughout a part or the whole of a poet's oeuvre. In reference to the latter case, one can cite Michael Allen's study of the use of iambic stress patterns in Michael Longley's early work;[9] or, similarly, in

Longley's later work, the frequent use of nominative lists in poems such as 'The Ice Cream Man' and 'The Greengrocer'.[10] In a similar vein, one can compare Longley's classicism to Heaney's use of Dante as a structural backdrop; or Longley's lists to Heaney's use of compound nouns. The stylistic habits of McGuckian have most often been characterised in terms of a linguistic hermeticism, or as a poetic idiolect: this style, in turn, seems contingent upon the particular habits of perception that inform her poetry, habits such as the use of iconic patternings and of imagistic, rather than semantic, associations as a structural organising principle. In each case, Longley's classicism, Heaney's use of Dante, and McGuckian's hermeticism, all may be seen as habits cultivated as a way of negotiating between the particular needs of poetry and the larger demands of the environment in which that poetry finds its place.

This type of negotiation, between the particular and the environment, between the poet, poetry and community, also occurs through the incorporation of practices of repetition and action external to the field of poetry: the inclusion in a poem, for example, of habitual patterns of speech or gestures of a community. Michael Longley's 'Wounds',[11] for example, turns around memories associated with certain communal patterns of speech: in the first case, the phrases cited in the opening lines, 'Fuck the Pope', 'No Surrender', 'Give 'em one for the Shankill' – phrases remembered from a father's participation in World War I yet still persistent in contemporary communal language – figure as pre-reflective habits, drained of meaning except as an almost gestural accompaniment to 'bewildering' violent action. These ritualised phrases are played off against another phrase at the end of the poem – 'sorry missus' – a phrase equally recognised as belonging to communal speech habits, yet one indicative of a different, meliorative ritual action: although as semantically empty as the first phrases, and disempowered as a speech act as those first phrases are not, it yet performs affectively a potentially healing, sensical gesture in the midst of a violent, nonsensical situation. In a similar vein, the inclusion of habitual speech patterns in Seamus Heaney's 'Station Island' – Kavanagh's 'good man yourself'; 'sure I might have known once I had made the pad, you'd be after me ...' in section v, for example, – can be seen as a way of negotiating between the claims of differing communal linguistic habits, between those, as section XII's encounter with Joyce implies, who would say tundish instead of funnel, and the artist's claim, pronounced by Heaney's Joyce, that 'the English language belongs to us'.[12]

It might be said that Heaney's 'Station Island' as a whole can be read as a poem of memory as much as of poetic vision, enacting, with its Dantean references, a purgatorial journey involving a process of cleansing, forgetting and redemptive remembering. The river Lethe of the Dantean Purgatory may be seen to be invoked by the water images of sections VII and VIII, sections concerning guilt and responsibility for real or imputed wrongs; and Dante's river Eunoe seems figured by the image of the fountain in section XI, the central image of an affirming recitation of faith. But it is section III of the poem that most exemplifies a mode of interaction between the two types of memory already discussed, between the type of memory incorporated through immediate sense perception, and a more mediated type of memory constituted by time-based objects, between institutionalised habitual action and individually cultivated habitual action. A close analysis of the first line of section III, for example, reveals how echoic memory feeds into memory as repetition and action. With, 'I knelt. Hiatus. Habit's afterlife' (*SI*, 67), the poet performs a gesture that has been incorporated as an habitual unconscious reflex solicited by the poet's immediate, pre-reflective perception of his environment. The tone and rhythm here perform the trance-like state indicative of the automatic nature of the gesture, effectively forcing attention to the iconic and echoic patterns of the words rather than to their hermeneutic potential. The iambic rhythm of the words is slowed by the pauses between them, pauses that repeat the iambics silently, like a measured inhale of breath before its release with the aspirate 'h's of 'hiatus' and 'habit'; the repetition of these aspirates, of the long sighing 'i' sounds in I, hiatus, afterlife and of the short 'a' sounds in habit/afterlife, furthermore, demonstrate a high recurrence pattern indicative of the formalism of ritual language and create the expectation of iconic and echoic reinforcement in the next lines.[13]

In the following lines, however, where the descriptive content indicates a conscious recognition of the environment that inspired the habitual genuflection, a different sequence of auditory and visual patterns emerge:

> I was back among bead clicks and the murmurs
> from inside confessionals, side altars
> where candles died insinuating
>
> slight intimate smells of wax at body heat.
>
> (SI, 67)

Compared to the first line, there is an awkward, plodding heaviness in the rhythm of the lines here, an instability that is only partially resolved in the iambics of the last line of the stanza and, after the disruption of the line break, in the final beats of the first line of the next stanza. The relative instability of the rhythmical patterns sits oddly with the highly recurrent tonal patterns – the repetition of heavy b sounds (back/bead/body) and the close proliferation of hard and soft s's (was/clicks/murmurs; inside/ confessionals/side/altars; candles/insinuation; slight/smells). These tonal patterns merge with the patterns of visual imagery to give the impression of a close, warm darkness bearing down. The rhythmical awkwardness of these lines, especially compared to the smooth weight of the first line, seem indicative of an effort to throw off this weight, as though marking the incongruence between the actions of unconscious habit of the first line and the poet's discomfitting recognition of the environment that had initially solicited this habitual action. This disturbance – given by the overall lack of equilibrium in the iconic and echoic patterns of these first lines – might be said to signal an effort to re-establish equilibrium between the poet's individual thought and action and his environment. The effort to re-establish equilibrium, in turn, opens a space to another level of memory: against the impression of the almost claustrophobic closeness of the first lines, the visual patterns of the next lines indicate an airy, upward-moving lightness:

> There was an active, wind-stilled hush, as if
> in a shell the listened-for ocean stopped
> and a tide rested and sustained the roof.

> A seaside trinket floated then and idled
> in vision, like phosphorescent weed,
>
> (*SI*, 67)

The series of recollections that follow are occasioned not by immediate sense perception, but occur around another, mediating object of memory, the image of a seaside trinket. This object – 'a toy grotto with seedling mussel shells / and cockles glued in patterns over it' (*SI*, 67) – is associated with another kind of habitual action, perhaps tangential to, but not bound by, institutionalised religious commemoration: namely, the poet's personal habits of commemoration for a dead girl he once knew. In one sense, this shell as an object of memory figures metaphorically for the empty housing that memory provides for something once perceived immediately as a lifelike presence. Its hollowness as an object provides a mediating distance, a proximity without the equivalence that would compromise the poet's self-possession. On another related level, this object of memory, and the recollections it gives rise to, may be said to function as a coping mechanism, one brought into play to mediate disturbances between present perceptions ('bead clicks and murmurs / from inside confessionals') and the action this environment had incited ('I knelt'). This is indeed how Bergson describes the movement from habitual memory, sparked by immediate, unconscious sense perception, to a more mediate, and mediating, type of memory. Unconscious habitual action ordinarily allows us, he writes, to 'act our recognition before we think it'; memory as a mediator, in the form of images called up from the past, is normally dormant, 'always inhibited by our consciousness of the present moment, by the sensori-motor equilibrium of a nervous system connecting perception with action'. It only comes into play as a result of an incongruence between perception and action: 'this memory [memory as images called up from the past] merely awaits the occurrence of a rift between the actual impression and its corresponding movement to slip in its images'.[14] Between memory as unconscious habitual action and memory as the more or less involuntary recollection of images from the past, however, the differences are less striking than the similarities: in both, the subject is relatively passive, although the movement from the former to the latter is marked by increasing demands upon psychic energy. Both incarnations of memory, furthermore, have a coordinating function, in that the movement from memory as habitual action to memory as recollection is indicative of an attempt to negotiate an increase in the differences between the individual and the environment.

At this point, the specificity of the relation between poetry and memory, between Mnemosyne and the muses, can be described with more precision. On one level, the recurrence of sound and visual sequences in poetry can be seen as inherent to the facilitation of memory: this recurrence reduces the possible selection of tones, rhythms, images and words and coordinates them according to one or two general patterns, rather than to multi-faceted, un-patterned, and inherently ambiguous categories of meaning. The interruption of these sound and visual sequences, then, can be seen as blocks or complications to the functions of memory which, as modes of forgetting, might serve to move memory down a different path. Memory as repetition and action also relates specifically to poetry, although perhaps on a less evident level:

poetry not only may incorporate recurring behavioural sequences as habitual speech patterns, ways of seeing, gestural habits, and coordinate these into a cohesive form, but it can also be said to *perform* this coordination. Indeed, that the rhythmical sound patterns characteristic of poetry may induce a sort of bodily coordination has been proposed before: 'the simultaneous use of rhythmic speech', one study argues, 'facilitates the coordination of body movement among different individuals; it allows them, metaphorically speaking, to become a "collective subject"'.[15] Poetry in this way can be seen as a type of ritual action, the recurring patterns, not only of rhythm, but of tone and image, having an affective impact that may facilitate coordination between vehicle and recipient(s), poem and reader, speaker and listener.[16] Thus, poetry can be said to have a function analogous to that of the types of memory identified through our reading of poems thus far. Poetry and memory both may be said to perform the negotiation of complexity by first, reducing the number of different elements making up that complexity through pattern repetition, and second, by establishing possible levels of coordination between these elements and patterns, whether this coordination be physical, psychic, linguistic, or societal.

The tension between the poetic offspring of Mnemosyne and memory as written or narrated history might be said to be embodied in Medbh McGuckian's poem 'Slips', a tension that plays itself out more through the oppositions of iconographic patternings that structure the poem, than through what the poem offers to direct interpretation. Indeed, that the poem may have anything to do with memory is evident neither from the title nor from the first stanza, which seems simply a series of contingent, loosely associated images:

> The studied poverty of a moon roof,
> The earthenware of dairies cooled by apple trees,
> The apple tree that makes the whitest wash ...[17]

Only the qualification set up by the opening line of the second stanza, 'But I forget names', calls the reader's attention to the possible import of the first lines – as though demanding that the reader too engage in an act of recollection that would give shape and perhaps significance to the images already slipping from view with the ellipses that close the first stanza. In an odd, but striking manner, the shape that recollection confers upon this series of images is one that would seem to embody recollection itself: recollection as a series of collected objects that themselves figure as shelters, coverings or containers for a certain type of memory. The opening line of the poem, for example, 'The studied poverty of a moon roof', offers the moon as lunar shelter, the anthropomorphic attribution of 'studied poverty' to this shelter indicating a certain style of dwelling, an aesthetic or affective restraint, rather than a pecuniary impoverishment. Similarly, the second line of recollected images – 'The earthenware of dairies cooled by apple trees' – also fuses the organic, natural world with the human; but the sheltering image given by 'apple trees' is now chthonic rather than celestial, and implies a certain rich solidity that the moon roof in its 'studied poverty' lacked. The sheltered object itself is an earthen container, the image of whiteness once associated with the moon in the first line now perhaps transferred here in the dairy whiteness of that which the earthenware vessel holds. If these images are indeed memories, the third line points us towards the particular nature of the recollection: the image of the apple tree is here repeated – 'the apple tree that makes the whitest wash ...' – and the associated whiteness reappears incongruously attributed to the action of washing. Although these recollected images bear a certain homely solidity, a marked sensual presence, the meaning that might be attributed to them seems to have slipped away, washed white into a blankness despite (or because of) their containment of, or their dwelling in, the fullness of a perceptual recollection.

If the first stanza indicates the atemporal presence of images recollected through perceptual memory, the second is marked by the intrusion of a mutable temporality, and by an unstable, inorganic type of memory:

> But I forget names, remembering them wrongly
> Where they touch upon another name,
> A town in France like a woman's Christian name.

The opening of this stanza brings us into the realm of nomination, but a nomination that has lost its Adamic power: names here are easily misremembered, slipping from their referent, 'touch[ing] upon another'. The names in question, unlike the 'moon roof' and the 'earthenware of dairies', appear as nonessential, arbitrary coverings for human subjects or collectivities, coverings that cannot properly contain their contents.

Such arbitrary coverings for human subjects or collectivities reappear in the third stanza, not as names, but as narratives, narratives into which periods of time in the life of an individual or community are collected and, to a certain extent, preserved:

> My childhood is preserved as a nation's history,
> My favourite fairytales the shells
> Leased by the hermit crab.

'Childhood' stands on a level of equivalence to 'a nation's history', both of which are preserved as 'fairytales', fantastic fabrications that with the passing of time one no longer believes in, but which nevertheless provide a framework against which the past may be remembered. The metaphorical equation of these frameworks with 'the shells leased by the hermit crab', habitations that the living presence of an individual or community outgrows, leaving only the empty shell of memory, makes use of what appears to be a common trope in the poetics of memory. We have already seen its use in Heaney's 'Station Island', where a 'seaside trinket' made of 'mussel shells and cockles', precisely in being emptied of the living presence it nevertheless marks, serves as a mediating object for the poet's individual commemoration. These shells mark, in both poems, what Pierre Nora has termed 'lieux de mémoire': sites of memory, intentionally constructed memory frameworks which serve as surrogates for what he terms 'milieux de mémoire', or 'real environments of memory', where memory forms an organic part of a community's (or individual's) life cycle. Nora, too, makes use of the figure of the sea-shell to describe 'lieux de mémoire':

> if history did not beseige memory, deforming and transforming it, penetrating and petrifying it, there would be no lieux de mémoire – moments of history torn away from the movement of history, then returned; no longer quite life, not yet death, like shells on the shore when the sea of living memory has receded.[18]

For Nora, these 'lieux de mémoire' occur as signs of a culture's decay, the last vestige of 'real' or 'living' memory before instrumental history dominates all connection to the past and memory becomes simply a store of archival fragments detached from any living relation to the community or the nation: 'lieux de mémoire' are thus for Nora somewhere between memory and history. For Heaney and McGuckian, the sea-shell and the 'lieux de mémoire' it may be said to signify, suggest much more positive, and certainly more complex, relations to memory and to history. McGuckian's 'lieux de mémoire', the 'shells leased by the hermit crab', and the movement this image signals of a living presence slipping away from its habitual coverings, work in at least two ways. This movement may be seen as closure, as given by the image in the following lines, of 'my grandmother's death as a piece of ice', where death is the cold melting away of the coverings of life. But it may also occasion an opening into new life, a movement into a new habitation, as implied by 'my own key slotted in your door –'. Indeed, as the last stanza implies, the moments that will perhaps next live in memory are created precisely from the movement of a living presence slipping out from its coverings:

> Tricks you might guess from this unfastened button,
> A pen mislaid, a word misread,
> My hair coming down in the middle of a conversation.

These 'tricks' are life's sleight of hand as it discloses itself from the coverings of the everyday, from our conscious constructions and intentioned fabrications. As with 'an unfastened button', a bodily presence slips out from beneath the habitual coverings of clothes. With 'a pen mislaid, a word misread', motivating thoughts emerge from behind the coverings of language; or with 'hair coming down in the middle of a conversation', an unruly physical presence intrudes upon the effort to communicate, an intrusion which may, in itself, communicate in ways mere conversation does not allow.

Jean-Luc Nancy writes that:

> Art forces a sense to touch itself, to be this sense that it is ... by leaving behind the integration of the lived, it also becomes something else, another instance of unity, which exposes another world, not a 'visual' or 'sonorous' world but a 'pictorial' or 'musical' one ... This is the force of the Muses.[19]

Tracing through these poems a type of memory based on perception, repetition and action, recollection and 'lieux de mémoire', clarifies at least some aspect of the particular relationship between poetry and memory, and thus points towards that space of silence between Mnemosyne and the type of memory that cohabits the space of poetry: the inscribed memory of a collective or universal history. But perhaps that silence may only be filled by the poet, who, with a properly mislaid pen, finds a new way of writing into being the presence of something that may be sensed but never adequately communicated.

RICHARD KIRKLAND

Ways of Saying/Ways of Reading

Materiality, Literary Criticism and the Poetry
of Paul Muldoon

> No degree of knowledge can ever stop this madness, for it is the
> madness of words.
>
> PAUL DE MAN[1]

In the introduction to what appears to have been an after–dinner speech by Gayatri Chakravorty Spivak from 1985 she remarks upon our tendency to think of experience as story shaped, to 'read life and the world like a book'.[2] This compulsion extends from the 'so-called "illiterate"' to 'the politicians, the businessmen, the ones who make plans', and such is its significance to Western society that without it there would be 'no prediction, no planning, no taxes, no laws, no welfare, no war'. At one level this argument may appear to be little more than a mischievous inversion of the expressive realist fallacy that reads a book as if it were the world, but, as she develops her case, it is clear that this underplays the complexity of her parallel. In fact, for Spivak, the real difficulty with reading the world in this way is that we invariably imagine it as the wrong sort of book. We construct our consciousness and environment as if they were chapters of a rational textbook when, in fact, 'the world actually writes itself with the many-leveled, unfixable intricacy and openness of a work of literature'. Addressing her audience of Arts and Humanities academics directly, her conclusion is stark: 'if, through our study of literature, we can ourselves learn and teach others to read the world in the proper "risky" way, and to act upon that lesson, perhaps we literary people would not forever be such helpless victims.'

Even if one were unaware of the date of Spivak's talk, its description of the literary critic as some kind of abandoned waif locates it quite precisely as one of those crisis interventions about the state of literary studies that were much in vogue during the early 1980s. However, just as it reminds us of the ways in which all criticism takes place within the process of the institution, it also (and perhaps more interestingly) reveals something of Spivak's own intellectual inheritance. Inscribed in her sense that we read the world as if it were a book is a version of what Paul de Man famously termed the 'aesthetic ideology': our subconscious urge to shape disparate, stubborn and random events into a narrative of significance. Indeed, to develop the comparison, if the aesthetic ideology equates with the world as textbook, then the 'world as literature' to which she invites us to aspire is derived, in turn, from de Man's sense of 'the literary' as the resistance that is encountered in the reading of the specific text: that which prevents that work from becoming a mere illustration of a preconceived aesthetic position. It is the 'literary' that inserts itself as a disruptive force, an irreducible materiality, within those teleological models of criticism whose final judgements endorse an existent knowledge. For this reason, Spivak's sense of reading the world as literature, following de Man, is 'risky' because it has to allow for the materiality of language itself, that which creates 'unfixable intricacy' and which ultimately offers itself as a mode of resistance to formalist criticism and its assumptions. It is the materiality of the literary that forces us into inevitable misreadings, that troubles our sense of the critical enterprise and that keeps us awake at night.

Spivak, of course, has never been reluctant to acknowledge her debt to de Man's thinking but one of the reasons why her 1985 intervention is of interest is because it constitutes a rare attempt to apply his resolutely literary-critical thinking to a socio-political issue. Indeed, one way of gaining a perspective on de Man's overall critical project is to see it as an extended mediation on the relationship of ideas to the institution in which those ideas emerge. It is perhaps for this reason that one can detect in his work a continual anxiety about the effect unfettered thought might have on an academic career. As he notes in a comment only intensified by its ironic possibilities: 'Better be very sure, wherever you are, that your tenure is very well established, and that the institution for which you work has a very well-established reputation. Then you can take some risks without really taking many risks.'[3] This suggests that the individual act of reading that preoccupies de Man's later work can be better understood as an institutional act of reading; an analysis of what happens when the certainties of tenure – or what one should say when one is tenured – collide with the resistant, ultimately unteachable, text. It is for this reason that while de Man's work reveals to us a universe of misreadings, it ultimately lacks the grandiloquent ambition often found in the ethical (or, in de Manian terms, aesthetic) discourse of Cultural Studies. Instead, the borders of an individual's imaginative universe coincide with the intellectual parameters of the discipline; one containing the other.

That said, de Man's most significant critical legacy to Cultural Studies is his specific perception of materiality as refined in his later work. Indeed, for Terry Eagleton in a recent polemic, the dominance of the term has become symptomatic only of a 'suitably disenchanted' postmodernism. As a result, our concept of the 'material' has become so over-extended that 'it has now been stretched beyond all feasible sense', reaching a point where 'if even meaning is material, then there is nothing which is not, and the term simply cancels all the way through'.[4] Understood in this way, the overuse of materiality as a touchstone in textual analysis indicates only a dishonourable institutional discourse designed to say nothing while appearing to say everything: a way of finding a voice when one has nothing to say.[5] Although Eagleton's attack on the materiality of meaning clearly has a form of de Manian materiality in its sights, it would be unfair to place de Man's actual usage of the idea alongside the subsequent abusage that Eagleton identifies. In de Man's work, materiality is in fact a highly refined concept, and it is no great exaggeration to suggest that it becomes the key that allows us to decode his formidable late essays. However, in a twist typical of de Man, if we are to attempt such an enterprise we first have to invert our commonsensical notions as to what the 'material' is. As J. Hillis Miller has observed, in de Man's work materiality 'does not name the solid substance of physical materiality, open to the senses, nameable and manipulable at our will. It names a radical alterity that is not phenomenal, that is not the object of a representable intuition, that cannot be confronted or referentially, literally named. Other displaced names for this de Manian other are "death" or "the impossibility of reading".'[6] In this conception, materiality retains its familiar opposition with ideology but only insofar as it is, to return to Spivak, 'unfixable'. The 'bottom line', as de Man insists, remains 'the prosaic materiality of the letter'. Further consideration is futile as 'no degree of obfuscation or ideology can transform this materiality into the phenomenal cognition of aesthetic judgement'.[7]

How, then, does materiality disrupt the formal teleology of an aesthetic reading? Although the material aspect of language is precisely that which we cannot make known, its presence is identifiable by inadvertent linguistic slips, puns, and the random interconnections of words. As de Man observes, it is felt in 'the play of the letter and of the syllable, the way of saying . . . as opposed to what is being said'.[8] In these terms, materiality is that which evades the energies of aesthetic ideology but it is also the irreducible presence that provokes such ideology in the first instance. We can glimpse this process in our initial encounter with a text as that which flashes past us before we begin to 'read' (or perhaps I could say 'aestheticise'), but significantly we will always fundamentally misrecognise it. This is because we are the victims of what de Man calls an 'aesthetic education' that 'inevitably confuses dismemberment of language by the power of the letter with the gracefulness of a dance'.[9] As this implies, de Man is not concerned with the play of words and intentions that we call creative writing as such a discourse only gestures towards a greater absence that it cannot comprehend. Instead, an aesthetic education fools us into believing that the process of non-meaning revealed by reading is something we can contain and explicate. This is the 'dance' of reading, 'the fencing match of interpretation', that becomes 'the ultimate trap, as unavoidable as it is deadly'.[10]

It is clear that in de Manian terms, the materiality of a text can only draw attention to our persistent misreadings, to that which we are unable to say. However, while the imposition of the aesthetic ideology on the act of reading is an inevitability ('as unavoidable as it is deadly') and, as such, not an issue that one can take an ethical position on, de Man is much more scathing about those reading acts that are formalised within the institution – or, in other words, what we call literary criticism:

> The systematic avoidance of the problem of reading, of the interpretive or hermeneutic moment, is a general symptom shared by all methods of literary analysis, whether they be structural or thematic, formalist or referential, American or European, apolitical or socially committed. It is as if an organised conspiracy made it anathema to raise the question,

perhaps because the vested interests in literary studies as a respectable intellectual discipline are at stake or perhaps for more ominous reasons.[11]

While this slightly bizarre attack constitutes another example of the way in which de Man's thinking never moves too far from institutional politics, it also reveals his absolute confidence in his ideas. It is inconceivable that institutionalised literary criticism will not heed his warnings because it does not agree with them, instead such neglect must stem from secret motives and dubious alliances. The paradoxical nature of literary criticism derives from its necessity to uncover that which was already evident. It is in this way that criticism is an epiphanic activity in that, as de Man defines an epiphany, 'it reveals and unveils what, by definition, could never have ceased to be there ... it is the rediscovery of a permanent presence which has chosen to hide itself from us'.[12] The arrogance of the literary critical project means that it must find itself everywhere, must understand everything, but it can only do this by ignoring all that its practices cannot encompass.

It is, of course, hardly necessary to point out that this is far from what we *think* we are doing when we read. Rather than de Man's sense of reading as an agonising series of deceptions, when we encounter a difficult poem we hope that prolonged exposure to its seeming mysteries will result in a sudden moment of revelation, a glimpse of perfect understanding. In this process, the length of time expended attempting to understand the initial confusion of words is a necessary part of the overall reaction and in direct relation to the satisfaction we may ultimately take from the reading. As Wlad Godzich notes, such a model 'opposes the immediately apprehensible darkness of the sensible to the eventuality of the great clarity of the intelligible, yet makes the first the condition and the means of access to the second'.[13] This suggests that every act of reading re-enacts the defeat of a text's materiality (what Godzich also terms 'its verbal component') by the forces of rationality and formalism but it achieves this not by asserting that the verbal component is an irrelevance but rather by incorporating it into an overall aesthetic principle. Rather than being the uncovering of that which it has previously concealed, as de Man has suggested, literary criticism instead becomes a process of constant exploration and renewal. This is why, for Godzich, 'the eye remains trained on the darkness knowing it to hold a secret that the flash will disclose. The flash is not the secret but the occasion of the moment when all is in the light; the reward for peering into the dark.'[14]

One of the most interesting recent encounters with this allegory of reading has been in the poetry of Paul Muldoon. His poem 'Something Else' from 1987 is a text that conducts itself knowingly, or rather it displays the materials of its own unknowability and invites us to gaze upon them in the hope of a sudden (en)lightening:

> When your lobster was lifted out of the tank
> to be weighed
> I thought of woad,
> of madders, of fugitive, indigo inks,
>
> of how Nerval
> was given to promenade
> a lobster on a gossamer thread,
> how, when a decent interval
>
> had passed
> (*son front rouge encor du baiser de la reine*)
> and his hopes of Adrienne
>
> proved false,
> he hanged himself from a lamp-post
> with a length of chain, which made me think
>
> of something else, then something else again.[15]

In terms of Godzich's model of reading, 'Something Else' can be understood as a text that initially appears entirely impenetrable but that also, and simultaneously, offers the promise of a sudden enlightening at which point all that was previously dense will be revealed as ordered. As such, the 'verbal component' of the poem, its materiality, is that which has to be overcome if meaning is to emerge. Before the conscious act of 'reading' occurs, we attend to the text's muddle of word associations, half-rhyme and alliteration and glimpse de Man's 'play of the letter and of the syllable' as the barely perceptible shift of 'weighed' to 'woad' takes place in lines two and three. As I have already noted, when the moment of inspiration takes place the previous chaos of this play is not seen as an unnecessary distraction, something that has inhibited us, but rather as an integral precondition for the final achievement. However, this does not adequately account for the ingenuity of the work which lies instead in its reluctance to give up this transitive mode. 'Something Else', in fact, is a poem that sees settling upon a point of meaning to be no more than a version of death envisioned in both de Manian and literal terms.[16]

This suggests a particular form of critical reading. Our search for the solution to the maze of words (or, to use a Muldoon term, the 'key' to the poem) has to be enacted solely within the parameters of the text itself and, for this reason, one way of approaching 'Something Else' is as a wry comment both on this mode of formalist reading but also on the idea that there is a materiality to the text that such formalism cannot encompass. Understood as such, the 'key' to the poem – its moment of insight – is the sudden realisation we get that all its fleeting connections, its metamorphoses and its absences, occur as part of a strategy of avoidance: a solipsistic and futile attempt to avoid the awareness of death. The poem becomes a version of the classic Tolstoy conundrum that asks whether it is possible to stand in a corner for one hour and not think about a white bear. In cognitive psychology this mode of thought suppression is termed 'the rebound effect': the fact that when we deliberately try to suppress a thought we guarantee only its increased incidence.[17] This becomes a recurring strategy in forms of obsessive compulsive behaviour: an automatic response to an upsetting or damaging thought. The cognitive process that this suggests is not linear but rather one that jags backwards and forwards between the taboo thought and its immediate suppression. The more the protagonist tries to distract his mind from the imminent death of the lobster the more it is drawn back to the contemplation of the death itself so that, for instance, as the image of the reddening forehead occurs in line ten of the poem, so at that precise moment the lobster too is turning red; the moment of its death. As a result of this, 'Something Else' appears to dramatise the extreme mental state of an obsessive compulsive's preoccupation with death.

Discussing the reading strategies of 'Something Else' like this suggests that it is a poem engaged in the search for an ideal reader: a quest that typifies Muldoon's poetry in its entirety. Such a figure varies from work to work and from poem to poem: the questions asked of the child reader in his nursery poem *The Last Thesaurus*[18] are at least as daunting in their context as the examination faced by the adult (maybe highly trained) reader of *The Annals of Chile*.[19] Perhaps for this reason the ideal literary critic of Muldoon's work appears equally elusive. Anyone who has read Muldoon's own formidable, if engrossing, critical work *To Ireland, I*[20] will appreciate the intensity of the scrutiny he sees as integral to the discipline. As a result of the book's circuitous exploration of Irish literature, James Joyce's 'The Dead' is effectively reconstituted not as an autonomous text but rather as one whose significance derives from its location as a (albeit crucial) node in the vast web of texts and intertexts that constitute the canon. In this way Joyce's story is seen to enable a literary tradition (although Muldoon himself would never use such a portentous phrase) but only by distorting it. This is because Muldoon's criticism insists on the simultaneity of all the texts he considers. Their interdependence functions synchronically rather than diachronically and thus all are present at the scene of reading. For our purposes, the obvious value of such a deliberate literary critical strategy is that it suggests a method of reading Muldoon's own poetry, as well as inferring, perhaps, that previous criticism of Muldoon's work has not necessarily approached it in the ways that he would wish.[21] However, Muldoon's emphasis on what I have termed the synchronic reading does accord with Clair Wills' perception that the ideal reader of Muldoon's poetry must travel '*across* the canvas of the poem', must be 'open to contingent unpredictable encounters, taking pleasure in *accidental*, serendipitous *interconnections* of language' (emphases added)[22] – a strategy that takes us back to de Man's recognition of the materiality of the word and its 'play of the letter and of the syllable'.

A case can be made that the emergence and development of this synchronic tendency marks a crucial transformation in Muldoon's poetry that takes place in his three major volumes from 1983 to 1990: *Quoof*, *Meeting the British*, and *Madoc*. Centrally placed among these, *Meeting the British* can be seen as a transitional collection that charts Muldoon's move from a preoccupation with the relationship between politics and literature (that I am tempted to term the Longleyite reading[23]) towards a mode of poetry more amenable to the criticism of de Manian deconstruction.[24] While the former is illustrated by early Muldoon poems such as 'Lunch with Pancho Villa'[25] – and indeed has its valediction in the long poem '7, Middagh Street' from *Meeting the British* itself – the latter tendency is exemplified by the strategies of 'Something Else' from the same collection. I have already noted how in this poem 'weighed' and 'woad' function in de Manian terms as a moment of textual play but just as this comes within an act of reflection ('*When* your lobster [. . .] *I thought* of woad'), so the poem's engagement with de Manian reading paradigms as a whole is similarly double voiced. Wills has noted that 'Something Else' is a poem preoccupied with 'ways of articulating movement, the slippage from one state to another'.[26] For this reason, the 'madders' and 'fugitive' inks are 'reminders of disappearance, departure, things which do not last' just as they draw attention to the ink that marks the paper itself, the temporal position of the poem's status and perhaps its most obvious form of materiality. In these terms, the self-conscious deployment of an idea of materiality within the poem's structures (the 'Something Else' of the title) is based upon a reading of materiality as a concept which forces us to think about processes of change. As materiality draws attention to the act of things in process rather than the act of completion, so in this poem we are continually drawn not to the dead but rather to the act of dying – a distinction similar to de Man's sense of 'the way of saying ... as opposed to what is being said'.[27]

'Something Else', however, is more than just a playful dissection of the de Manian distinction between formalism and materiality. Just as this is a text constituted out of that which is left over after the moment of revelation, so it cannot enclose the readings it generates. To return to Godzich, the displacement of significance presented in the poem deflects attention 'away from itself onto the surrounding darkness whose internal composition it reveals'.[28] Our reading of this poem, as with any reading, draws our attention not to the coherencies we may assert but to the chaos we have ignored, or rather, cannot see, in order to frame it. This is where the knowing, ironic, structure of the poem deserts us. 'Something Else' is both a fifteen line sonnet (or rather a sonnet with a line attached) and, in a typically Muldoon way, a single sentence.[29] We are invited to find a position outside the boundary of the sonnet, a place from which we can begin meaning but this, in turn, is a place marked only by the 'something else' of the supplementary line. It is for this reason that the dialogue that begins the poem ('When *your* lobster') gives way as the nominal addressee is abandoned. These tensions are rendered most explicit in the poem's ending which constitutes a form of crisis as the active elements of the transformation (the dying as opposed to the death) run up against the formal necessity of having to make an ending, a conclusion. Not for nothing does Miller equate death with the de Manian 'impossibility of reading'.[30] This suggests one final definition of materiality. In financial accountancy the concept has its own precise usage defined as 'the magnitude of an item's omission or misstatement in a financial statement'.[31] While this is a definition that de Man would surely have approved of, it is one that also seems bizarrely appropriate to this poem in that this sense of materiality attempts to quantify the scale of an absence. The ultimate irony of 'Something Else' is that the flash of inspiration we may ultimately stumble upon is almost entirely useless – it points us only to 'death' and refuses to offer us any other form of wisdom, any kind of comforting narrative, in which this death can be accommodated. In these terms, the 'magnitude' of the poem's 'omission' is extremely great. As de Man suggests, all texts ultimately make us aware of such an unknowability, aware of that which lies beyond and threatens our reading, but it is the role of the aesthetic to at least offer some form of consolation, some strategic lie which tells us that the wisdom we have arrived at will at least enable us in some way.

In reading the poem in this way I am, of course, demonstrating nothing more than my own bewilderment. I have been bewitched by the dance of words into thinking that the play of the letter is something other than a brutal dismemberment. The aesthetic ideology is a trap into which we fall no matter how often we are warned of its dangers. 'Something Else' can no more reveal the darkness of what lies beyond it than any other text, but its significance, perhaps, lies in its lack of concern about this dilemma. It is a poem that lodges itself between mystification and knowledge, aware of its own collusion with formalist readings but also of the inevitable failure of such readings. Despite the fact that we always read as critics, always find narratives of significance, the lobster's death is discrete and will remain discrete no matter how many similar acts are forced to interconnect during the process of the poem. The aesthetic ideology that makes itself known through these violent couplings can only point to something beyond itself: its own lack, its failure to conclude.[32] Indeed, the inevitability of this process suggests in turn the futility of any attempt to evaluate its ethical dimensions. Our critical consciousness reconstitutes the narrative into which the lobster's death is placed for no other reason than because we are unable to do anything else. The point at which we think ourselves most in control, most able to read the world, is, in actuality, the moment when we yield what small amount of resistance we may once have possessed.

This awareness suggests something of the limits of the literary critical project as de Man understood it and perhaps also indicates why, for Spivak, 'literary people' remain 'such helpless victims'. Literary criticism is the pursuit least able to discover the riskiness of literature because of its necessity to discover in any individual text a certain a priori knowledge. As the epistemology of every critical school is rooted in the history of the institution from which it developed this could hardly have been otherwise. An aesthetic education is persistently reconfirmed and renewed by exposure to seeming challenges to its authority; threats which will inevitably be assimilated into its practices. In turn, such threatening texts (of which

'Something Else' is a good example) are reconstituted as good teaching material. Perhaps this explains why the nihilism of de Man's vision has gained relatively little purchase beyond the humanities faculties of American universities. If criticism is located in a place where representation is, instead, a contested, fragile and ultimately scarce achievement, or if one lacks the means to hold or negotiate power, de Man's positing of an ultimate unknowability, a boundary of non-understanding, may not provoke an excited shiver but rather a moment of despair. The paradox of the aesthetic as de Man posits it lies with the fact that the liberation of finding a narrative it provides is immediately compromised by the realisation that we are unable to shape it to our own ends. In this way, criticism becomes analogous to a dance in that it is a mode of freedom made manifest in preconceived moves. In fear that the dance will stop, that the literary critical enterprise will crumble, our readings will always find 'something else, then something else again'.

PAUL MULDOON

News Headlines from the Homer Noble Farm

I
That case-hardened cop.
A bull moose in a bog-hole
brought him to a stop.

II
From his grassy knoll
he has you in his cross-hairs,
the accomplice mole.

III
This sword once a share.
This forest a fresh-faced farm.
This stone once a stair.

IV
The birch crooks her arm,
as if somewhat more inclined
to welcome the swarm.

V
He has, you will find,
two modes only, the chipmunk:
fast forward; rewind.

VI
The smell, like a skunk,
of coffee about to perk.
Thelonius Monk.

VII
They're the poker-work
of some sort of woodpecker,
these holes in the bark.

VIII
My new fact-checker
claims that *pilus* means 'pestle'.
My old fact-checker.

IX
The Rose and Thistle.
Where the humming bird drops in
to wet his whistle.

X
Behind the wood-bin
a garter snake snaps itself,
showing us some skin.

XI
Like most bits of delf,
the turtle's seen at its best
on one's neighbour's shelf.

XII
Riding two abreast
on their stripped-down, souped-up bikes,
bears in leather vests.

XIII
The eye-shaded shrike.
BIRD BODIES BURIED IN BOG'S
a headline he'll spike.

XIV
Steady, like a log
riding a sawmill's spill-way,
the steady coydog.

XV
The cornet he plays
was Bolden's, then Beiderbecke's,
this lonesome blue jay.

XVI
Some fresh auto-wreck.
Slumped over a horn. Sump-pool.
The frog's neck-braced neck.

XVII

Brillo pads? Steel wool?
The regurrrrrrrrrrrrrrrrrrrrgitations, what,
of a long-eared owl?

XVIII

The jet with the jot.
The drive-in screen with the sky.
The blood with the blot.

XIX

How all seems to vie,
not just my sleeping laptop
with the first firefly.

NICHOLAS ALLEN

Free Statement

Censorship and the *Irish Statesman*

George Russell, poet and author, was editor of the *Irish Statesman* from 1923 to 1930. W.B. Yeats, George Bernard Shaw, Sean O'Casey, Frank O'Connor and Sean O'Faoláin were all contributors to this internationally distributed weekly report of cultural and political trends. Russell used his editorial position to inspire Irish intellectual support for the newly independent Free State. Cumann na nGaedheal was founded in December 1922 and formed its first administration under the leadership of William Cosgrave in September 1923. Russell believed that official acknowledgement of the Literary Revival's national importance was key to the state's foundation. But the Irish Statesman's defence of Cumann na nGaedheal was conditional. The government's introduction of the Censorship Bill in 1928 upset Russell's assumption of official sympathy as legislative regulation of literature threatened his coterie's critical authority. Russell attacked censorship on the grounds that his Irish literary project alone was responsible for the cultivation of moral order in the post-nation state.

State stability was a current question in Ireland in 1928. The Free State's political dispensation had been radically altered the previous year with the foundation, and first entrance into the Dáil, of Fianna Fáil.[1] The Republicans' return coincided nearly exactly with the murder of the

Minister for Justice Kevin O'Higgins. James Good, assistant editor of the *Irish Statesman* and columnist in the *New Statesman*, sensed that the Censorship Bill was a government attempt to outmanoeuvre Fianna Fáil: 'The fear of the Government is not that they have gone too far, but that when the Bill comes before the Dáil next month Fianna Fáil may strive to score at their expense by insisting that the screw has not been tightened sufficiently.'[2] Such a Bill offered the Free State government an opportunity to reclaim the radical political tradition that Fianna Fáil threatened to appropriate. Good, again, caught the wider mood in his reproduction in the *New Statesman* of a popular air:

> One widely circulated ballad thus describes the Cumann na nGaedheal candidates: 'Once I pictured John Bull as a knave and a liar. / But never, no never will do so again; / Garryowen is a tune that I used to admire, / But "God Save the King" has a greater refrain! / I will pull down the structure by Griffith erected, / Uproot the foundations and alter the plan; / Nor rub shoulders with those with foul treason infected, / Live rich and respected – a practical man.'[3]

The slight to the *Irish Statesman* that the Censorship Bill involved was not lost upon its editors. Ever perceptive, Good noted in the *New Statesman* that the Bill's first draft was published on the day that the recipients of the literary awards were announced at the 1928 Tailteann Games.

In these, Yeats was recognised for his achievement in *The Tower*, Shaw for *St Joan* and Father Dineen for his Irish language dictionary. That Yeats and Shaw were two of the most prominent Irish writers to voice their opposition to state censorship in the *Irish Statesman* is further evidence of the intimate nature of the controversy. Good interpreted the simultaneous publication of government and Tailteann proclamations to be significant of a shift in Cumann na nGeadheal thinking. He wrote of the Tailteann Games that:

> Most of the Irish writers have worked hard to achieve its success, and some of them flattered themselves that it might serve as the nucleus of an Irish Academy of Letters. This project, which had advanced so far that negotiations were in progress to induce the Free State Government to accord recognition to a representative body of creative literary artists, had been blown sky-high by the Censorship of Publications Bill.[4]

The loss of administrative support for a proposed literary academy signified more than a lack of government imagination. A split between political and aesthetic considerations in the practice of independent statehood was, to Russell, a disaster. By robbing his voice of authority, the state left a void to be filled by the clamour of an under-educated mob. His detractors' general lack of cultivation made them amenable to subversion and the effects of political manipulation. In rhetoric reminiscent of that used against Republicans during the Civil War, and in line with his reactionary mistrust of democracy's capacity for self-regulation and reliance on popular authority,[5] Russell asserted his position by stressing that the study of literature was a professional practice, open only to its initiates. His opponents were accordingly a 'group of fanatics incapable of exercising a critical spirit about literature and shouting vociferously about books whose purpose they are incapable of understanding'.[6]

Russell's ability to use the *Irish Statesman* as a forum in which to criticise government policy is symbolic of the institutional influence at his command. Far from being the isolated and unread voice of intellectual opinion, the *Irish Statesman* was an instrument of cultivated judgement, enjoying an educated and well-connected readership. Even if there were doubts as to the devotion of the journal's readers, the list of benefactors to the *Irish Statesman* in 1929 is a formidable collection of Free State luminaries.[7] Russell's political orthodoxy rested on his belief that cultural institutions could influence state development. Intellectuals were guardians of the national faith and any attack made on their integrity was equally an attack on the nation. To Russell the equation was simple, if arcane:

> Let beauty fade, and in some mysterious way, public spirit, sacrifice, enthusiasm, also vanish from society. Its foundations of its morale have been obstructed. If we destroyed in Ireland our National Gallery, our Abbey Theatre, our Feis Ceoil, and our poetic and imaginative literature, the agencies by which the mysterious element of beauty filters into national consciousness, we are certain that in fifty years the nation would be corrupt or dead.[8]

Russell's appeal was made to a government well aware of the propaganda value of Ireland's literature to the state's international status. The institutions that Russell lists in the above passage are 'agencies' able to popularise concepts of Irish political identity. Indeed organisations like the Abbey Theatre were important enough to the function of the Free State to receive official financial patronage. A Cumann na nGaedheal government that included such able media manipulators as Desmond Fitzgerald could not be slow to realise the damage that a rebellion by Irish writers might cause. Furthermore, the government was so anxious about Fianna Fáil's efforts to raise funds for a party paper, *The Nation*, in America that it despatched Cosgrave there to publicise the Free State. Among his engagements was a Foreign Policy Association meeting that also hosted Russell, who spoke positively on Cosgrave's behalf.[9] The government's predicament in 1928 meant that Ministers were willing to risk such international support from previously sympathetic intellectuals regardless of the media consequences. What Cumann na nGaedheal did not appreciate was the degree to which Russell imagined the executive powers of the state to be coterminous with the operations of the nation's creative intellects. The collapse of negotiations over the funding of a proposed Academy of Letters is typical of the misunderstanding between the government and the intellectual coterie surrounding Russell that resulted in the bitterness of debate over the Censorship Bill.

The Irish Free State had adopted in 1922 the entire body of British common law.[10] There was no difference between Irish and British legislation on the control of obscene literature in the immediate post-Treaty phase. The first divergence was the Censorship of Films Act in 1923. The censorship of printed matter was in one sense the next logical step for the Free State government to take, but it should be noted that such legislation was aimed specifically at popular entertainment, rather than literature or art. Neither was censorship simply a subject for debate in the Dáil. A number of religious organisations involved themselves in the agitation for stricter moral control of newspapers and books, among them the Irish Vigilance Association and Catholic Truth Society. Determined to regularise the state's approach to the censorship of printed matter, the government instituted a Committee of Enquiry on Evil Literature in 1926. Its report was delivered to the government in December of that year and its details published in the spring following. This document formed the basis of the Censorship Bill first published on 13 August 1928.

The Bill was first referred to in the *Irish Statesman* on the eighteenth of that month, leaving the journal six weeks to respond to Deputies and public opinion before the Dáil resumed sitting in October. In his first report Russell was moved to admit of the Bill 'that we do not like it, that there are provisions in it that by obscurity of wording may lead to grave interference with liberty of thought.' The *Irish Statesman* further questioned 'the wisdom of these 'recognised associations' referred to in the Bill.[11] Such associations were a legacy of the report of the 1926 Committee on Evil Literature and described organised groups of concerned citizens. Each association was able under the terms of the draft Bill to refer offensive or indecent publications to the Minister for Justice. Such publications could then be censored if necessary. Russell had by this early stage identified his two main objections to the Censorship Bill. The first was its imprecise wording, with the possibility that censorship might be more indiscriminately applied by a subsequent administration than its then supporters envisaged. The second was that the recognition of associations of concerned citizens, unlicensed except by virtue of their collective morality, threatened individual liberty.

Both these objections, however, revolve around the same preoccupation, that of control. For Russell was not an advocate of unfettered free speech. During the Civil War little mention was ever made by him of the regular suppression of the republican press. Equally, the *Irish Statesman* was itself susceptible to a form of censorship from its American investors; the critic Ernest Boyd was unable to become the journal's American correspondent because of their influence.[12] What Russell is concerned with in his criticism of the Free State censorship is less the freedom of speech than with the method of its control. He refers to the criminal law as the appropriate method of censorship as its authority rests in a system that, if not impartial, is at least accessible. Legality affords Russell a critical ally in his attack on the Censorship Bill as its rulings are based on precise renderings of the written word. In this area above all Russell had an advantage over his adversaries. It is no coincidence that the phrase the *Irish Statesman* most often uses to refer to recognised associations is 'semi-literates'. To label these groups with such a tag is to associate them with the mob and identify them as enemies of a state dependant on legal precedent and formal association for its very existence. One need only think of the Anglo–Irish Treaty itself, and the battles fought over it, to realise the implicit rhetorical power of Russell's legalistic strategy.

Russell invoked a fear of revolution throughout his articles on the Censorship Bill in late August and September of 1928. In the leader of 25 August, 'The Censorship Bill', Russell asked of the recognised associations if they were 'associations of intelligent and cultivated men? Or are they associations of fanatics, the associations which have been clamouring for a censorship and seizing and burning excellent journals like the *Observer* and *Sunday Times*?'[13] Both these publications were illegally destroyed because of their publication of information on birth control. Russell does not mention this qualification but rather concentrates on the fact that:

> We have to be very precise in our definitions. There are thousands of books we read without approving of the ideas. But a disapproval to lead to suppression – that would be revolutionary. Men would conspire against the orthodoxies of opinion the State would impose upon them.[14]

The identification with the state through the pronoun 'we' is significant. Russell, and by extension the *Irish Statesman,* is the voice of authority, responsible not only for the moral state of the general public but actively engaged in the moulding of its national consciousness. His greatest fear since independence was the anarchy that might result from the separation of the creative intellect from state power. To Russell, both formations have a shared responsibility to act on behalf of a population that is incapable of self-regulation. The Censorship Bill is an intrusion into a shared nexus, an unwelcome repudiation of the mutual understanding that was previously held to exist between the *Irish Statesman* and certain sections of Cumann na nGeadheal.

Accordingly, Russell reserves his sharpest criticism for the functionaries who would replace him as official censors. He felt their situation would be 'very unhappy – their intelligence made transparent to the world'. 'We wonder,' he wrote, 'what kind of people will have courage to go upon the Board to supervise the reading of their betters?'[15] September ended in disillusion for Russell, as he feared that the Dáil would ratify the Censorship Bill with little opposition, with Fianna Fáil, the party that had pressed for a quick introduction of censorship throughout 1928, only worsening its terms. 'We confess,' he wrote, that 'we have not much hope of modification, for the Opposition in the Dáil, so far as we can judge by the utterance of their leaders, are upon this point more illiberal than Ministers who introduce the Bill.'[16]

Seeking to prevent a rout, Russell published an inflammatory article by Yeats in the *Irish Statesman,* fiercely critical of the censorship. Yeats's article was a clear attempt to destabilise the Bill before it reached the Dáil. The government was at pains throughout the entire debate to stress that the censorship was entirely non-sectarian in nature. This position was difficult to maintain, especially after the Lenten pastorals of 1928, vigorous in their dismissal of all immoral forms of public expression. The publication of the Censorship Bill also coincided with a Free State census that showed a huge apparent decline in the Protestant population of the twenty-six southern counties since 1911.[17] While the government tried to present the censorship as the expression of a homogenous public morality, Russell published Yeats's article, 'The Censorship and St Thomas Aquinas', to embarrass the government over the religious aspects of its legislation.

Yeats obliged Russell by referring initially to the definition of 'indecency' offered as the standard for censorship by the government. Yeats noted that the Bill declared 'in its introductory section that "the word 'indecent' shall be construed as including 'calculated to excite sexual passion'"'. Yeats was further 'convinced that this definition, ridiculous to a man of letters, must be sacrilegious to a Thomist. I cannot understand how Catholic lawyers, trained in precision of statement and ecclesiastics, could have committed such a blunder.'[18] Yeats's appreciation of the finer points of Catholic dogma is less the point than is his sly ability to introduce religious dissension into the debate. The Minister for Justice, James Fitzgerald-Kenney, was himself a lawyer and Yeats's attack was personal enough for the Minister to take sarcastic note of it in his introduction of the Bill to the Dáil on 18 October 1928:

> One gentleman of very high literary ability, whose only fault as a literary man is, I think, that he does not write enough, and who has a great store of personal information, has attacked this definition ... on the grounds that the words 'calculated to excite sexual passion' are entirely heretical. I would venture to point out that I, personally, can hardly follow the criticism which has been passed upon the use of these three words in this definition, because I cannot understand the class of book which would excite some person just to proper love and might not excite others towards unlawful lust.[19]

Russell had in the meantime capitalised on Yeats's article by subsequently publishing Padraic Colum's religious criticisms of the Bill. Just five days before Fitzgerald-Kenney was to make his remarks to the Dáil, Colum predicted that censorship would expose the religious authorities to 'resentment and mockery'. Censorship would result in the 'moment that countries predominantly Catholic have most to fear – an anti-clerical movement. This means a division of the people deeper than any division we know of.'[20]

By publishing two separate criticisms of the Censorship Bill for its exercise of religious prerogative, Russell hoped to create as much controversy about the Bill as possible. But behind this propaganda screen there was offered simultaneously to the government the possibility of the *Irish Statesman*'s adoption of a more moderate approach to censorship. So in the very same issue that Colum predicted religious catastrophe, the journal noted that since 'a censorship in some form seems inevitable, we think there should be concentration upon the amendments of the most indefensible clauses'.[21] The editor's sanguine tone is in sharp contrast to Colum's depression at the thought of mass religious dissociation. The ethics of utilising religious controversy to make one's political point are dubious but the publication of Yeats and Colum in debates on this matter was effective enough to ensure that the Minister responsible for the Bill had personally to reply to their criticisms in the Dáil.

The Minister for Justice was surprised at the anger that his Bill aroused. He imagined perhaps that Russell and his associates would realise that they were, by virtue of their status, practically immune to the effects of the proposed censorship's prohibitions. The Minister made a great effort in the Dáil to separate the functions of the Bill from that of a draconian literary censorship. He cited a number of texts to make his case, not altogether convincingly. Thackeray's *Vanity Fair* would be ignored, despite the fact that the character Becky Sharp was not 'entirely a moral woman'. *Othello* too was immune, despite some 'very objectionable expressions'. The Minister continued: 'In a famous modern book of verse – 'The Shropshire Lad' – there is a poem which ... advocates suicide. It would not come under that definition of "contrary to public morality" because it would be entirely different from what this Bill is actually dealing with. This Bill deals solely with questions of sexual morality or sexual perversion.'[22] The Minister specifically remarked that the Bill 'has been attacked ... by extremists, demonising it as an unwarrantable infringement on the liberty of the subject and of the rights of free citizenship'.[23] The *Irish Statesman* was quick to respond to the Minister's criticism by replying the following week that:

> Our protest was made because of the kind of literature attacked by the fanatical reformers and the recognition given by the Bill to associations which were not content to attack the baser sort of journal, which destroyed books by great writers who had never been regarded as indecent, books which could only have been burned because of philosophical or economic or religious ideas which were not those of the reformers. To permit this to go on would represent a grave danger to the intellectual life of the Free State.[24]

The conciliatory tone of the above passage is matched the following week by the appearance of a new series of articles in the *Irish Statesman*, published under the title 'As Others See Us'. Essentially a propaganda vehicle for the journal's opposition to the Bill, the subject of the first instalment of 'As Others See Us', a series of interviews conducted by Russell's French confidant Simone Téry,[25] was the Taoiseach himself, William Cosgrave. A blunt and none too subtle reminder of the public projection of the government that the *Irish Statesman* could make, the next interview was with the Minister for Agriculture, Patrick Hogan. This panegyric labelled the Minister as 'the hardest working member of the Cabinet',[26] and continued the praise that the *Irish Statesman* had reserved for Hogan since his appointment. As Minister for Agriculture, Hogan was often congratulated in the journal for his appreciation of Horace Plunkett's co-operative ideals.[27] As Hogan's Agricultural Bill passed the Dáil without division in 1927, for example, the *Irish Statesman* noted with pleasure that: 'It is by the proper co-ordination of State aid and voluntary organisation, as Sir Horace Plunkett said, that our agriculture would become prosperous. That co-operation he desired is now becoming a reality.'[28]

Russell's strategy was to split the Cumann na nGeadheal cabinet over the question of censorship. Hogan's interview with Téry was published the very week that Hogan resumed debate over the second stage of the Censorship Bill to the Dáil.[29] Russell's policy had some effect as the Minister stated to the assembly that the Bill should instate 'a censorship which is limited in the most stringent and specific way'.[30] Like Russell in the *Irish Statesman*, Hogan felt that it would be 'extremely difficult [in this country] to get anyone . . . fit to censor books'.[31] Having offered these provisions the Minister went on to deliver a witty and savage attack on the morality of the opposition Fianna Fáil party, questioning their ability to perceive the truth of an argument after their abandonment of principle to enter the Dáil: 'I listened to this debate very carefully. We were all very virtuous and anxious to make the other fellow virtuous . . . I suppose the next time we are taking an oath we will call it an empty formula and push the bible two feet away.'[32] Hogan's sally was a public attempt to obscure the divisions that Russell so clearly perceived to exist within the government party. As the *Irish Statesman* noted the next week, Hogan was one of the Ministers who listened to the Minister for Justice's ensuing speech in 'a scornful silence'.[33] Satisfied that he could embarrass the government by pursuing such tactics, Russell consistently vilified Fitzgerald-Kenney in the following months for his inability to construct a suitable censorship. The Minister for Justice was unfortunate in his choice of enemy as Russell's derision excluded Fitzgerald-Kenney from the support more generally offered Cumann na nGaedheal by the *Irish Statesman*.

Russell was not foolish enough to imagine that his journal enjoyed a popular support strong enough entirely to disable the censorship. What he managed to do was to identify individual elements within the government, isolate them and then reduce the force of their personal authority. This tactic suited perfectly Russell's growing belief that ministers were themselves conduits for a new Irish identity, prompted by independence to an appreciation of state efficiency. Russell had noted in 1927 that 'the tendency to bring about an organic unity in the national being has become the most noticeable thing in the Free State' and further that 'atoms or cells seem to be modelled by some overwhelming instinct which imposes its law upon them. It operates primarily through Ministers.'[34] Russell reifies the function of elected representatives into a paradigm of general order. The *Irish Statesman*'s cultivation of Hogan, the Minister for Agriculture, is indicative of Russell's understanding that the government is the proper conduit for the dissemination of Russell's own ideals. This in turn modifies the understanding Russell had of democratic government, as electors choose only the means by which they will be ordered rather than the means by which order might be changed. In this complex, the Minister for Justice's recommendation in the Censorship Bill that certain associations of lay people be recognised as the first implements of a state censorship is anathema to Russell's belief that regulation should be the preserve of an enlightened elite. His opposition to censorship once again reverts to his disagreement with the Minister for Justice over the means by which media control is to be exercised. The concern over the Censorship Bill's deregulation of state authority to recognised associations was then symptomatic of his broad concern that cultural authority might pass from the directors of the Literary Revival.

As the Censorship Bill progressed through the Dáil, Russell kept pressure on the Minister for Justice by publishing a further attack on it by George Bernard Shaw on 19 November. This was the first major article that Shaw had contributed to the *Irish Statesman* since its first issue in September 1923. Shaw himself had followed a personal interest in the operation of state censorship since the first decade of the twentieth century. Called before a Joint Committee of the British Parliament in 1909, Shaw, like Russell later in the *Irish Statesman*, argued that censorship must only be exercised under the due process of law. Censorship of drama was at the prerogative of the Lord Chancellor and Shaw found it grossly unfair that this official had 'absolutely at his disposal my livelihood and my good name without any law to administer behind him'.[35]

One of Shaw's interrogators in this committee was Hugh Law, one time Lord Chancellor of Ireland. Law's son became a Free State Deputy and spoke against the censorship in the Dáil in 1928. The younger Law was also a close associate of Russell, who wrote the preface to his 1926 study, *Anglo-Irish Literature*. Speaking in the Dáil, this latter Hugh Law informed the Minister for Justice that he had made it his 'business' to consult about the censorship 'a great number of people ... including writers, a body which I am myself a very modest, humble member'.[36] Since Law had contributed to the *Irish Statesman*, the inference is that Law speaks with knowledge of Russell's opinion on the subject. More than that, his associations suggest the degree to which Russell, through figures like Hogan and Law, was able to exert pressure on the Dáil by virtue of having access to members sympathetic to his ideas.

Russell meanwhile exerted pressure on the government from the pages of the *Irish Statesman* by his publication, in November, of Shaw's essay. Shaw first appealed to the Catholic Church to distance itself from the Bill, if only to reassure the Protestant North. Shaw, like Colum, predicted that if this did not happen, a clerical backlash would follow, because 'when all these monstrous follies are being perpetuated by way of purifying Ireland the Church will be blamed for it. Already it is said on all hands that the Censorship Bill is the Church's doing.' Shaw finished by suggesting that if Ireland

> having broken England's grip on her ... slips back into the Atlantic as a little grass patch in which a few million moral cowards are not allowed to call their souls their own by a handful of morbid Catholics, mad with heresyphobia, unnaturally combining with a handful of Calvinists mad with sexphobia (both being in a small and intensely disliked minority of their own co-religionists) then the world will let 'these Irish' go their own way into insignificance without the slightest concern. It will no longer even tell funny stories about them.[37]

This passage marks a critical point in the *Irish Statesman*'s response to the Censorship Bill. Shaw's rhetorical geography consists of a world whose first boundary is England and whose mass is the civilisation of Europe beyond it. The image of Ireland slipping back into the Atlantic, lost beneath a wave of religious dogma, is a powerful one. But it is also the product of a political sleight of hand, as Shaw takes onto himself the voice of arbiter between the

Irish nation and the outside world. States of course operate through treaties and association, the Free State itself having taken an important role in the League of Nations by the time Shaw's article was written. The *Irish Statesman* too was aware of the influx of outside capital into the Free State: the journal was peppered throughout this period by adverts from the American oil company Texaco.[38] Each advertisement celebrated the arrival of this multinational conglomerate in the Free State by angular diagrams of sophisticated machinery and reports of new flight records set by aeroplanes using Texaco fuel. The *Irish Statesman*'s readership was also well aware that Ireland was in no danger of economic isolationism under the administration of Cumann na nGaedheal, not least because of the favourable and regular reports that the Ford factory in Cork received in the journal's pages.[39]

What Shaw proposes then is a myth of the Free State's potential regression. It is a myth created to empower Shaw, and writers like him, with a prophetic voice by which to influence the politics of a state within which writers had as yet found no formal place. We noted earlier the surprise with which James Good reacted to the publication of the Censorship Bill since the government had been in discussion to set up an Academy of Letters, the very mark of state authority for literature. This move collapsed, leaving Shaw to deride a nation for its inadequacy, when in fact the nation's transition to statehood already made such criticism anachronistic. Shaw's article is a masterful piece of polemical writing but it fails on one critical point. It reads, in the context of the adverts for Texaco petrol and Ford tractors, as out of date, an echo without substance.

The proof of Shaw's irrelevance is that Russell, after the publication of Shaw's article, committed his energy to lobbying for change to the Censorship Bill rather than to Shaw's demand for its complete dismissal. In this Russell was successful. To follow the progress of the Censorship Bill through the Dáil between October 1928 and March 1929 is to notice that the areas of the Bill which were most contested were those brought to public attention by the *Irish Statesman*. There were now three specific problem areas for Russell. The first was the definition of indecency. As Russell noted in the *Irish Statesman*, the problem might arise from such a broad definition of the term that a secular theory such as evolution might be banned from schools, as it had been in parts of the United States. The second was the power of private associations to refer obscene literature to the Minister for Justice. Finally, Russell was concerned over the number of censors to be elected to the board, primarily because he felt, like Milton before him, that since so few would be qualified to judge, it would be difficult to appoint worthy candidates.[40] On the first point, Russell was reassured by the time the Bill passed through the Dáil. The *Irish Statesman* accepted the Minister's assurances that the Bill would be applied sparingly to literature. Its assistant editor, James Good, reported in the *New Statesman* that 'it is expected that books will be handled cautiously, with the exception of birth-control literature, which is to be automatically banned without reference to the Censorship Board'.[41]

Russell's support of this aspect of the Bill's most illiberal provision is interesting, especially in the context of Oliver St. John Gogarty's submissions to the Senate on the matter. Russell had long favoured Gogarty, and Yeats gave him a poetry award at the 1924 Tailteann Games.[42] Gogarty published frequently in the *Irish Statesman* throughout the latter part of the 1920s, even going to the length of conducting personal exchanges with Russell through verse.[43] Crucially for Russell, Gogarty had also been a Senator since 1922, using his position in the Senate to support his associates' attacks on the censorship. Like Russell, he fiercely denounced aspects of the Censorship Bill that affected creative literature but was, again like Russell, more circumspect when the question of birth control arose. Gogarty in fact noted that:

> No one who has any care for a nation's welfare can for one moment countenance contraceptive practices, which are a contradiction of a nation's life. In England the condition of the miners and the unemployed is as it is because England has allowed its capital to go into yellow, brown and black labour, so that the Government tolerates clinics for education in the practice of contraception.[44]

A diagnosis of Gogarty's racism is suggestive of the dubious assumptions that underpin his subsequent opposition to a literary censorship. Gogarty, Russell and Yeats all shared the idea that the cultivated could be trusted to read even the most morally doubtful texts. What is interesting in Gogarty's speech is the way in which the shared assumption of national purification is made explicit through his discussion of birth control, an illiberality that is concealed by the rhetoric of detached criticism when he refers to literature. It is hard not to draw the conclusion that many of the opponents to the Censorship Bill were, like Gogarty, motivated to their defence of free speech by a reactionary desire to retain control of the outlets for critical debate from the power of the state.

Russell was himself most satisfied with the Dáil's rejection of the recognised associations. The 'number of Deputies, Fianna Fáil, Cumann na nGaedheal and Labour,' he observed, 'who resisted these proposals and defeated them was a pleasant surprise'.[45] The *Irish Statesman* now found that the 'Bill is much more reasonable in its post-Dáil form than most expected who saw it in its first monstrous infancy'.[46] Russell was especially pleased about 'the amendment which swept out of the Bill the Minister's preposterous "recognised associations". This was absolutely the worst aspect of the Bill.'[47] It should be noted however that, despite his praise of the Dáil as an effective democratic body in its amendments to the Censorship Bill, many of the Deputies who spoke most cuttingly of its weaknesses were friends of the *Irish Statesman* or associates of its editor.

In the Dáil, the Bill's chief critic was William Thrift, Professor of Physics at Trinity College Dublin, and former member of the Committee on Evil Literature, who held a University of Dublin seat. Unionist in politics, he was also a friend of the *Irish Statesman* contributor and Trinity Fellow Walter Starkie's father. Thrift was Provost of Trinity from 1937 until his death in 1942. One of the *Irish Statesman*'s main contributors on the matter was Edmund Curtis, Professor of History at the same university. Russell was himself awarded an honorary doctorate at Trinity in July 1929, proof, if it were needed, of the private circles that represented public interest in the Free State. Furthermore, Hugh Law, as previously mentioned, spoke against the Bill, as did Bryan Cooper, an independent member of the Dáil whose unionist background did not affect his desire to serve the new state efficiently. Cooper's letters were occasionally published in the *Irish Statesman*, and Lennox Robinson, one of the journal's directors, wrote his biography.[48]

In the Senate, Sir John Keane lamented Yeats's absence and tried to make up for his loss by aping the controversial tone of Yeats's article in the *Irish Statesman*.[49] Combined with Keane was Gogarty and the former speaker of the Senate, Sir James Douglas, also a director of the *Irish Statesman*. With associates like these, Russell may well have praised the efficacy of the Free State parliament, not least because it contained some of his closest political allies.

Russell felt his authority secure after the censorship controversy, the *Irish Statesman* having proved to be a suitable vehicle for intellectual interference with state regulation. Generally a register of Russell's cultural interests, the journal was able successfully to focus political opposition in times of public dispute. Examination of the censorship controversy exposes the intimate relations between literary authority and political power in the early Irish Free State. As editor of the *Irish Statesman*, Russell was at the centre of transactions between the two. Recognition of this fact redefines our understanding of him, a writer whose guileful agitation in the *Irish Statesman* belies his posthumous reputation as an abstract idealist.[50] It also leaves us with a final view of Ireland in the first decade of independence as subject to vigorous competition between authorities, cultural, political and religious, determined to secure their influence within the new dispensation. Russell took his place among these factions and successfully protected, for a short time at least, his literary and political investment in the state by the *Irish Statesman*'s re-negotiation of the Censorship Bill.

EDNA LONGLEY

Ulster Protestants and the Question of 'Culture'

I want to discuss three interrelated issues: some applications of the term 'culture' to Northern Irish affairs; the perceived 'culturelessness' of Ulster Protestants; how this perception, together with cultural stereotyping, has affected literary criticism – especially the criticism of poetry. In December 1999 I attended a Belfast book launch on the day when ministerial posts in the precarious Northern Ireland executive were being horse-traded. The novelist Glenn Patterson rushed up and said: 'Great News! The Ulster Unionists have taken Culture.' Like other Protestants concerned with cultural matters (Patterson was then a member of the Arts Council of Northern Ireland), he had despaired of unionist politicians realising their significance. Such anxiety is usually not on behalf of unionism itself. Rather, it denotes the intellectual fear, by no means confined to Protestants, that a mono-cultural ideology might prevail by default. Indeed, the political pundits had revealingly assumed that 'culture' was a nationalist thing. As it turned out, the Ulster Unionist Party had covertly targeted Culture all along, thereby frustrating Sinn Féin's desire to hold both the ideological ministries (Culture and Education). Today Michael McGimpsey runs the Department of Culture, Arts and Leisure (DCAL) spelled out as: 'Arts and culture; sport and leisure; libraries and museums; Armagh Planetarium; Ulster Historical Foundation; inland waterways;

inland fisheries; Ordnance Survey; Public Record Office; language policy; lottery matters; millennium events and companies; visitor amenities.'

McGimpsey's brief is wide (not to say miscellaneous) as regards the mediation and consumption of culture, but that difficult word itself is scarcely in focus. From an anthropological angle, for instance, its inclusiveness should subsume the ministry's other components – and, indeed, all the other ministries. Yet the anthropological definition is not universally agreed. Marxist theorists like Terry Eagleton and Francis Mulhern have recently criticised the appeal to 'culture', even in its 'multicultural' guise, as a denial of politics whose mystificatory purpose is itself highly political. Stefan Collini argues, however, that the transcendental right wing appeal to high culture and the 'Cultural Studies' appeal to popular culture do not exhaust the ways in which culture, as a combination of practice and signification (the meaning attached to cultural practices), might be understood: 'the impulse of self-conscious appeals to culture has rather been to introduce and make effective in public discussion the kinds of consideration that the instrumental and present-driven world of purely political discourse habitually underplays or neglects.'[1] On this premise, culture secretes reinventions and renovations of politics – 'places where a thought might grow', to quote Derek Mahon.

The theoretical argument impinges on dialectics about Northern Ireland because Northern Ireland is one of its contexts or subtexts. Here the difficult word marks a difficult spot where communities select certain cultural practices for heavy-duty signification, for symbolic functions of self-definition and self-defence. The 'Arts' potentially re-order the symbolic domain by complicating the cultural field, whereas the local *Kulturkampf* limits 'culture' by yoking it to 'identity'. Amin Maalouf speaks for individuals who are 'arenas for allegiances currently in violent conflict with one another', who inhabit 'a sort of frontier zone criss-crossed by ethnic, religious and other fault lines'. This might also be the locus of artworks that run counter to 'a narrow, exclusive, bigoted, simplistic attitude that reduces identity in all its aspects to one single affiliation, and one that is proclaimed in anger'.[2]

Maalouf's scenario fits a symptomatic row (in early 2000) about City Council funding for a St Patrick's Day parade in Belfast. A parade organised by a group from Catholic west Belfast had taken place in 1999. There had been objections, not only from loyalist quarters, to the number of tricolours carried in the saint's honour. As a result, the Alliance Party, which holds the balance of power in the Council, blocked funding for the 2000 parade. Funding was also denied to a St Patrick's proposal from a Protestant group as not being inclusive enough either. Councillor Tom Campbell explained the Alliance stance: 'The organisers were invited to agree to the rules applying in the Down District Council area which ensure the parade [there] is non-sectarian and inclusive ... One of the most vocal supporters of the Belfast parade is the *Andersonstown News*, which claimed ... "Irish people are not going to stop flying the Tricolour on *their special day* [my emphasis] any more than others will fly [their flag] on the Twelfth". The "them and us" attitude ... is precisely the problem ...' An adjacent letter, however, attacked 'sinister elements blocking the funding' and Catriona Ruane, one of the organisers, accused the blockers of 'anti-Irish racism'.[3]

This incident epitomises three basic points about the Northern Irish cultural question in general: (1) the magnetic convergence of culture, identity and politics at both the conceptual and practical level, commemoration being a prime site of this convergence; (2) resistance to negotiation and regulation; (3) the problem of getting cultural weapons decommissioned. All three points are dramatised by rival forms of public self-assertion: Orange parades are not the only provocative show in town although they may be the most objectionable. Instead of pondering the complexities evoked by St Patrick (long-claimed by the Church of Ireland, for instance), Ruane proposed the hyper-political solution that all thirty-two Belfast members of the new Assembly should lead the parade – quite a breastplate.

These events were typical sectarian skirmishes in a longer, wider culture-war whose modern phase began around 170 years ago. At its nastiest, combatants in the Irish *Kulturkampf* 'murderously' seek to erase not only the cultural presence but cultural memory of the perceived 'other'. Hence the attacks on monuments, memorials and cemeteries. Hence the desire to inferiorise the culture of another group or to deny that it possesses culture at all. 'Irish people' is a verbal form of erasure matched by Ian Paisley's 'the people of Ulster'. Thus a genuine peace process requires a cultural process too. This has been the objective of the government-funded Cultural Traditions (now Diversity) Group, which oversees the cultural work of the Community Relations Council. (One fruit of the kind of consciousness promoted by the CDG was the launch in February 2001 of a multi-million pound St Patrick Centre at Downpatrick to which even Ian Paisley contributes a voice-over.) Liberal appeals to culture often base themselves on a reopening of cultural arguments and spaces allegedly foreclosed by events between 1912 and 1923. This was the burden of Roy Foster's address to the first Cultural Traditions conference, *Varieties of Irishness*, in 1989: 'round 1900, an inclusive, energetic cultural debate was opening up between brokers of the different cultural traditions in Ireland'.[4]

Yet not every cultural or literary critic reads 'Ireland after Parnell' (the title of one Yeatsian retrospect) as a cross-sectarian window of opportunity. Attention to this period is itself conditioned by events since 1969. And, outside the academy, after thirty years of promoting segregation the Troubles have shifted to an intensified cultural front where they figure as ethnic cold war. Aodán MacPóilin argues that, while the peace process 'is unlikely to produce a convincing version of normal democratic politics, certainly in the short term ... it provides ideal conditions for the politics of outrage, swagger and emblematic posturing'. He continues: 'For this reason alone, cultural politics and the politics of identity are likely to become increasingly prominent.'[5] 'Community arts', for instance, can be either an agent of peace or a theatre of culture war. Some activities are cross-community and exploratory; others feed local preconceptions. Again, the Cultural Traditions concept has long been attacked as either unionist or nationalist 'social engineering', and its vocabulary hijacked. Thus the magnetism of culture by politics reappears in the 'Two Traditions' political model and in defences of political coat-trailing (parades etc.) as cultural practice. The CDG's fear that they were simply producing better-educated bigots resonates with Derek Mahon's line 'the bigots shrieking for their beleaguered "culture"' (*The Yellow Book*, VII).

Culture is further compromised at the very moment of its proclamation when it becomes a product to be funded, commodified and sold. Discussing the DCAL report, *Unlocking Creativity*, Jim Smyth contends that on all political sides 'culture is conceptualised as cultural assets: cultural assets and activities promote a dynamic image of a region, attracting people and investment, thereby propelling further development'.[6] The project director of the St Patrick Centre has tourists in his sights: 'We are promoting a product which is already internationally recognised.'[7] The space for culture just to happen or cultural 'thought to grow' (signification), then, is squeezed by culture as propaganda and by culture as capitalism. Meanwhile, Northern Irish people do all kinds of things – often the same things – that never acquire symbolic or significatory status.

Of course, this essay itself stakes out a position in the cultural field. Writing on 'Colonialism and Academic Representations', David Miller rightly stresses that no academic is above the conflict. This point is conveniently exemplified by Miller himself. Despite criticising social scientists who study unionism for being 'unable to distinguish between understanding a social phenomenon and identifying with it', he dedicates his book to the 'silenced and repressed', and views 'British propaganda, unionist ideology and revisionist "scholarship" ' as a single and hegemonic formation.[8] Colin Irwin, concerned with how anthropological research might inform public policy, ponders academic detachment from a different perspective: 'Resistance to integrated education has also come from those in the academic community who tried to predict the inevitable institutional or social failure of such an enterprise ... Perhaps research on conflict in deeply divided societies should only be undertaken in collaboration with "outside" scholars, who might be less inclined to dismiss new social opportunities and possibilities out of hand.'[9] Yet it remains hard to determine who is 'inside' and who 'outside', and 'divided societies' is itself ideologically loaded. Further, different academic disciplines as well as different political dispositions read 'culture' through incompatible lenses. Miller, a researcher into media, understands culture as one among several communal loci indexed to power and representation: 'the economic, social and *cultural* (my italics) inequalities which underlie the conflict'.[10] For anthropologists, however, culture is 'not a residual category when everything else is sifted out, something left behind when more obviously "economic", "ecological" and "political" factors have been dealt with but a key element which inflects the entire social field.'[11]

To place culture before politics can be read as not only right wing but unionist. For Eagleton, culture must wait. In the guise of postmodernism, culturalism 'licenses certain readings of Irish politics while suppressing others'.[12] In Ireland 'culture' constitutes the language of anti-colonial resistance to metropolitan hegemony essentially because that hegemony has masked itself in the language of cultural transcendence. To split culture even fractionally from politics ignores the realities of power: like other discredited groups, 'the more astute Ulster Unionists have learned to speak the language of multiculturalism'.[13] Bill Rolston (one of Miller's contributors) also criticises the 'multiculturalist agenda' as state-sponsored 'social engineering': 'History, colonialism, inequality, sectarianism are all reduced to relatively simplistic explanations which rest on social psychology, postmodernist discourse and wishful thinking.' Rolston then identifies culture with politics, when he celebrates 'nationalist culture' as 'a culture of resistance' and says: 'From their position of subordination, nationalists and republicans have more to say, more to dream, and can see themselves expansively as part of an international fraternity of subordinate groups resisting colonialism, imperialism and oppression. Unionism ... because of its real or aspirational superiority has more to lose, less to articulate, and feels itself isolated in an increasingly unsympathetic world.'[14]

Whatever else may be going on here, Eagleton and Rolston identify the common tendency in Ulster unionism and the British state towards transcendental cultural ideology. Cultural ukanianism (after Tom Nairn's coinage 'Ukania') strategically evades awkward local specifics that might introduce 'Irish' cultural traces. Hubert Butler often attacked the invocation of 'broad horizons', still weakly present in some unionist rhetorics.[15] Current Irish nationalist rhetoric of 'the diaspora' has similar features, while it also turns the historical tables by stigmatising 'Britishness' rather than 'Irishness' as parochial. (There is an equivalent theme in contemporary literary criticism.) Yet the trope has older roots, as when the newly elevated Cardinal Connell said: 'Ireland is European because of Rome. Because of the church, Ireland is a worldwide community.'[16] Alan Finlayson sees little functional difference between contemporary nationalist and unionist cultural rhetorics: 'lending primacy to culture is central to strategies of hegemony in the North; the appeal to culture and cultural identity, and to its capacity to "transcend" the merely political, has been the basis by which authority and claims to political right have been legitimated by various political and class factions.' Finlayson argues that academic study should focus on 'the undecideability of the relation between culture and politics and, in this sense, see the establishing of a particular version of that relationship as a deeply significant political operation.'[17]

Yet the content of 'particular versions' counts too. If culture is seen as a nationalist thing, if nationalism is seen as having 'more to dream', if writers from Ireland are generally conscripted into the 'national' culture, this stems from the traditional – and mutually determining – idioms of cultural nationalism and cultural unionism. Irish cultural nationalism (whose historical fissures are less apparent to what is really a northern neo-nationalism) has, like cognate European formations, chiefly stressed distinctive expression such as language, literature, myth, music. Unionism, in its cultural defence of the status quo, has switched between ukanian themes and 'Ulster' variations. Here distinctiveness chiefly depends on history, religion and kinship. Gillian McIntosh (in whose work 'culture' mainly signifies the cultural propaganda of the Stormont régime and its outriders) highlights the degree of conflict – not necessarily contradiction – between Ulsterness and Britishness:

many unionists were overtly anglophobic or were, at the very least, hostile towards the British government. Moreover, their sense of history was of a decidedly 'Ulster' variety, and throughout this period they argued for a history which was rooted in Ireland as well as Britain, and specifically in Ulster, focusing on the uniqueness of Ulster and the 'Ulsterman'. In addition to the planter tradition, their connection with Britain was highlighted in terms of war contributions made by Northern Ireland in the First and Second World Wars ... [also] represent[ing] their war-time experiences as unique within the United Kingdom.[18]

Inter alia this implies continuity with, as well as variation on, pre-1920 Irish Protestant themes. Thomas Bartlett has noted how eighteenth-century Protestants defined themselves 'against two "Others", the inhabitants of the mother country and the native Irish'.[19] And Colin Kidd finds 'dual strategies combining both appropriation and denigration of the indigenous culture as a means of ensuring territory-specific legitimacy'.[20] If Ulster unionism has usually been less appropriative and more denigratory *vis à vis* both the Gaelic and the Catholic, this is because its Anglican component has been modified by competition and alliance with Presbyterianism. Dublin-centred Anglicanism has been better placed to invoke the Irish-speaking Old English as legitimising ancestors – and hence to claim St Patrick.

Of course Irish nationalism has also stressed history, kinship and religion; while ukanian unionism might well stress linguistic, literary or musical commonalities with the rest of Britain. Indeed, it has done so in the past, and is significantly doing so now when older ukanian themes – Protestantism, industry, empire – have lost their context and clout (see below). Conversely, Irish nationalist cultural propaganda has not always disguised its Catholic foundations: for Marianne Elliott, Catholicism has been so profoundly internalised as the ground of that community's politics as to have become invisible.[21] Yet the dominant historical / religious emphases of unionist rhetoric permit the counter-attack that Protestants lack culture (in the cultural-nationalist sense) on which to base their arguments. Patrick Grant finds that, despite the best pluralist intentions, John Hume makes no 'distinction between political unionism and the varieties of cultural Protestantism', and offers 'no critical assessment of Catholicism' or awareness that it might underpin 'Irish identity'.[22] Up to a point, the self-deracinating mode of rhetorical unionism has only itself to blame.

With important exceptions,[23] the prevailing emphases of academic research on Northern Ireland underplay Catholicism and Protestantism as culture or as mentalities. Alan Megahey seeks to fill one gap:

> the wilder shores of Ulster Protestantism have attracted perhaps more than their fair share of attention. But the Protestant Churches themselves have been neglected. Perhaps 'church history' or 'ecclesiastical history' is regarded as *passé*. Perhaps it is too confusing, and too disruptive of analytical procedures, to analyse institutions which, while central to the 'Northern Ireland problem', are all-Ireland in their dimensions ... Apart from the more obvious distortions – Marxist analysis for example – there has been a tendency to look at the Irish churches as if they ought to be like the English churches; that, somehow, modern English Christianity is normative.[24]

To anticipate a later stage of this essay: other neglected areas listed by Megahey include 'the influence of Protestantism on, or its symbiotic relation with, literature and art'.[25] Here too, as in the critical writings of Tom Paulin, the wilder fundamentalist shores have generally proved sexier than mainstream Anglicanism, Presbyterianism and Methodism. John Wilson Foster's essay on John Hewitt and W.R. Rodgers, '"The Dissidence of Dissent"', is a rare exception.[26] Even Barry Sloan's welcome *Writers and Protestantism in the North of Ireland* (2001), which seeks to show how the work of certain writers 'has been conditioned by Protestant influences' and to contest 'oversimple notions of the nature of Protestant culture', highlights the Calvinist legacy and marginalises Anglicanism.[27] Sloan's subtitle (a quotation from W.R. Rodgers) is *Heirs to Adamnation?*

One factor may be that Anglicanism is less easily corralled inside the boundaries of Northern Ireland, even though its character there may be affected by symbiosis with nonconformism. (Hence current tensions within the Church of Ireland over the Drumcree issue.[28]) Anglicanism gives Northern Irish Protestants both southern Irish and English contexts. It places poets, for instance, in a heritage that includes George Herbert and W.B. Yeats. And – perhaps more problematically for some observers than the link with Presbyterian Scotland – it defines Ulster Protestantism as cultural Britishness in an 'English' mode. The point is illustrated by the vulnerability of all Ulster Protestant emigrants to so-called 'ethnic fade' when they cross the Irish Sea as well as the Atlantic. Especially in England (though even in Scotland), they merge into wider WASP culture, while the Catholic Church still serves as a locus for cohesion whatever its secular transmutations. Protestant 'fade', however, may be partly a matter of perception; in the academic sphere, the result of over-concentration on post-famine Catholic emigration to cities like Liverpool or Boston. Donald M. MacRaild argues that emigration from Ulster to Britain imported Orange-Green tensions on a wider front than is usually supposed; and that it influenced indigenous Tory and Labour politics well into the twentieth century: 'From this broadened chronological and cultural base, we can learn that the tensions which rose *between* Irishmen over issues such as religion and Home Rule were *as* important as native hostility in fostering robust and competing senses of Irishness.'[29] The invisibility of Irish Protestants in English contexts, including academic disciplines, may be correlated with reluctance to think about *English* history and literature in terms of religion, region or ethnicity rather than class.

If 'fade' renders Irish Protestantism invisible, 'fragmentation' renders it obsolescent. The relation between the multiplicity of Protestant denominations and unionist politics is another area where commentators put the political cart before the cultural horse. McIntosh finds that fragmentation was always an issue: unionist rhetoric of monolithic cohesion depended on repressing (theological and cultural) divisions among Protestants as well as on denying Catholic alienation from the state. Public 'performances of consensus', such as royal visits, were designed to cover 'underlying tensions'.[30] Colin Coulter seems too present-minded and class-minded when he portrays Northern Irish politics as contingently touched by, rather than grounded in, 'religious practice'. Also, his language of a 'collectivity' that 'dwarfs' schismatics takes a somewhat papal line with unionism's centrifugal tendencies:

distinctive forms of religious practice ... shape everyday life and experience in ways that may have some political significance ... Catholics living in Northern Ireland attend mass with remarkable frequency. As a result, members of the nationalist community ... tend to meet their co-religionists on a regular basis ... at certain crucial moments all nationalists who happen to attend church are exposed to similar sermons on critical moral and political issues ... These significant ties may offer one possible explanation as to why Northern nationalists have been able to survive the upheavals of the last three decades comparatively unfragmented ... The diverse creed of Protestantism is characterised by a lesser emphasis on religious observance and a propensity to schism. When a Protestant goes to church she communes with a fraction of her wider ethnoreligious community that is dwarfed by the collectivity formed by Catholics at prayer. [Hence perhaps] the tendency ... for unionists to bicker and fragment.[31]

'Fragmentation' ('discordant and oddly jarring' elements) is also a theme of Declan Kiberd's essay on Louis MacNeice in *Irish Classics*: 'Inevitably, the experience of being an Irish boy at Marlborough compounded this fragmentation of personality.' Kiberd also offers as a reason for the 'widespread perception that the central traditions of ... Irish poetry are somehow less readily available to writers who grew up in the embrace of Protestantism' the 'consideration that it is not in the nature of Protestant or even post-Protestant writers to form movements, much less traditions. The still small voice of the individual often prefers to be heard on its own.'[32] So much for Yeats. The frameworks of Catholic commentators or cultural nationalists may prove more relevant to such a perception.

I have quoted several negative images of Ulster Protestants. Although one size never fits all, most stereotypes are partly based on fact: Ulster Protestantism undoubtedly includes extreme fundamentalism, extreme bigotry and extreme violence. Yet even Orangeism may not wholly 'deserve' the mural reproduced on the cover of *Rethinking Northern Ireland* which features a Ku-Klux-Klans/ Orangeman terrorising a peaceful dolmen, inscribed with the word 'Garvaghy'. The mural is headed 'Not all traditions deserve respect'. More attention might be paid to stereotypes of the Ulster Protestant: their sources, target-audiences and effects. (The Ulster Society was moved to publish a pamphlet called *The Demonisation of the Protestant Community*.[33]) Celticism has been much rebuked as patronising Irish Catholics, but the fortunes of this stereotype have proved more positive than those of the Celt's binary Other, the Saxon, modified in Ulster to the Saxon-Scot, Ulster Scot, Ulsterman. Once self-eulogised as tenacious, industrious, honest, independent, progressive, loyal, this characterisation has been negatively inverted not only in nationalist discourse but by events, historical change and media images. In 1999 I was asked to explain unionism to the bewildered readers of the *Frankfurter Allgemeine Zeitung*. Someone responded: 'I very much like the idea that nationalism is sexier and easier to sell than unionism. You are absolutely right about the romantic view we have of republicanism and the unfortunate images of unionism that stick in the mind (bowler hats and Ian Paisley). Disagreement about who is the victim is naturally something that Germany is familiar with from our own experiences of unification.'[34]

'Disagreement about who is the victim': the current Protestant sense of victimhood includes a feeling of being not only misrepresented but unrepresented. Some observers and researchers would agree. Fintan O'Toole has discussed the 'notable absence' of Protestants from Troubles films, partly because these must be simple enough for the American market.[35] Alan Parkinson comes to a similar conclusion: 'Due to the dearth of analytical coverage and the media's insistence on presenting the Irish problem in a simplistic fashion, unionists continue to be misunderstood in Great Britain.' Parkinson notes the predominance of negative or stereotypical images and the marginalisation of unionist politics as compared with the high profile of nationalism / republicanism. After the first phase of the Troubles, 'the British (despite the occasional misdemeanour) took on the mantle of the "Good", the IRA and Sinn Féin became the "Bad" and the increasingly less significant Protestants became the "Ugly" group'.[36] A sign of more recent shifts is Rolston's paradoxical tone of triumphalist victimhood and the publication of books with titles like *A Precarious Belonging: Presbyterians and the Conflict in Northern Ireland* (John Dunlop, 1995) and *Northern Protestants: An Unsettled People* (Susan McKay, 2000). Hence, too, Ruth Dudley Edwards's championing of *The Faithful Tribe* (1999).

Gregory Campbell speaks of 'a people so vilified and so misrepresented that they must seek a refuge that will not betray them'.[37] When Dunlop more reflectively explains the culture of Prebyterianism, the largest Protestant denomination in Northern Ireland, he hopes to catch the ear of 'international interpreters who seem to have been persuaded that there is only one story to be sympathetically heard and that is the Irish Catholic story'. But he adds: 'The challenge is how to tell [the Presbyterian] story, which contains elements of achievement, of critical self-examination and of grievance, without attempting thereby to be the sole occupant of the moral high ground, or failing to acknowledge that, as well as being victims, we have made other people victims.'[38] Even Protestants who are less religious, less political, less unionist, or simply less inclined to moan, often resort to an ironic tone which implies the unlikelihood of their being understood by the wider world. Hence Glenn Patterson's 'ABC of Northern Ireland for Tourists' which includes such items as 'W/ West Belfast: Area that extends further south than much of south Belfast and excludes some westernmost, inconveniently Protestant, districts. Its festival, in a spirit of inclusiveness, coincides with Internment commemorations.' And 'F/ Fence: The place where all those who did not subscribe to the orthodoxies of nationalism and unionism were said to have been sitting all these years. Very commodious, in my experience, and heavily populated.'[39] Since the 1920s irony, pointed in two oblivious cultural and political directions, has been a recurrent trope of writers from Irish Protestant backgrounds.

In default of clearcut signals (such as the Irish dancers and Gaelic athletes on republican murals) much cultural investigation starts from (usually bad) Protestant political behaviour. This is the trajectory of McKay's *Northern Protestants*. The cover features a photograph of a union jack and a tattered red hand of Ulster flag attached to a withered branch at Drumcree. McKay's 'Prologue' tells the harrowing story of two sectarian murders committed by Protestants 'not because such violence is typical ... but because it represents the worst outcome of a type of strong political Protestantism'.[40] This approach strikingly contrasts with the more empathetic, though not uncritical, complementary work by Fionnuala O'Connor: *In Search of a State: Catholics in Northern Ireland*. Perhaps, in stressing the worst, McKay personifies (like some of her interviewees) the self-critical conscience of Ulster Protestantism angrily at odds with its pharisees. Although McKay's conclusion echoes Dunlop on victimhood, it contradicts the predominantly dark impression left by her book, and her language is more didactic: 'There are monsters which have to be faced down, but there is much to be proud of too. There is honest ground to stand on.'[41]

But even if *Northern Protestants* is itself culturally revealing, as is its conceptual distance from the communitarian spirit of *In Search of a State* (O'Connor's interviewees are not individually specified or indicted), 'honest ground' rarely appears in cultural terms. There is little sense of cultural history or cultural ideologies. McKay's interview with the playwright Gary Mitchell elicits from Mitchell an (inaccurate) self-image as a lone pioneering Protestant in 'theatre and media' where 'it is easy to talk about nationalism and republicanism and the great strides they are making ... Continually I hear the word "sexy" whereas in terms of Protestantism it is seen as very boring and nasty and dreadful.'[42] This illustrates how unionists / Protestants sometimes internalise the undermining nationalist charge that Protestants have 'no culture' or 'have less to articulate'. Even close to the Progressive Unionist Party, where the series of *Island* pamphlets has taken the culture-war to Sinn Féin's assumptions about Irishness and Britishness, a representative 'referred to "the insurmountable difficulty" in "actually *defining* what specifically constitutes our particular cultural identity"'.[43] This also internalises nationalist assumptions about the monolithic nature of culture and nationalist elisions of religion as a cultural force. Once again, Ulster Protestants effectively 'fade' into a range of Britannic and European cultural practices which render them invisible (even to themselves) except for the Orange bits, just as only a portion of 'Irish' culture gets green paint. Thus when Orangemen see Orangeism as *itself* the 'culture' they are defending, they have backed themselves into a corner.

Yet, as already indicated, there are also historical reasons why Protestants should now be so bad at explaining themselves to the world, and even themselves to themselves. They clung to cultural ideology which had cemented the UK during the eighteenth and nineteenth centuries – that 'Britishness' which Linda Colley puts in its most positive light when she writes that Protestantism 'gave the majority of men and women a sense of their place in history and a sense of worth . . . It gave them identity.'[44] Other UK regions, such as South Wales or Lanarkshire, have lost cultural identifications bound up with the old Britishness. That includes working-class socialist identity – which also once contributed to Ulster Protestant self-understanding. This explains why the Scottish and Welsh Left have made hitherto unthinkable compacts with cultural nationalism. But history blocks that route to Ulster Protestants since it would (seemingly) compound rather than resolve the weakening of Britishness. Mervyn Long, one of McKay's interviewees, says: 'Working-class Protestants have become so dull – they live in these sprawling housing estates and are not involved in anything.'[45] Thus a demoralised corner can become a limbo.

Perhaps Ulster Protestants currently serve as scapegoats for all the ugliness in the history of Britannic Protestantism. The English, for instance, blench at embarrassing ghosts from their own past. According to Ted Hughes's origin-myth, puritanism, industrialism and imperialism violated a Celtic, pre-Reformation unity of English being.[46] But there may be a link between the Ulster Protestant dilemma and contemporary agonising – if agonising it be – about Englishness. Just as unionism has overstressed, on its shaky frontier, the pillars of the metropolitan state; so the centre now notices a vacuum. Tom Nairn links 'Ulster-unionist atavism' with the general 'archaism' of the UK polity.[47] Ian McBride represents this interdependence of frontier and centre more enquiringly when he says: 'What is missing [from most discussions of Ulster unionism] is any consideration of "the British nation" itself.'[48] However, Nairn's recent article, 'Farewell Britannia: Break-Up or New Union?', views archipelagic redefinition as potentially reaching from the frontier into the centre and out again:

I would argue [that] both the redefinition of Sovereignty inherent in the new Ulster accords and its support structures, like the British-Irish Agreement, do suggest – albeit in a partial or shadowy way – something quite different from and potentially better than the old imperial state ... Our collective stake in the archipelago is far too high for most people to think of abandoning it *altogether* ... Where the old fabric was thinnest and most contested, it has begun to give way and already begun to turn into something else.[49]

For Graham Walker, however, the question is whether the British–Irish Council 'will help to revitalise British identity in any form' and promote archipelagic multiculturalism or 'give a fillip to separatism and contribute to the actual dissolution of the Union'.[50]

The object of this essay is neither to predict nor prescribe: cultural nationalism and cultural unionism will continue their symbiotic manoeuvres until the culture war has a victor or intercultural peace, together with new kinds of signification, prevails. But the full British Isles context would surely inform the latter scenario; and the more complex Protestant thinking prefers this to the corner or limbo of Little Ulster – the difference between cultural survival and an apocalyptic dead end. McGimpsey's ministry, it seems, rejects cultural ukanianism, accepts the Cultural Traditions philosophy, and promotes mixed regional, Irish and archipelagic horizons (the Agreement's North-South, East-West). Elsewhere, as in the political foreground, there is a struggle between regression and an emergent revisionism ready to 'turn into something else'. For example, the Irish-British Peace Park at Messines, a public revision of exclusivist historical narratives (as yet ahead of Northern Irish communal mentalities), contrasts with the Orange Order's partisan obelisk at Thiepval. Similar choices appear in the Ulster Protestant invocation of ancestral Scotland. Latterly focused on Ulster Scots dialect, this can figure as an introverted concern – more Ulster than Scots – with beating Sinn Féin at the language game. Hence the breach – as in Irish language circles – between Ulster Scots' academic / cultural and political wings.[51] Nonetheless, Ulster Scots now figures along with Gaelic in the new North-South language body. But what of East-West? Scotland's linguistic (and religious) complexities present an archipelagic challenge that, like emigration, cuts both ways. This is evident in relations between poetry from Northern Ireland and from Scotland. Yet Ulster Protestants will need to work at knowing a changing Scotland that may not want to know.

In *Intimate Strangers* Graham Walker discusses the long 'reluctance of Scottish political parties to involve themselves in debate about Northern Ireland'.[52] This reluctance understands and represses sectarian dynamics in Scotland itself. Devolved Scotland's current attraction to the Irish Republic (or Celtic Tiger) also shows signs of caution or denial. 'Don't mention Northern Ireland' characterises most Scottish contributions to 'Scotland and Ireland', an extensive *Irish Times* supplement which marked the official opening of the Research Institute of Irish and Scottish Studies at the University of Aberdeen (November 1999). For instance, the late Donald Dewar refers euphemistically to 'our shared history and our shared culture'. Meanwhile Bertie Ahern affirms 'Shared elements of Celtic ancestry, language and traditions'. It is left to John Dunlop to suggest the particular cultural meaning that an Edinburgh / Belfast axis might potentially have for Ulster Protestants:

> [On a visit toEdinburgh] I had once again the strong impression of being at home, being given space to stand up and be myself without having to hug the clothes of my northern Irish Presbyterian identity about me to keep me warm from the chill winds of those in Ireland who deem my double belonging to be absurd.[53]

Not that an archipelagic 'Presbyterian identity' is an asset in the sphere I am about to discuss. Before turning to how simplistic or stereotypical notions of Ulster Protestantism have affected poetry criticism, I would stress that readings of Scottish literature have been similarly affected – a connection more often noted than explored. Matthew Arnold, as usual, is to blame. John Wilson Foster underlines the influence of a critic, 'for whom dissent and genuine culture were mutually contradictory', on perceptions and self-perceptions of Ulster Protestant 'philistinism';[54] while Cairns Craig indicts 'the sources of [Edwin] Muir's conception of Scotland in the model of "culture" which linked thinkers from ... Matthew Arnold, through the work of Eliot and F.R. Leavis'. Craig questions Muir's influential polemic *Scott and Scotland* (1936) and its explanations of Scottish cultural 'emptiness': namely, lack of a 'homogeneous' language; discontinuity of literary tradition; Knoxian Calvinism. On Muir's model, the latter

> rather than an expression of national identity, comes to be the negation of the nation's once authentic culture. Muir's presentation of Knox is the culmination of a long process in which the iconic founder of the nation

came to be viewed as its subverter and destroyer.[55]

Craig's 'challenge to those readings of the nation which have seen in Calvinism nothing but a negation of the imagination and the creative potentialities of the nation' becomes more problematic, however, when applied to Ulster. Not only must 'other religious and intellectual traditions' (Craig) be continuously reckoned with, so must the contested 'nation'.[56] A positive rethinking of Calvinism-as-culture might indeed modify what in the Scottish context has been termed 'inferiorism' but it can have no agreed *national* literary-critical outcome. John Hewitt's essay 'The Bitter Gourd: Some Problems of the Ulster Writer' (1945) echoes the subtitle of *Scott and Scotland* (*The Predicament of the Scottish Writer*) and is strongly influenced by Muir's ideas. Yet, for Hewitt, Scotland not only lacks Ulster's 'problems and cleavages' but can show a linguistic-literary coherence and a 'creativity' that (Protestant) Ulster has yet to attain:

> Scots has been a literary instrument since the days of Dunbar and Gawain Douglas ... We have no such literary heritage, no such ancient language ... our best men are the Lawrences, Kelvin, Hart, Bryce, extroverted men of tremendous energy, skill and integrity but deficient in creative genius ... Sensitive not tough-minded persons ... finding themselves in an extroverted stubborn inarticulate society with well-defined values and, for the most part, a rigid creed, revolted against their condition, became minority minded, perpetually and consistently in opposition ... and fled.[57]

Ironically, Muir's model of 'a central and homogeneous' literature is Irish literature in the terms of Yeats's original Revival.[58] The felt experience of Muir and Hewitt cannot be dismissed as wholly subjective any more than can a theology that distrusted art and (for good as well as ill) promoted 'externalised energies' (Hewitt). Yet just as, according to Craig's argument, the metropolitan absorption of Scottish writers into English 'tradition' asset-strips and 'fragments' the periphery, so the enduring canonical and cultural force-field of the Irish Revival subsumes writers from Protestant Ulster. Because of its vaguely apprehended proximity to cultural nationalism, Irish Catholicism – which has been equally hard on sensitive literary minds – gains where Ulster Protestantism loses. And perhaps both the Anglo-Catholic and Anglo-Irish versions of 'tradition' have been more user-friendly to Irish Catholics than to dissenting Scotland or to the Calvinist guilt-by-association that touches every 'Ulster Protestant' writer.

I have been arguing that representations of Ulster Protestants' 'culture' can depend on discursive tropes and biases that are partly propagandist, partly the product of unexamined assumptions. The varying ratio between religious or post-religious and secular cultural expressions, or between North–South and East–West horizons, is slippery to grasp as contrasted with (perceived) homogeneity elsewhere. Nor is the situation helped by the asymmetry whereby Protestantism rather than 'Britishness' (or, indeed, Protestant Irishness) is highlighted in one quarter, 'Irishness' rather than Catholicism in another. Further, post-ukanian Britishness needs to be broken up too. Steven Matthews not only fails to analyse the cultural complexities of discussing Yeats in relation to a range of Irish and British poets: all his 'British' poets are (undifferentiated) English. Again, Barry Sloan quotes anti-Calvinist poems by Iain Crichton Smith and R.S. Thomas without registering how these poets – like Hughes in west Yorkshire – dramatise quarrels with themselves over cognate conditions in their own backyard. *Some* structural factors that influence poetry from these islands, including poetic forms, can only be fully understood in the context of archipelagic dynamics. In an archipelagic anthology poems marginalised by the category of the 'national' may take on new meanings that reflect back on poems which supposedly vindicate it. This applies, in ways that Matthews inadequately conceptualises, to the most significant figure in modern poetry from these islands. Following Homi Bhabha's 'problematic of colonial representation', Matthews concludes: 'Yeats's invention of an eclectic 'tradition' offers a partial form of identification, partial because its oblique take on Anglo-Irish cultural temporality estranges any immediate access to originary identity be it Irish or British.'[59] Again, the problematic may be in the beholder's eye. As Christopher Prendergast observes, in a review of Pascale Casanova's *La République mondiale des lettres*: 'a monolithic image of "nation" can mask all manner of divisions and constituencies'. Disagreeing further with a work that over-stresses relations and competition between national literatures, Prendergast argues:

> It might make more sense … to speak of literary 'negotiations', itself of course a diplomatico-commercial term, but with the implication of at least a modicum of cooperative rather than competitive transaction. This need not necessarily mean that the negotiations constitute a cosily eirenic exchange; they may well be fraught with tension and ambivalence.[60]

The cultural fine print of poetic negotiation makes additional demands on close reading. The addressee of this *Festschrift* is one critic who meets these demands. Peter McDonald, questioning the literary-critical uses of 'identity-discourse', is another. McDonald observes, for instance, that 'finding a poet who can serve to articulate the essence of the Protestant tradition is not perhaps all that simple a process'.[61] Although critical complexity on the point has advanced during the past decade, certain patterns persist – and in the writings of some influential commentators. An essay by the novelist Ronan Bennett exemplifies the interface between culture war and literary criticism. In 'Don't Mention the War: Culture in Northern Ireland' he states:

> The Protestant North has produced art, but rarely is it art that celebrates the world that spawned it. More often it is an angry reaction to the prevalence of bigotry, claustrophobia and paranoia ... Unsurprisingly, most artists and writers who have emerged from Ulster Protestantism have tended to move away – physically and mentally – from the world that bred them.[62]

Bennett's language is tinged by race, and he adds art-as-culture and culture-as-art to the unitary nationalist identification of culture with politics. Thus he assumes that non-celebratory art produced by Protestants has both rejected 'its' culture and accurately described 'its' totality. Bennett contradicts himself when he condemns as 'propaganda' the fiction of Robert McLiam Wilson which does not particularly celebrate the Catholic 'world that spawned it'. He also assumes that dissent and critique are not primary literary causes. Patrick Grant, whose book compares texts by writers from different backgrounds – a surprisingly rare procedure given all the 'negotiations' – contrastingly proposes that 'literature and its assessment are part of an educative process by which an unravelling and deconstruction of traditional binary opposites might patiently be effected'. But because writers in Northern Ireland 'are not exempt from the conditions of their own upbringing ... [a comparative] arrangement ... can help to show how persistent are the mythologies of ethnic identity, as well as the complexity and variety of ways in which people "go between" the binary opposites.'[63]

'Persistent mythologies', it must be stressed, are mutual. But I will conclude by summarising a few more instances from writings on Irish / Ulster poets from Protestant backgrounds, even though a time may be coming when these no longer need to be nailed to the door. The point is that reductive readings of the 'Protestant poet' prevent understanding of how intricately poetry negotiates the cultural field and creates new kinds of signification.

Such readings include the too ethnic, too Calvinist, too counter-cultural, and too colonial. First, an amusing ethnic (cultural-political) stereotype of the Ulster Protestant emerges if we conflate some notes in the 'Contemporary Irish Poetry' section of *The Field Day Anthology of Irish Writing* (1991). The Ulster Protestant poem is: 'self-deprecatory', 'astringent', 'self-effacing'. It exhibits 'dry good humour' and is 'elusive of all categories'. It looks to the 'semi-detached suburban Muse of Philip Larkin' or aspires to be 'a parsimonious Northern lyric' since its author 'writes with a self-imposed parsimony, as if he had committed himself to a doctrinaire "northern" reticence of feeling and expression'. It constitutes 'studies in a dying culture' and 'messages from an Ulster Protestant sensibility that has decided to go it alone': 'a strand of Ulster that identifies itself as British and asserts its rights to the English lyric'. Declan Kiberd, inventor of this portrait of the artist as doomed Ballymena Man, continues the good work in his essay on MacNeice in *Irish Classics* where 'the Protestant imagination' figures as 'ever more wryly self-mocking'.[64] Although this notional creative agent has indeed much to be wry or dry about, the adjective, like all Kiberd's terms of obsolescence, marginalises what it identifies as marginal.

Admittedly, some Ulster 'Protestant' poets have themselves taken the ethnic route and countered the accusation of cultural emptiness by half-subscribing to stereotype rather than trusting to poetry. John Hewitt, up to a point, transposes the character of the "Ulster Scot" into an aesthetic: 'a native mode to tell/ our stubborn wisdom individual' ('Once Alien Here'). His ethnic self-definition can be seen as a response to the same pressures that prompted Yeats's Anglo-Irish people-of-Burke-and-of-Grattan pose. Some of Tom Paulin's poems combine an ethnic focus and ethnic persona with a myth of Protestant history (a fall from Enlightenment ideals to barren provincial fundamentalism) in a manner that often seems more thematic than structural. Paulin contrasts a sectarian Ulster Protestant *ethne* with a redeemed characterisation which his own poetry, it is implied, adumbrates in the radical stylistic habits he identifies with a positive nonconformism: 'Provisional, exploratory, mercurial, eagerly engaged'.[65] In 'Mahon, Paulin and the Lost Tribe' Peter McDonald argues that Mahon's poetry 'constantly in debt to Beckett ... touches on areas of Protestant identity which are far more complex than the politically accessible aspects so common in Paulin's writing'.[66] Paulin is to be commended for placing the question of Protestantism in the cultural foreground. It might be noted, however, that his narrative of fall and salvation has as biblical a structure as Muir's narrative of Scottish literature.

Paulin has influenced other critical views of what Ulster Protestantism as ethnicity owes to Ulster Protestantism as religion. I have suggested that Barry Sloan's book, welcome as it is, overstresses the cultured and devotional contour of Calvinism. There is also a fine line to be drawn (which depends on specific close readings) between McDonald's wariness of critical identity-mongering and Sloan's 'effort to understand how priorities and preoccupations learnt or inherited from Protestant theology and cultural practices in Northern Ireland have affected and influenced particular poets'.[67] Yet Ulster Protestantism is both internally diverse and defined by the most intense proximity to Catholicism in these islands (Catholicism, in turn, being culturally influenced by that proximity). The effects of all this on poetry may be as dialectical as singular. Thus what Sloan terms 'the rigid austerities of [MacNeice's] northern Protestant background'[68] are perhaps more accurately seen as a perceptual complex formed by an interplay between his father's Anglican ministry, exposure to local fundamentalism, and distinctive autobiography. Similarly, as I have argued in an earlier essay, Mahon's poetry is informed by personal history and Anglican liturgy conjoined with a disturbed sense of more extreme religious fervour.[69] But perhaps the main gap in explicating Ireland's 'Protestant' poets is theological and metaphysical. We need to map the post–Darwinian cognitive fallout: the circulation of spilt Protestantism, including its impact on forms and on constructions of selfhood, and how the Irish case compares with aesthetic consequences elsewhere.

Bennett assumes that critical Protestant writers have *de facto* left the tribe: that they are counter-cultural apostates. While this may betray pressures to repress criticism within either nationalism or Catholicism, it seems a literal reading if Protestant self-criticism functions only as Catholic–nationalist self-vindication. Fran Brearton remarks of Mahon: 'the whole picture must include the poetry that claims to stand outside it'.[70] A critical and self-critical Protestantism does exist, as in the churches' internal critiques of 'civil religion' or 'religious nationalism'. Johnston McMaster writes, for instance: 'To deal with the past, [all] the churches individually and together will have to name and acknowledge their failures and their negative contributions to a dysfunctional and failed community. Until the churches are prepared to name publicly their cultural sins, there will be no release of prophetic imagination required to build the new future.'[71] The underlying problem with Paulin's poetic critiques may be that, unlike Mahon's, they lack 'prophetic imagination'. They fall into the trap that for MacNeice, in a passage that equates criticism with 'conscience', marks the nemesis of critical poetry: at its 'extreme development' it becomes 'propaganda', 'the defeat of criticism'.[72] There is convergence between the ideas that poetry is alien to a philistine Protestantism; that critical poetry cancels its author's Protestant cultural origins; and that the redeemed or saved Ulster Protestant poet serves as an example to the people. Susan McKay illustrates this convergence in that she tends to cite poetry by Protestants as transcending the communal failings.

Finally, behind the hazy ethno-Calvinist, counter-cultural image of the Protestant poet may lurk the familiar belief that Irish / Ulster Protestants are ultimately defined by nothing more spiritual than colonialism. Yeats is more often 'Anglo-Irish' than post-Christian. This has curious results in some discussions of poetic form: the 'well-made poem', urbanity or civility as a kind of fortress or bawn. Seamus Heaney refers to Yeats creating 'a fortified space within the rooms of many powerfully vaulted stanzas'[73] in a manner that perhaps outruns Yeats's own symbolic uses for his tower. Steven Matthews refers to Mahon's neo-Yeatsian 'stylistic and formal fastnesses'.[74] Declan Kiberd characterises MacNeice and his northern (Protestant) successors in terms of a 'professional training in classical scholarship' that produced 'rigour of form and clarity of outline as mildly moral stays against chaos'. MacNeice also engages in 'an urbanely amused' 'construction of a self'.[75] The Protestant poet's forms slide between denoting a big house, a siege mentality, an over-civilised pose, and suburban hedge-clipping – all of which contrasts with the implied cultural vitality of the natives.

Heaney's 'Frontiers of Writing' (1993), like Kiberd's essay, is generously pluralist in intent, and similarly makes Louis MacNeice the locus of that generosity. Heaney sets out to conceive 'at-homeness' all round these islands. Here poetry figures Ulster Protestants and the question of culture. Heaney represents MacNeice as 'offering a way out not only for the northern unionist imagination in relation to some sort of integral Ireland but also for the southern Irish imagination in relation to the partitioned north'. Yet the fancy whereby Heaney attaches Protestant poets to a quincunx of castles or towers (MacNeice to Carrickfergus Castle) seems telling. Heaney also speaks of MacNeice's 'bilocated extraterritorial fidelities' and sums him up as 'an Irish Protestant writer with Anglocentric attitudes who managed to be faithful to his Ulster inheritance, his Irish affections and his English predilections'. Heaney makes 'fidelity' a principle that carries MacNeice over what appears stretched and fissured terrain. Thus a remaining difficulty might be that

MacNeice's inheritance, affections and predilections (do the last two words differ in nuance?) are not quite seen as constitutive, mutually complicating, an epitome of archipelagic cultural and poetic dynamics. And the shape whereby Heaney includes MacNeice '*within* the symbolic ordering of Ireland' (my italics) might itself be regarded as an exercise in 'fortified space', and one that runs counter to MacNeice's own fluid aesthetic.[76]

ELMER KENNEDY-ANDREWS

Antic Dispositions in Some Recent Irish Fiction

Robert MacLiam Wilson's *Ripley Bogle*, Patrick McCabe's
The Butcher Boy and Eoin McNamee's *Resurrection Man*

Polonius's advice to his son – 'To thine ownself be true' (*Hamlet*, I, iii) – seems like common sense. However, its assumption of the existence of a single self is challenged by postmodern psychology's claim that identity is a series of masks which one puts on in response to different situations and people; and 'Once donned, mask becomes reality'.[1] Hamlet's announcement that he 'shall think meet / To put an antic disposition on' (*Hamlet*, I, v) recognises the polymorphous self, and indicates that the 'antic disposition' need not be pathological, but can be a functional or strategic style of identity. According to the *Hamlet* paradigm, the 'antic disposition' is a feature of historical periods that are 'out of joint', the recourse of those who find themselves powerless or threatened. Rather than being a sign of psychological disturbance, it can be understood as adaptive or even innovative. Hamlet, interested in acting and adept at wearing masks, gives notice of fluid personal boundaries which may be liberating, revitalising or self-protective, and which others may find threatening or confusing.

Hamlet's unstable self represents a style of identity prominent in our own period of social and technological upheaval which Robert Lifton has dubbed the 'protean style'. 'The protean style of self-process, then, is characterised by an interminable series of experiments and explorations, some shallow, some profound, each of which can readily be abandoned in favour of still new, psychological quests.'[2] Protean man is to be distinguished from older definitions of identity: 'For it is quite possible that even the image of personal identity, in so far as it suggests inner stability and sameness, is derived from a vision of culture in which man's relationship to his institutions and symbols is still relatively intact – hardly the case today.'[3] And hardly the case in Wilson's *Ripley Bogle*, McCabe's *The Butcher Boy* or McNamee's *Resurrection Man* whose protagonists illustrate many of the key features of protean man. Among these are: 'a profound inner sense of absurdity which finds expression in a tone of mockery', stemming from 'a breakdown of a fundamental kind in the relationship between inner and outer worlds'; a feeling of guilt – 'hidden guilt: a vague but persistent kind of self-condemnation ... a sense of having no outlet for his loyalties and no symbolic structure for his achievements'; a feeling of being 'uncared for, even abandoned', which prompts 'diffuse fear and anger'; a pervasive 'nostalgia' for 'a mythical past of perfect harmony and prescientific wholeness', combined with 'massive disillusionment'.[4] However, Lifton stresses the positive as well as negative sides of the protean style. Protean man is driven by 'strong ideological hunger. He is starved for ideas and feelings that can give coherence to his world, though here too his taste is toward new combinations.'[5] Change always contains the possibility of renewal: 'The principle of death and rebirth is as valid psycho-historically as it is mythologically.'[6]

The term 'antic disposition' refers to behaviour which, from the perspective of the social centre, is aberrant, grotesque, subversive. Transposed to an Irish context, its connotations of strangeness are recognisably part of traditional colonial discourse: English colonialism justifies itself by invoking an Irish racial 'antic disposition', the Other of itself, which needs to be civilised. *Ripley Bogle* deconstructs all such binarisms as the 'civilians and barbarians' opposition, all totalising explanations of history, society or identity, and looks to the potential of protean, hybridised consciousness to produce a plural self. In McCabe's novel the centre is the oppressive official culture of small-town Ireland, which constructs its Other in the image of the insubordinate butcher boy. Francie's insurgent 'antic disposition' is a reaction against the degraded culture of Irish nationalism which, as Seamus Deane says, has simply reproduced imperialism to become 'a copy of that by which it felt itself to be oppressed'.[7]

Lifton also recognises a tendency which seems to be precisely the opposite of the protean style – a 'closing off or constriction of self-process . . . a straight-and-narrow specialization in psychological as well as in intellectual life, and . . . reluctance to let in any "extraneous" influences'.[8] This kind of 'one-dimensional' self-process is essentially 'reactive and compensatory', requiring deliberate effort 'to fend off protean influences which are always abroad', and is not to be confused with earlier essentialist notions of the self. The type of man Lifton recognises is what, following Brian Friel, we might call 'fossilized' man, those people who have closed themselves off to the complexity of life.[9] Such is McNamee's 'resurrection man', Victor Kelly, who has immured himself in the claustrophobic world of Loyalist gangsterism and its cult of violence, seeking transcendence in, as Lifton puts it, 'the way mystics always have, through psychic experience of such great intensity that time and death are, in effect, eliminated'.[10]

In these novels we have three versions of the contemporary crisis of identity. Together they highlight some of the challenges facing (post)modern man: How independent can the self be from its culture, environment, society? How can it engage with external reality without being only fluid and protean and losing itself in that reality? How can the self pursue its own realisation without losing itself in its own desires?

In *Ripley Bogle*, the 'antic disposition' is an effect of the narrator's displacement and alienation: situated on the margins of society, distanced geographically, intellectually and ideologically from his west Belfast, Catholic, nationalist, working-class origins. Throughout his life he has known homelessness of one kind or another. Rejected by his family and peers, he describes himself in significantly textualising terms: 'I was merely ignored, neglected, edited, tippexed really.'[11] Seeking escape from his community and culture he goes to Cambridge, but his misconduct leads to expulsion and to life on the streets of London, which he finds more agreeable anyway.

Ripley Bogle would seem to be the latest in a line of Irish tramps, a figure of Irish dispossession and exile. Indeed, this is the way – or, rather, one of the ways – in which he likes to see himself:

The world did me wrong by making me an Irishman. I've kicked hard but Micksville packs a boot like a donkey. When you think about it, I'm practically faultless – a victim of circumstance, timing and nationhood. It's Ireland's fault, not mine. (272)

But try as he may to present himself as a Joycean victim enmeshed in the nets of nationality and religion, his situation is much more complex than that of simple 'victim of circumstance, timing and nationhood'. The course of his life is determined by his own actions and decisions at least as much as it is by social and historical factors. His life is inscribed within a system of representation which Bogle exuberantly writes as much as he is written by. He acts the part of the barbarian, but resists any simple essentialist labelling. If he is tramp and 'boor' (190), his character is not to be read in terms of natural degeneracy or colonial stereotyping, but in terms of mockery, parody and menace which both recognises and disrupts colonial authority.

Through Ripley Bogle, Wilson reproduces a type of colonial subjectivity characterised by ambivalence, mimicry and hybridity. Boglean identity is heterogenous, changeable and ambivalent, split by othernesses within, and hybridised through contact with the external Other. As Homi Bhabha explains: 'The fantasy of the native is precisely to occupy the master's place while keeping his place in the slave's avenging anger. "Black skin, white masks" is not a neat division; it is a doubling, dissembling image of being in at least two places at once.'[12] Wilson reconfigures monolithic categories such as race and class in terms of crossings, interstitial spaces, splits and joins, and uses notions of plural identity and cultural hybridity to challenge the oppositional identitarian politics of both nationalism and colonialism.

Bogle delights in evading all fixed positions. He refuses to conform to any social institution or communal organisation, whether family, school, or Cambridge. Early on he claims a hybrid identity that cannot be accommodated within existing formulae. On his first day at school this 'all-inclusive type of chap' insists on calling himself 'Ripley Irish British Bogle' in the face of coercive social forces and more straightforward categorisation: 'She stressed with some vigour that no matter what anyone else were to call us, our names would be always Irish' (14). Bogle's hybrid parentage is 'part Welsh and part Irish', and this, he says, is 'a fucking dreadful thing to be' (7). Whatever the positive possibilities of such hybridity, it also leads to the absurd situation where his 'maternal grandfather was having his legs and most of his testicles blown off at Passchendaele while fighting for the British nation against the German Army – while his brother (my greatgranduncle?) was having his head blown off in O'Connell Street while fighting for the Irish nation against the British Army in the Easter Rising' (7).

The first part of Bogle's narrative adopts the child's fresh, defamiliarising perspective, from which events are emphatically human before they are political: 'the stoning of army vehicles is experienced as schoolboy entertainment long before it is perceived as political activity. Set-piece descriptions of a soldier being shot . . . and of a local girl tarred and feathered . . . are presented in vivid cinematic detail, but in the context of childhood horror and voyeurism rather than adult condemnation'.[13] Bogle's memories of Internment Night are informed, not by political outrage, but a child's excitement, especially at the sight of a West Indian British Army soldier standing in his kitchen: 'Boy, was I chuffed or what!' (27). Internment Night 'was all much too good to miss' (28). This perspective displaces the received Irish Catholic Nationalist perceptions of Internment Night, and offers an alternative narrative of the Troubles. These new perceptions emphasise a child's sense of the force and wonder of the actual. This play with viewpoint is one of a range of narrative strategies whereby Wilson attempts to break down fixed boundaries and create a MacNeicean world: 'suddener than we fancy it / . . . crazier and more of it than we think / Incorrigibly plural'.[14]

Adopting the exile's perspective and a superior attitude, Bogle challenges the fixed identities and received narratives and histories of his benighted homeland. He reduces the historical process to the stark outline of tragic farce in which all is ridiculed:

> Soon, however, will come the Civil Rights marches. The Protestant lot will get annoyed. They (reasonably, I feel) would rather like their civil rights to remain exclusively Protestant. So, the British Army will be drafted in to protect the catholic minority from the brutality of their Proddie countrymen. Maladroitly enough, the British Army will then shoot a little bunch of unarmed Catholic civilians, clerics and toddlers on Bloody Sunday. In their turn, the Catholics grow rather peeved and start exterminating a whole plethora of soldiers, policemen, prison officers, UDR men, Protestants, Catholics, English shoppers, Birmingham pubgoers and men who make the mistake of editing the *Guinness Book of Records*. (83)

Bogle's satiric denunciation of the dominant discourses of Ireland continues through parody and pastiche, which simultaneously remind us of the constructed nature of the novel as a series of literary conventions. His Deirdre story is an ironic re-writing of both the *Book of Leinster* and Joan Lingard's *Across the Barricades*; his Maurice Kelly story is a deliberately exaggerated imitation of a Troubles thriller; the account of Bogle's birth echoes Beckettian narrative; the account of Bogle's hallucinatory encounter with the four brothers and a 'Harridan' in a Kilburn pub plays intertextually against Joyce's 'Nighttown' episode in *Ulysses* and Flann O'Brien's ironic treatment of the themes and tropes of Irish revivalism in *At-Swim-Two-Birds*. Bogle reacts particularly venomously against the conventionally sentimental discourse of romantic nationalism: 'All that old Irishness crap promoted by Americans and professors of English Literature. Menace and cupidity. All balls . . .' (160).

The narrator's re-location to Cambridge University allows him to switch attention from one of the categories of colonial subjectivity – 'Irishness' – to the other – 'Englishness', though he retains his liminal position. England, which historically has constituted Irish identity in the demeaning terms of the barbarian 'other', is itself now seen, as a site of constructed identity, to be vulnerable to post-colonial manipulation. Post-imperial England, Bogle opines, is in a state of terminal decline: 'Remote, impersonal, disengaged. Easy pickings for the dark, concocted vitality of the Celt (i.e. me)' (171). The English lack power and vitality. Traditional English values and institutions, as presented by Bogle, are hopelessly degraded, disfigured by an encroaching popular culture and blighted by endemic violence and racism. Yet Bogle's narrative is always ironically self-subverting and ambivalent. He, himself, is culpable of horrifying violence (as in his fight with another mad, drunken derelict who accosts him in Hyde Park), and, for all his disaffection with Cambridge, he freely admits his susceptibility to English 'charm', personified by Laura, an idealised image of bourgeois Englishness: 'For a time, for a very short time, she made me a little like her. She dragged me halfway up to meet her. By jiminy, it was awfully nice up there with all that charm and discernment. I'm grateful for the jaunt' (228). He may savagely mock 'Englishness', but his consciousness is shaped by English literary culture, from Dickens and Orwell to Shakespeare, Shelley and T.S. Eliot. Bogle's bravura polyvocal discourse is a powerful representation of counter-domi-nation: yet behind the impressive verbal display lies a contradictory mixture of feelings, among them uncertainty, self-consciousness and inferiority as well as defiance and self-assertion.

Bogle is a 'mimic man'. For Bhabha, mimicry is ambivalent because it requires 'a difference that is almost the same, but not quite'.[15] Irish Bogle is like the English coloniser but remains different. Bogle's near-duplication of authority, in Bhabha's analysis, might be construed as oppositional to the extent that it contains within it uncertainty and the threat of subversion. Mimicry disturbs by displacing and problematising the coloniser's 'authenticity'. Bogle's double vision (both Irish and English) makes him a figure of suspicion, but the challenge he poses to the power and difference of authority pushes beyond mimicry and mockery to explicit menace: 'I persisted in going too far. I picked fights, skipped lectures, told lies, got pissed, taunted dons and made fewer friends. I fucked everyone off in a big way' (206). As Bhabha notes: 'The ambivalence of colonial authority turns from *mimicry* – a difference that is almost nothing but not quite – to *menace* – a difference that is almost total but not quite'.[16] This is the menace confronted by Dr Byron, the Senior Tutor, before whom Bogle is arraigned for his insubordinate behaviour. Byron attempts to neutralise Bogle's menace by stripping from him the mask of rebel and misfit: 'Whether you like it or not, when you came to Cambridge you signed yourself up as a member of an élite ... Egalitarians don't come to Cambridge. Not real ones' (211). Colonial control relies on the capacity to appropriate the Other and to produce the colonised as entirely knowable: 'His (Dr Byron's) little smile was full of kindness and the promise of future kinship. Inclusion. It made me want to puke' (211). Refusing to assimilate, Bogle resists the colonialist discourse as he had resisted the dominant narratives of decolonisation: he prefers an interstitial position from which he can interrogate both Englishness and Irishness. Wilson elaborates a displaced postmodern discourse of fragmentation and hybridisation in preference to a totalising narrative which aims for traditional effects of unity, identity and closure. Boglean postmodern post-colonialism is characterised by what David Lloyd calls 'adulteration' (similar to Bhabha's 'hybridity' – a 'stylisation of the hybrid status of the colonised subject as of the colonised culture'[17]) and by what Luke Gibbons calls 'allegory' (the articulation of 'a fugitive existence on the margins between the personal and the political'[18]). Eschewing the abstraction of essences and a classical dualistic logic, Wilson emulates Joyce, the master of heterogeneity, parody, 'adulteration', and 'allegory'. Wilson's text is contentious because its ambiguity is disruptive of fixed identities, whether colonialist or nationalist.

Identity is an ever-revisable script, subject to 'revision', 'erasure', 'arbitration' (269–70) and other kinds of radical fictionality and textual play. Bogle's narrative is full of omissions, suppressions, evasions, deviations and additions. He indicates explicitly those stress-points where he was 'spoofing' and candidly considers his reasons for playing games with his reader. 'I wanted you to like me', he confesses. By suppressing certain facts and inventing others, he seeks to construct a more sympathetic, more romantic, even heroic, narrative of himself; but at the end, he re-writes his story, hoping to attain 'some kind of wisdom' (270). The novel, in its picaresque form and subversive comedy, is a carnivalised text. Bogle, through his behaviour and language, undercuts the established order through an unruly, carnivalistic energy. But at the end Bogle arrests the carnivalistic play by confronting the need for an authentic textuality. The novel, as Bakhtin would say, is a site of conflict, a heteroglossia of contending voices and identities. In Bakhtin's model, the text is in a state of internal tension between centripetal and centrifugal forces. Wilson favours the centrifugal tendencies by adopting the narrative perspective of the indecorous tramp situated on the extreme margins of the official world, by constructing Bogle's narrative out of a profoundly self-conscious speech diversity, and by turning Bogle into a playfully unreliable narrator. Bogle is an impresario of alternatives and false identities, his masquerade functioning both as survival technique and as virtuoso display of his own creativity. The danger is that in assuming and discarding many masks he loses any sense of a coherent self. So, working against the centrifugal energies are centripetal forces which finally require honest self-confrontation and an end of 'evasion'. At the end, the narrator, a kind of 'resurrection man', experiences a momentary epiphanic quietude, in which the value and beauty of the material instant make themselves fully felt. 'Starved for ideas and feelings that can give coherence to his world', he looks forward to an authentic existence founded on 'new combinations': 'That's it. The end. I'm glad it's over. I was running out of evasion ... Things aren't so bad. Perhaps the situation may be resurrected' (272). Though he likes to blame his present situation on his Irish background, Bogle is not passive and helpless. The sheer energy and variety of his linguistic performance asserts the self's essential freedom from historical determinism. *Ripley Bogle* is a statement of both the positive and the negative potential of an aesthetics and politics of postmodern fictionality. The novel's concept of textuality dismantles oppressive hegemonic discourses and suggests the positive possibilities of post-colonial political and ethical revisionism and reconstructivism. However, a text where all meaning is seen to be an effect of rhetoric, where there is no stable condition of identity, may also be a demonstration of the postmodern capitulation to performative pragmatism. The novel affirms the transformative power of the creative imagination, but there is little reason for seeing its celebration of artifice, its self-reflexivity, its ideological fluidity, as anything more than a manifestation of an immature and irresponsible ethical relativism, the triumph of the culture of the simulacrum.

At the centre of Patrick McCabe's *The Butcher Boy* is the radically alienated consciousness of Francie Brady whose voice is doubly estranged in being both the voice of a child and the raucous voice of the deranged. The novel is concerned with how a degenerate culture distorts identity into 'antic disposition'. McCabe wants us to recognise the pain that lies behind the violence, the disfiguring social forces that have produced such a monster.

As an exemplar of 'protean' identity, Francie doesn't really have a 'character' or 'personality', both of which suggest fixity and permanence. More appropriate for describing Francie would be Lifton's term 'self-process', with its connotations of change and flow.[19] Lifton stresses two historical developments as having special importance for creating protean man, and both of them are relevant to Francie:

> The first is the world-wide sense of ... *historical* (or *psychohistorical) dislocation*, the break in the sense of connection which men have long felt with the vital and nourishing symbols of their cultural tradition – symbols revolving around family, idea systems, religions, and the life cycle in general. In our contemporary world one perceives these traditional symbols ... as irrelevant, burdensome or inactivating, and yet one cannot avoid carrying them within or having one's self-process profoundly affected by them.[20]

In revealing the dark, unruly energies lurking in human consciousness, McCabe both re-writes the Wordsworthian innocent child of nature and unearths a hidden Ireland very different from anything envisioned by post-revolutionary Irish nationalism. The novel is strategically set in 1961. Francie's personal breakdown is explicitly related to the the apocalyptic backdrop of the Soviet Missile Crisis as well as to crisis and transition within Ireland itself. McCabe re-writes the official national narrative of the family, church and state. The family, recognised in the 1937 Constitution as 'the natural primary and fundamental unit group of society' whose rights were guaranteed 'as indispensable to the welfare of the Nation and State' is defined in terms of a hapless, suicidal mother and a drunken useless father whose degradation serves as a savagely ironic comment on the promise of post-independence Ireland. The conjoint patriarchal authority of church and state is figured as a variety double-act ('Father Bubble' and 'Sergeant Sausage'). Written in the wake of a series of sex scandals involving members of the Catholic clergy, the novel reflects a profound disillusionment: at the Industrial School run by Father Bubble, Francie is sexually abused by Father 'Tiddly' Sullivan, but the only concern of the authorities is that Francie's complaints are hushed up. The essential Ireland is no longer the Literary Revival's idealised countryside but a small-town backwater exhibiting the divisive class rivalry precipitated by the rise of the *arriviste* urban middle class represented by the Purcells and the Nugents. The literary icon of the pure peasant is replaced by a radically dislocated psyche which takes its cues, not from the Irish past, but American Westerns and gangster stories. The rural myth has been de-Gaelicised and Americanised: 'We'll ride out to the mountains Joe and there we can track for days. We can listen to the coyotes in the night'[21] – this American presence undermining further any essentialist notions of a pure and fixed identity. The novel is set in the period following T.K. Whitaker's *First Programme of Economic Development* (1958), which outlined a plan for supporting native industry and encouraging foreign investment. However, in the depressed environment of the novel, the only employment on offer is in Leddy's abattoir. At the same time, socio-economic change has disrupted people's connections with traditional values which had given their lives direction and purpose. Mother Ireland is invoked in the souvenir from Dublin which Francie buys with stolen money for his already dead mother – a slice of tree decorated with shamrocks and bearing the picture of an old woman rocking by the fireside, with the motto 'A Mother's love's a blessing no matter where you roam'. The subject in McCabe's novel inhabits the universe of the simulacrum, attempting to live off an outmoded past, which nevertheless continues to be reproduced with no reality any more but that of the cannibalised image.

Lifton's second historical development which has had a special importance for creating protean man is the spread of mass communications:

The second large historical tendency is the *flooding of imagery* produced by the extraordinary flow of post-modern cultural influences over mass communication networks. These cross readily over local and national boundaries, and permit each individual to be touched by everything, but at the same time cause him to be overwhelmed by superficial messages and undigested cultural elements, by headlines and by endless partial alternatives in every sphere of life.[22]

Alienated from his social world which is unable to help him sustain a stable and coherent self, Francie moves in and out of a series of fragmented fantasies from television, cinema and comics: he is 'the Time Lord', 'Green Lantern' and 'the Fugitive', John Wayne or Kirk Douglas. He's Algernon Carruthers. He fantasises about being a great footballer. He thinks of himself and Joe as being Huck Finn and Tom Sawyer. Not all are masterful roles: he's also 'Bogman', 'Pig', 'Butcher Boy', 'Brock King of the Town'. He can't resist mimicking the Industrial School's gardener, or the town drunk. Unlike Ripley Bogle, who knew when he was 'spoofing', Francie has little self-knowledge or control over his unstable selfhood.

At one point he breaks into Philip's house, puts on Philip's clothes, assumes Philip's name. The product of a dysfunctional family, Francie longs for a normal family life, such as Joe Purcell or Philip Nugent enjoys (59). This episode is typical of the novel's highly subjectivised narration: everything is focalised through Francie. The presentation of Francie's thought is varied and complex, combining fantasised narrative, Francie's free direct speech and quoted direct speech of other characters. None of the characters' direct speech is marked off by conventional speech marks, and the direct speech that is given to the Nugents is permeated by Francie's own intentions – humour, mockery, irony. All the other characters are denied autonomy, their voices subsumed in Francie's. The distinction between Self and Other, reality and fantasy dissolves. The narration becomes a babel of different voices which merge and overlap in the narrator's troubled stream of consciousness: the 'self' becomes diffused in all the roles it plays. So, Francie sheds his 'Philip' mask and, as effortlessly, dons that of the schoolmaster to teach Philip and Mrs Nugent a vicious lesson on pigs. It is a tribute to McCabe's prose that it renders so effectively the elisions, tensions and contradictions in Francie's free-flowing 'self-process'.

Superficially, Francie's direct, intuitive narration resembles that of Huck Finn (another notably protean figure and one deliberately invoked in the novel), and is conveyed in a similarly fresh, energetic vernacular which defies conventional grammatical structures, the attempt to 'sivilize'. Francie, however, has an aggressive, demonic streak which makes his speech disturbing as well as entertaining. Like Huck he confronts a corrupt and hostile world, but where Huck seeks to preserve individual freedom and integrity through flight from society, Francie is committed to violent negotiation with his social world.

One of the important features of protean man is what Lifton calls the disappearance of the classical superego, 'the internalization of clearly defined criteria of right and wrong transmitted within a particular culture by parents to their children. Protean man requires freedom from precisely that kind of superego – he requires a symbolic fatherlessness – in order to carry out his explorations'.[23] With the death of his father, the disintegration of Francie's own moral base accelerates: laying claim to a dangerous freedom, he murders Mrs Nugent. But if the death of his father creates the space wherein Francie can explore new freedoms, being fatherless also makes him more exposed to the coercions of environment: he is arrested and incarcerated in a mental home. Francie is seemingly forced into total submission, but he still represents that ineradicable residue of humanity, elemental and distorted though it may be, which serves to bring culture itself under criticism and keeps it from being absolute.

The ending allows only a minimal optimism. With Joe's final rejection of him, Francie begins to disintegrate psychically: 'I started to feel myself draining away'. He enters a state beyond language: 'I was now the dumbest person in the whole world who had no words left for anything at all.' With Joe gone from his life for good, Francie 'went off into the dark' (50). After 'twenty or thirty or forty years' in solitary confinement in the mental hospital, he is told he is to be returned to the society of the other inmates. 'How can your solitary finish? That's the best laugh yet' (214), he replies. Yet, the final image of Francie hacking at the ice on a puddle (symbolic of restored fluidity?) with a fellow inmate (215) reprises Francie's first meeting with Joe. The ending refuses to foreclose on the flowing power of the imagination, and may thus suggest the possibility of renewal, the beginning of a new socialisation and human bonding. Equally, it may be intimating a process of recurrence and useless fantasising. The narrative looks back to the trauma of the past: by beginning at the end, it enacts the central trope of Gothic tradition – resurrecting the disturbing apparition of the past in the present.

Eoin McNamee's *Resurrection Man* is based on Martin Dillon's documentary account of the Loyalist killer gang which terrorised Belfast in the 1970s, *The Shankill Butchers*. McNamee takes the historical personages and the actual events and tries to understand and explain the perverse impulses and fantastical violence that lie beneath the orderly surfaces of civilised life and seem to defy all rational explanation. The focus of McNamee's attention is

Victor Kelly, a character based on the gang leader, Lenny Murphy. McNamee's opening gambit by way of explaining Kelly's behaviour is psychological rather than political. Although ostensibly sectarian, the violence is not seen as deriving essentially from religious bigotry. Some of the most brutal acts of savagery are perpetrated by Protestants on Protestants. Clearly, McNamee wishes us to consider other more fundamental factors involved in accounting for such savage violence. Thus, the novel opens as ironic *bildungsroman,* sketching Victor Kelly's socially disadvantaged and psychologically deformed background. The relationship between mother and son is unhealthily close. His Oedipal mother-fixation prevents him from forming normal relationships with other women. His father is a silent shadow whose most significant contribution to the family has been the burden of a Catholic surname. Identity becomes Victor's dangerous obsession: uncertainty about his own identity is what drives him to the violent assertion of one.

Declan Kiberd shows that 'the Irish father was often a defeated man', and that the 'over-intense, clutching relationship between mother and son' often implied 'something sinister about the Irish man, both as husband and father. Women sought from their sons an emotional fulfilment denied them by their men.'[24] The preoccupation with father-figures 'is the tell-tale sign of a society which is unsure of its ultimate destiny. Its rebellions are conducted not so much against authority figures as against their palpable absence. These gestures rehearse not the erosion of power so much as the search for a true authority.'[25] Due to his preoccupation with father-figures Victor 'always took up with older boys, men sometimes, who were not concerned about his moral welfare'.[26] Eventually he finds a father substitute in the manipulative Nazi sadist, Billy McClure, who pretends to become his minder, and betrays him to his death. Through violence Victor seeks 'a true authority' in a world of 'palpable absence'. The knife attacks involve the mutilation of the tongue ('the root of the tongue had been severed'), as if in revenge against the silent father whose throat the son would like to cut when he's shaving him at the end.

Kiberd's Freudian account of the production of rebel sons seems relevant to the presentation of Victor Kelly:

Children with problems have traditionally been described as mother-dominated, but such problems may often be attributed to the father's refusal to assume full responsibility ... By asserting his due authority over his children, the father allows them to explore their own anger until they can control it at will and learn to stand up for themselves. Even more importantly, the father teaches the child that other people have needs too, and that everyone functions as a member of wider and wider groups. When such family authority is not asserted, the child may become a self-indulgent subversive with no respect for the configurations of the larger community ... in other words, a rebel ... If the father does learn to assert himself ... the child can begin the task of achieving a vision of society as a whole and the even more exhilarating challenge of framing an alternative.[27]

Without a positive example of manliness, Victor emerges as a 'self-indulgent subversive'. His actions serve only personal needs, not any kind of social project. With no defined centre of self, he looks to popular culture for desirable identities, heroic images of masculinity on which he can model himself: 'Before they got in bed he took out his big gun he had stuck in his belt and spun it around in his hand all the time watching himself in the mirror on the wardrobe with an expression of being somewhere else completely' (44).

Victor is a product of the postmodern culture of the simulacrum, and, as Frederic Jameson remarks, 'the disappearance of the individual subject, along with its formal consequence, the increasing unavailability of the personal *style*, engender the well-nigh universal practice today of what might be called *pastiche*'.[28] Extending beyond the characterisation of the protagonist, the stylish depthlessness of postmodern culture characterises the whole world of the novel. McNamee foregrounds the intertextuality of 'real' life through pastiche of a range of popular forms and genres, including the American gangster thriller (in his use of the figure of the lonely, single-minded investigator, and a narrative voice modelled on a characteristically understated Chandlerese), the comic-strip (as in the comic-strip names of Victor's gang members – 'Hacksaw McGrath', 'Flaps McArthur', 'Biffo Barnes', 'Big Ivan'), children's television programmes (in recreating the 'Romper Room' as the gang's interrogation and torture room), *film noir* (from which he takes his imagery of urban desolation and the pervasive atmosphere of doom and darkness), and Gothic horror stories (in his conception of the gang as 'resurrection men').

Victor's simulacral, pastiche 'self' is also a 'performing self'. In the scene where Frames McArthur is executed, terrorism is theatre. Victor makes a dramatic entrance, approaches 'the cone of light in which the chair sat' (164) and adopts the language and style of an evangelical preacher: 'He was talking in a style that his audience were accustomed to. The preacher's formal madness' (165). To McClure, the scene 'seemed distant, a televised roadside execution coming intact from a far-off war'. It has no more reality to Victor: 'This must be a simulation of death, a poor rehearsal'. After Victor departs from the expected script and actually kills Frames, the onlookers 'exchanged puzzled glances then moved to do as he said, standing for a moment to gaze on Frames' unconvincing corpse' (166). Victor experiences his own death in terms of gangster films, and is perplexed by the way reality contaminates the simulacrum. Leaving his mother's house and returning to his hide-out, 'he felt an expression cross his face like in a film, something's wrong'. Victor 'knew the moves', but the reality doesn't match the familiar script:

> He wanted them to be serious-minded men who shouted out a warning. He wanted words full of allure and danger to shout back. Never take me alive. The rifle fire had a flat industrial sound. Victor felt the bullets force him back against the door. Victor knew the moves. Struggle to raise the gun. Clutch the breast and lean forward in anguish. His face hit the pavement. He did not see one of the men leave cover and walk over to him and put his foot in his neck and shoot him through the back of the head with a snub-nose revolver. There were no words, got him at last. No last rueful gangster smile, goodbye world. (230)

'Thus perhaps at stake has always been the murderous capacity of images, murderers of the real, murderers of their own model,' writes Baudrillard.[29] So the reality of Victor's death quickly loses out to its representation, and is converted to 'an "esthetic" hallucination of reality'.[30] Watching news coverage of Victor's death that night, Heather, 'felt as if she was watching something old-fashioned. Archive footage' (231). She reacts to the death as 'a staged murder, a minor spectacle with themes and digressions' (232). Similarly, the earlier episode when two of Victor's gunmen burst into the Shamrock Bar to exact reprisals for an IRA attack is presented in terms of Baudrillard's 'precession of simulacra': the shots 'did not fit into the perceived idea of gunfire'; 'a whole glamorous ethic was missing from this scene'. In other respects, reality lives up to fiction: the barman 'started to fall, tumbling down the stairs in a graceful, cinematic manner' (140). Back on their own territory, the gunmen 'were like heroes from a film with John Wayne' (141). As with Victor's death, the narration passes from the event to its re-presentation on television news. Again, McNamee focuses on what occurs in the mediating process, this time indicating a displacement of the real into the modalities of Gothic Horror: 'There was an atmosphere of disinterment, grim cloaked figures working by lamplight, poisonous graveyard vapours' (142).

Both the perpetrators of violence and the newspapermen who report it are disturbed by the unreality of media reports: Victor 'became distrustful of the narrative devices employed ... He heard accounts of events he had been involved in which conflicted with his experience' (39). Ryan notices 'how newspapers and television were developing a familiar and comforting vocabulary to deal with violence ... Atrocity reports began to achieve the pure level of a chant. It was no longer about conveying information' (52). Events are converted to text; the city to the giant ordnance survey map which covers Ryan's desk, and the internal street-map which Victor carries about in his own head: 'he felt the city become a diagram of violence centred about him' (11). Reality becomes its representation. To know the real is no longer to know something stable.

Just as Victor recognises the mismatch between occurrence and representation, so he is aware of a gap between external reality and his own perception of it. At the end, his weakening influence is indicated as an increasing disorientation in a rapidly changing world:

> They (street names) had become untrustworthy, concerned with unfamiliar destinations, no longer adaptable to your own purposes. He read the street names from signs. India Street, Palestine Street. When he spoke them they felt weighty and ponderous on his tongue, impervious syllables that yielded neither direction nor meaning.

The street names imprison the citizens of Belfast 'in a linguistic contour which no longer matches the landscape of ... fact'[31] (the history of Empire which they tell), rather than delineating the contemporary narrative of Belfast: the remapped city no longer corresponds to the deeply etched topographies of Victor's racial memory. His topographical disorientation betrays a deep uncertainty about identity, the authority of the self, the relation between self and world, and to ward off these troubling feelings, the names of Belfast streets are intoned like a mantra.

Lifton makes the following observation on the 'profound psychic struggle with the idea of change itself' which protean man (whether the willing or the reluctant role-master) experiences:

> He is profoundly attracted to the idea of making all things, including himself, totally new ... but he is equally drawn to an image of a mythical past of perfect harmony and prescientific wholeness ...

Moreover, beneath his transformationism is nostalgia, and beneath his restorationism is his fascinated attraction to contemporary forms and symbols. Constantly balancing these elements midst the extraordinarily rapid change surrounding his own life, the nostalgia is pervasive, and can be one of the most explosive emotions. This longing for a 'Golden Age' of absolute oneness, prior to individual and cultural separation or delineation ... sets the tone for the politically Rightist antagonists of history.[32]

Victor, too, while being attracted to the 'contemporary forms and symbols' of popular culture, longs for a 'Golden Age' of Belfast:

Victor found that he could see faint outlines of the old streets on the ground. If he squinted his eyes he could almost see the streets themselves, windscoured and populous. The coopers on the quay, the ropeworks, the bakery, men selling milk from the tin, the honey-wagon from the abattoir ... But these were not his streets and he found himself drawn back to the night-time rides ... and the sense that he had created a city-wide fear and put it in place and felt it necessary to patrol its boundaries. (202)

Situated midst 'the extraordinarily rapid change surrounding his own life', and caught between his 'restorationist' and 'transformationist' impulses, Victor finds that he has, quite literally, no ground to stand on. The landscape itself is imaged in terms of instability and danger. Victor's mother 'had told him that the city stood on a former marsh', and Victor grows up nourishing himself on dreams of mastery and stability (160). Later, his thoughts again return to his mother's obsession with life's threat:

Dorcas had warned him about the lough as a child; the sudden squalls, fast currents, sucking undertows. The sea to her was deadly and graceless – full of shifting bars and ancient murks that required a wariness beyond comprehension. (202)

The view over the city is equally demoralising. Even the city landmarks are unreliable and susceptible to change:

A different territory now that he was looking at it from this height, seeming unreliable with slithery, grey rooftops and the dominating bulk of the city hospital looking prone to moodiness, as if it were at any moment liable to become detached from its surroundings and begin a surly flotation seawards. (203)

For Victor, who experiences himself in a postmodern fashion – ungrounded, decentred, defined through others, lacking agency – violence offers the possibility of full presence. The outbreak of the Troubles in 1969 does not politicise him so much as allow him to complete an already ongoing 'self-process': 'In 1969 the streets began to come alive for Victor' (27). Where writers such as Benedict Kiely and Bernard MacLaverty show that self-fulfilment can only be realised in a private sphere of sexuality or domesticity dissociated from, although constantly threatened by, the world of political violence, McNamee explores the possibility of authentic existential fulfilment through violence. The private relationship between Victor and Heather reads almost as a parody of the romance plot as found in *Cal*. Victor, like Cal, is a version of frustrated and disaffected youth, but where Cal escapes into a passive and apolitical privacy, Victor asserts himself through acts of outrage and transgression, thereby seeking to transform himself from victim to 'victor'. *Cal* is a 'Catholic' novel of guilt, anguished conscience and penance, but in the nightmarish world of *Resurrection Man* murder has a salvationist glamour. The 'antic disposition' and its capacity for violent transgression become the basis for a projected authentic selfhood.

The newspapermen, Coppinger and Ryan, who follow the knife-murders, emphasise the uniqueness of these new forms of violence. Ryan imagines the strange new killer as 'an evangelist with burning eyes, a seeker after fundamental truths' (3). The violence 'declared itself different ... demanded a new agenda' (147). In the investigations of the first murder, they note, in a sentence that is repeated, that 'the root of the tongue had been severed' (15) and that 'new languages would have to be invented' (16).

McNamee effectively conveys the excitement as well as the hideousness of violence. In writing of hallucinatory power, he conveys a sense of dreaminess at the heart of the action. The unswerving, Hemingwayesque attention to objective detailing is accomplished with journalistic precision and vividness, without any explicit authorial attempt to guide or influence the reader. At the same time, the language, grounded in simple realism, gestures towards mysticism. Killing has both an aesthetic and religious potential. This is violence with 'a dark and thrilling beauty' (34). Victor's showdown with Darkie Larche is like 'choreographed movements leading to a duel' (41). McClure discovers 'the transcendent possibilities of silent suffering' (30); when Victor raises his gun, his victims 'looked like the members of a sect devoted to moments of urgent revelation' (48); Heather notes the 'mystic zeal' (135) in his eyes, and the effect he has on his followers: 'She had a sense of the huge faith they had invested in him. A devotion almost religious in its intensity' (93); the Resurrection Men 'were seen as favoured and visionary. Defenders of the faith' (145). When Victor confides in Heather, he speaks of the deep need that violence satisfies:

> He said little about the killings themselves but he managed to convey the impression of something deft and surgical achieved at the outer limits of necessity, cast beyond the range of the spoken word where the victim was cherished and his killers were faultlessly attentive to some terrible inner need that he carried with him. (174)

This is the 'need' of the man with no inner self who requires others to confirm his existence. Uniting the erotic, the sacred and the diabolic, Heather describes him as searching for some secret significance in life: 'Suddenly she pictured him crouched over a corpse holding a knife. The same intentness on his face that she saw in bed, seeking the pattern, the deep-set grain, with dreamy inventive movements' (175). Through violence, Victor momentarily obliterates doubt and uncertainty, and achieves order and control; his acts of torture and killing 'had formal structure' (29); a set of new knives is 'a rapture of design' (48). To the man who 'knew that ordinary speech was inadequate to the occasion' (52), violence offers a more meaningful form of self-expression, a way of writing himself – literally – on the body of the Other. The identification of knife and word is made explicit when Victor sees Willie Lamb's butcher knives: 'they looked like something inscribed on the counter, a word or versatile phrase of extinction' (132). Looking at photographs of Victor's victims, Heather notes that 'many were marked with knife-wounds on the torso and limbs, the marks regular, like the script of some phantom tongue' (197).

Ironically inscribed within the narrative context of 'slippage' are the figures of Victor and the resurrection men. Victor's situation is not as Gerry Smyth defines it – a protagonist who 'lacks any sense of self' inhabiting an essentialist world of 'evil, unchanging and elemental':[33] rather, he is a protagonist who, lacking any sense of self and inhabiting a shifting postmodern world, searches for a transcendent, essential self through monstrous violence. His fanatical commitment to this project of resurrecting himself from the fallen world of the simulacrum turns him into a grotesque – not a Christ-figure, more a body-snatcher. Reacting against the Protean forces, he prefers the 'imprisonment' of fixed outlines. He is happiest in prison:

The prison building was a geometric expression of rigorous morality ...
He was at home in closed societies with their stringent and predictable
codes of behaviour. At this time he felt his most powerful. His life was a
thing hedged with magic and the possibilities of renewal. (70)

Withdrawn from a changing world, the resurrection men are characterised in
terms of fixity and timeless recurrence. Part one ends with a description of
Victor and Biffo doing look-out duty on the roof of their hut in Long Kesh:
'motionless figures acquiring a permanence which seemed impervious,
amoral, immune to entreaty' (113–14). They are creatures of myth not
history, marooned amid the postmodern flux, monumental, unchanging,
unable to keep up with the flow.

The novel's original (and originating) 'resurrection man' is of course the
author. 'Resurrection' considered as a form of 'restoration' or 'reproduction'
gestures toward Baudrillard's idea of the 'hyperreal' where images replace and
determine the real. McNamee 'resurrects' the historical figure of Lenny
Murphy, through the mediation of a complex network of media references,
including Martin Dillon's book; through a range of 'resurrection' intertexts –
the Gospels, historical accounts of Burke and Hare, the myths of Orpheus and
Odysseus – and through contemporary representational forms. But
'resurrection' also has a 'transformational' connotation: it also expresses a
concept of magically reconstituted self-presence, an idea of escape from
(cultural and technological) determinism and the sepulchre of the
simulacrum. In this sense, the author need not share Baudrillard's notion of a
purely reproductive economy of the sign, but use the aesthetic (parody,
allusion, quotation, borrowing of styles) as a way of freeing cultural forms
from earlier identities and investing them with new possibilities. The author
himself becomes protean man whose 'innovations' may be thought of 'as new
combinations of old modes'. These redemptive possibilities of the aesthetic are
twice hailed in the novel: 'The root of the tongue had been severed. New
languages would have to be invented' (15, 16).

McNamee's 'new language' challenges the traditional discursive premises
of 'Troubles fiction', undermining 'reflectionist' or realist conventions of
literary form and the usual account of history as 'reflection' of a reality
which precedes it and determines the form of its representation. It
problematises the epistemological grounds of texts and, by insisting on the
postmodern awareness of the absence of centre or source, expresses the
constant slippage and unreliability of meaning. But even more striking and

controversial is its treatment of the violent 'antic disposition'. In adopting a narrative stance very close to that of his protagonist, McNamee runs the risk of encouraging the reader to identify the author with the character. At first reading it might seem, as Lionel Trilling said of Isaac Babel's collection of short stories, *The Red Cavalry* (1926), that the writing of *Resurrection Man* is itself 'touched with cruelty'. McNamee deals with extreme violence, yet describes it, as Trilling believed Babel did, 'with a striking elegance and precision of objectivity, and also with a kind of lyric joy, so that the reader cannot be sure how the author is responding to the brutality he records'.[34] As one reviewer described *Resurrection Man*: 'This horrible, brilliant book allows us both to condemn and also to understand the awful addictive excitement of violence, the bloody poetry of it.'[35] The relentless detailing of mutilation and murder ultimately evokes the predictable feelings of shock, horror and moral outrage all the more powerfully precisely because of McNamee's controversial postmodern style – its ironic detachment and objectivity, its apparent indifference to 'depth', 'meanings' and 'values', its refusal of explicit human sympathy, its mechanistic psychology and choreographed horror.

CIARAN CARSON

Dante: *Inferno*

CANTO I

Halfway through the story of my life
  I came to in a gloomy wood, because
      I'd wandered off the path, away from the light.

It's hard to put words to what that wood was –
      I shudder even now to think of it,
      so wild and rough and tortured were its ways,

that death, I'd say, must be akin to it.
      Yet many brilliant insights do I owe
      to it, which I will presently relate.

How I got into it, I still don't know,
      for I was well upon my way to sleep
      before I ever left the straight and narrow.

It seems I'd found myself at the foot of a steep
      hill; here, the valley formed a cul-de-sac;
      and there, I fell into depression deep.

Then I looked up. Clouds were riding pickaback
    on the high-shouldered peaks, as, bursting through,
    the sun pursued its single-minded track;

so was the lake of fear in me subdued
    a little, that had festered like a cyst
    all night, till I thought dawn long overdue.

And, as a sailor washed up by the tempest
    flounders gasping on the half-drowned shore,
    yet turns to watch the ocean's huge unrest,

so did my spirit, like a bold survivor,
    turn to view the dreaded mountain pass
    that no-one yet has overcome alive.

Tired limbs somewhat relieved, onwards I pressed
    across the wasteland, one foot firmly set
    below the other in iambic stress.

And then, behold! just where the mountainside
    began to rise, up sprang a lithesome leopard,
    splendidly arrayed in spotted hide,

who would not be faced down by me, but barred
    my every path, no matter where I went,
    confining me as in a prison yard.

It was now early morning, radiant
    with those same stars that had accompanied
    the rising sun, when in the Orient

they first were set by Love Divine; indeed,
    I was encouraged by that goodly light
    to think the prancing beast of spotted breed

might bear me no ill-will, and wouldn't bite,
    when suddenly, from nowhere, sprang a fearsome
    lion! Picture for yourselves the sight:

this animal with mane frizzed high and handsome,
    charging towards me, roaring oh, so loud
    the air around him trembled at the volume.

What next? A wolf, her body sunk and bowed
    with hunger, slunk into my view, like one
    well used to singling from a crowd

a weakling for her weekly dinner. Stunned
    with fear at this dread apparition, I
    tried to summon up the nerve to run.

Then like a venturer for whom the sky
    was once the limit, finding that his shares
    have reached an all-time low, and not a high,

he weeps, and wrings his hands, and tears his hair,
    I too was driven by that lupine brute
    to stagger back, as down a broken stair,

to where the sun becomes irresolute;
    and in that lower place, a shape appeared
    to glide across my vision, pale and mute

from long restraint, As through that wasteland weird
    he skimmed, I cried, 'O pity me, you shade,
    or man! Whate'er you be, please make it clear!'

'Not man, though formerly a man,' he said.
    'My parents, you must know, were Lombards true,
    for both in Mantua were born and bred.

Under Julius I was born, and grew
    to fame in Rome when good Augustus reigned,
    and bogus pagan gods were all we knew.

I was a poet, and to some acclaim
    I sang of bold Anchises' son, who sailed
    from Troy when Ilium went up in flames.

But as for you, why have you left the trail?
    Why look so down? Why don't you climb the Mount
    of Joy, where every happy thing prevails?'

'Are you then Virgil, that superior fount
    which spouts so generous a verbal brook?'
    I bashfully replied to his account.

'O you, to whom all other poets look!
    may that enthusiasm long endure
    which brought me first to scrutinize your book!

You are my paragon, my favourite author,
    and the very one from whom I stole
    the noble style that critics praise me for.

Behold the beast that kept me from my goal;
    O help me, famous sage! her very presence
    makes me shiver and my blood run cold.'

'You need to go another road from hence,'
    he answered, when he saw my tearful face,
    'if ever you're to bid this place good riddance,

for this rough beast will let no mortal cross
    her path, but she will harry them to death,
    and worry them to their eternal loss.

Her appetite is such, that every breath
    she draws enfevers her with lust for life;
    the more she feeds, the more she feels a dearth.

She's lain with many animals as wife;
    she'll breed with many more, until the Greyhound
    comes, who'll slay her after awful strife.

He'll not be fed by capital, nor found
    to take a bribe, but will be brave, and wise;
    he'll make a nation of the common ground.

All lowland Italy he'll galvanize
    to freedom, for which Turnus, Euryalus,
    Nisus, and Camilla gained the martyrs' prize.

He'll hunt the Wolf from every civic status,
    till she's once again confined to Hell,
    from which her wanton pride first set her loose.

But as for you, I think I will advise you well
    to follow me, and I will be your guide,
    to lead you hence into a place eternal,

where you'll hear the shrieks, unqualified
    by hope, of those who suffer so much pain,
    each wishes that he died a second time.

Next, you'll see those snug within the flames,
    for they have hope that some day they'll receive
    an invite to the heavenly domain;

and should you want its wonders to perceive,
    a female soul, one worthier than I,
    will take you when it's time for me to leave.

You see, that Emperor who reigns on high
    prohibits me from entering his state
    because I once opposed his polity.

There he rules as supreme potentate;
    his the city, his the sceptred throne;
    O happy whom he welcomes through his gate!'

'O poet, by that God who was unknown
    to you,' I said, 'I beg of you to lead the rout
    from this increasingly contentious zone,

and take me to that place you spoke about,
    to see St Peter's Gate Below, and find
    those dreary souls, and hear their dreadful shouts.'

So off he went; and I kept close behind.

WILLIAM WISER

'Poet's Corner'

from *The Circle Tour*

The Circle Tour was published in the US in 1988, following my time
as writer-in-residence at Queen's University Belfast from 1979 to
1982. Michael Allen's good offices in sponsoring me for the writer
in residence position at Queen's inspired the writing of
'Poet's Corner'.

The story is this: Michael read some short stories of mine published
in England without knowing me or knowing that I am a white
fellow, though the stories were about a black guitar player, told in the
first person. Michael thought he was recommending a black for the
position, and when I showed up at Aldergrove airport Michael was
there to meet me, but no black (with a guitar) got off the shuttle flight
from London. Somewhat disappointed not to be met, I made my way
(for the first time) into the heart of Belfast and to the Common Room
on campus. Michael later met me there, and carefully disguised his
shock at my unexpected color behind his usual goodhearted affable
manner. He took me downstairs to the Common Room bar to
introduce me to the Belfast poets and to my soon-to-be colleagues at
Queen's.

My three years at the Queen's University were perhaps the best of
my academic life, and the support and friendship of Michael Allen was
a large part in my delight and profit from those years. I am not an

academic, nor a poet (never having attended university, or written a poem), but I was made welcome in that social ambience in ways I have never known in France, where I have been a longtime resident, or in the US where I was born. Despite the anomaly – an American writer, living in France, hired to teach the Irish to write English – my tenure in Northern Ireland was rich beyond compare, and I remember the time, and my association with Michael Allen, with heartfelt nostalgic regard.

In *THE CIRCLE TOUR* a psychiatric aide at a hospital in Miami has attended the suicide-death of a patient (The Poet, or 'Gold') whom he has befriended. The Poet, before his death, was offered a post as 'Distinguished Writer in Residence' at the King's University in Belfast. No one at King's has known Gold personally, so the protagonist assumes Gold's identity and appears in his place at the university, where he is accepted as The Poet and made welcome in boozy celebration. These characters, all, are invented.

'Would debarking passengers who have had any contact with poetry please report to Immigration at the air terminal building.'

Poetry? The air pressure had gone to my hearing or they were on to me already.

Like those subway passengers in New York, in our collective guilt or fear of contagion we avoided one another's eyes. Who among us had come into contact with poetry? As we filed forth onto the tarmac, into the soft black rain of Aldergrove, I shoved the suspect collection of poems inside my jacket . . .

A woman in the crowd held aloft a notice scrawled in her own lipstick: *Prof.* GOLD. The D in GOLD had run off the edge of the cardboard. I took a breath, set my jaw and went straight to her.

'Professor?'

'Gold,' rolled off my tongue.

'Singh,' she sang and revealed her speciality: 'Ulster dialects'.

She placed a dark hand in mine. Despite the Western tailored suit in wool, and the study of dialects, her scent was redolent of the East. The lacquer on her fingernails perfectly matched the carmine lipstick. A foreign warmth in this cold place: the white teeth and innocent whites of her eyes in the dark setting of her face made me immediately aware – how had I got to this, so soon, in my daring? – of an erotic possibility, white on black.

There was an element of surprise in the air, but she allowed only her great puzzled eyes to show it. I swam in those liquid eyes, and at the same time wondered if she carried a photograph in her handbag. After the first hesitant question – 'Professor?' – she had covered with a jeweled smile. I knew all was well. I was in.

When I mentioned the bizarre announcement on the plane, she said, 'The stewardess must surely have meant poultry.' She spelled the word poultry for me in her crisp English, then announced, 'I've read your poems.' ...

I lowered my head in modesty. ...

As she drew me to the carrousel I could indulge the thought of her hand in mine under far less formal circumstances. I savored the suggestion of her hips beneath the woolen skirt and fell under the sway of that sway. I tried to imagine the effect of a visiting American, not so inconsequential at that – a poet, one that glittered like gold – placed in her care. Did she ever wear native dress in this rude climate? I imagined how she would slink beside me in a sari, if she chose to slink beside me.

They cared about titles over here, and my title bore a certain cachet. Distinguished Poet in Residence – it said so in a letter from a man named Bannister. My conniving extended to whatever treasure this title might attract. Then my poor bags came trundling around the carrousel horseshoe wrapped in their plastic shroud-pacs.

She assessed my meager dowry and commented: 'You must buy a brolly straight off.' A brolly was an umbrella.

Of course, I intended to place myself in her dark capable hands, be embraced by her and comforted ...

The barricaded airport might have been designed by an architect of penitentiaries. Barbed wire was strung along the outer limits of the parking lot, a persistent rain blew through the brutal searchlights. Farther along this moonscape in the beam of arc lights I saw what must have been control towers manned by machine gunners.

Her car was a Mini, to suit her demure and miniature self. We folded ourselves into her toy and adjusted out separate centers of gravity. It was like being safely packed inside an egg. Close as convention allowed, I was enveloped in her aura and attached to her hip. Her exotic scent was all the more overpowering in our confinement, her bared knees occupied my thoughts. We set off with a jerk of misapplied gears and a musical 'Sorry'.

She drove on the wrong side of the road until I realized the left side was the right side here. Her windshield wipers went on being frantic, but I at last relaxed. In the heart of the hostile black void I could make out the ghostly shapes of sheep, where sheep may safely graze, behind barbed wire. Dr Singh was giving me charming instruction in the pronunciation of the word eight.

'Pronounced h'eight, the person is probably Catholic.'

'Hate?'

'No, h'eight. H'it is the Protestant way of saying eight. Or a variation that sounds more like aight.'

'They both sound like hate.'

'But not at all.' Her heart would verily break to make me understand. 'You don't hear the difference?'

'The hate of one sounds like the hate of the other. To me.'

'It's the aspiration of the letter *h*.' Little she knew of my own aspirations. '*H'eight*. Or as the Protestants say, h'it. The closest a Protestant comes to the Catholic h'eight is aight.'

Ulster dialects were her world and she wanted more than anything in that world to instruct me properly. Her perseverance was endearing. I could have kissed her for it. But not yet. The car was brought to a stop at a roadblock. Dr Singh made her way warily over the corrugated treads to the metal gate where a young soldier with a rifle awaited us. The soldier thrust his cocky wet beret into her window, and she showed him some papers from the glove compartment. I was obliged to produce my passport. The soldier touched fingers to his eyebrow in a slack salute and allowed the barricade gate to be raised. As good as Gold. I had been accepted: the salute was my welcome to Northern Ireland.

We entered the city alongside a river she named the Lagan past the shadows of cranes and warehouses, the Queen's Bridge, then the Royal Courts of Justice and finally past the Queen herself guarding the floodlit City Hall. Victoria, formidable in stone but deceptively thin. A convoy of armored Army trucks slowed us at Donegall Square and a patrol of foot soldiers surrounded the Royal Courts. My fear of being shot by a sniper – or exposed as a counterfeit – was eventually dispelled by my beautiful chauffeur's complete aplomb and dispassionate lecture.

'People in Belfast have an ear for accents, especially in the ghettos.'

'Is this a ghetto?' I asked, for we had left City Hall behind and the streets had turned mean, though too dark to read the graffiti.

'This,' she said, 'is City Centre.'

O-apostrophe was generally a Catholic surname. From the first word out of a stranger's mouth – stranger to that ghetto, that is – he was known for what school he had attended, what church, what part of the city he was from. O'whatever was mostly Catholic and Mc's Protestant, but not always.

'Micks?'

'M-c. Like McDonnell and McDonald of Scots origin.'

I was not as dense as I pretended, or as interested, but wanted to keep the reassuring chat alive. She had a passion for explaining and I was delighted to play dumb. All down Great Victoria Street she differentiated for me the Conleys with single consonants from the Connellys with two *l*'s and two *n*'s and the Connallys with an *a*. As she went on about the significance of names I felt warm and secure and removed from my swindle.

'Dunne with an *e* is Catholic, without, Protestant – but not always.'

How could I keep from falling in love with her?

When we passed the brooding outbuildings of the King's University she made the cryptic announcement that we were expected at the belly.

The Belly she referred to was the Bellingham Park Hotel . . .

Originally I was to have been installed in the Staff Common Room on the university campus, but there had lately been a bomb threat against the Common Room, so my reservation had been transferred to this secure hostel. Now. Would she hand me the key to my exile in solitary or accompany me to the very door and perhaps beyond? The moment of truth was postponed: she kept the key and warmed my heart with the offer of a drink.

Then she added, 'The poets are waiting to meet you.'

'Poets. What poets?'

'The Ulster poets.'

Was I supposed to know them? I thought I was the poet here. My expression must have collapsed as thoroughly as my hopes, and I feared she would take offense. But talking to poets – so soon. What if someone asked are-you-Gold?

'Are you cold?'

'Not really. Someone just walked on my grave.'

'Is that an Americanism?' She collected such expressions. 'Here we say a goose has.'

'Has what?'

'Has walked on one's grave. You're not too fagged?' Fagged meant tired and fags were cigarettes here.

'Not really.' I had learned to say not-really in London.

'They are keen to meet you.'

I had also learned to say by-all-means when I meant the opposite, so I said, 'By all means.'

Her enticing hips moved ahead of me, and I concentrated on that sensual essential as I was drawn into a strangely noisome but soundproof lounge beyond the lobby ...

The poets looked no more like poets than I did. Not even the Poet looked like a poet, unless Ghandi looked like a poet. Anyway, what did a poet look like?

Pairs of low round tables were pulled together in figure eights laden with sturdy pint glasses of dark ale and delicate sherry glasses of white wine.

'Gold b'god should be given a drink.'

'The man hasn't had his hand shook. He hasn't sat down yet.'

Through the cigarette fumes and across the debris of drink we extended our hands as Dr Singh presented her damp Yank to the smiles and eyebrows. Several of the younger poets, consigned to students' tables, stood formally to receive my hand, shyly, but with frank blank stares and a touch of awe, as they might have received a monsignor. ....

The names Dr Singh had trained me in were there: Dunn – with or without an *e* I had no way of knowing – and a Mac- or a McDonald along with a Donald, given name, or Ronald, from Donegal. I would never have known Dr McDonald from Donald O'Donegal except that McDonald had a bristling military mustache and spoke an incomprehensible Scots while O'Donegal carried an Irish harp case with his poems in it, and had no mustache. At one of the students' tables was McDonald's son Donalbain from *Macbeth* and at the next table a cast of Lords, Gentlemen, Officers, Soldiers, Murderers, Attendants and Messengers from the same play.

A red-bearded Michael, or McMichael, gently asked, 'What will you have, Professor?'

'He'll have a drink,' said a drunk, 'for the love o'god.' ...

I was placed at the center table between two of the women, poets or critics or both, merry Mary of English and Deidre O'Dear or O'Dare, the latter something of a dumpling, the former with features as sharp as a blade. How wise and considerate of the Committee to dispatch their glamorous Indian princess to meet me at Aldergrove instead of married Mary (her husband was Rupert Bannister, of the Arts Council correspondence) or plumpish stumpy Deirdre, whose resemblance to Cookie of the Sans Souci was unearthly and disturbing.

Dr Singh sat opposite me, preoccupied and out of touch. Someone asked her, 'What does he drink?'

To survive here, it occurred to me, I need only drink with them.

'Whatever,' I said uncertainly.

'A whatever-and-water,' a wag said. They were not above putting me down but I trusted they would not put me out.

'Get the man b'god a whiskey and water.'

I sat not in the place of honor (that would have been, as far as I was concerned, beside Dr Singh) but two places away, for a place was left empty, in memoriam, for the Old Poet, my predecessor, who had dropped dead strolling through the rose trellises in the Botanic Gardens six months ago.

When I dared take a sidelong assessment of faces I could find no hint of suspicion or trace of outrage. Only a polite puzzlement, perhaps, in certain eyes as they tried to place a few of the mug shots of poets they had considered for this post. But all in all the gathering seemed glad enough to have me. I was hostage to their need for a poet-passenger to deplane in Ulster's alien territory.

'And with ice,' said a bard with a bird's chirp. He had been to America – he showed a Massachusetts driver's licence to prove it – where one and all, he declared, took ice in their drinks.

'Not ice,' said Deirdre with a shudder. 'Can you not see the poor man is chilled to the bone.' Her way of saying man and bone came very close to rhyme.

'A hot Powers wouldn't hurt him any,' proposed Mary.

'A hot Powers wouldn't hurt anybody.'

A man with long wet mustaches attached to his sideburns asked me if I knew John Powers or Paddy? Jameson's or Bushmills? But these were just names without faces.

'A hot Bush would put him right.'

'Get the man b'god a Bush and be done with it.'

'Indeed,' said Deirdre, 'a Bush. A wee Bush will put him right.'

'Not so wee as all that,' said the wag. 'Everything's bigger in the States.'

'And a lager on the side,' said the bard from Massachusetts. In America one and all drank a chaser.

Dr Singh gently translated into Cambridge English: 'They are proposing a Bushmills whiskey with a lager chaser.'

'Lovely,' said I addressing her rather than the question. Lovely was the term I learned in London pubs, all the barmaids used it.

Dr Singh would have a white wine. O'Donegal left his harp case of poems behind and went off with a wet tray to fetch a fresh round. . . .

Arts Council politely asked, 'What do you think of our emerald isle?'

'Man just got here for the love o'god.'

'Lovely.' I tried to remember some evidence of loveliness as I bathed my gaze in Dr Singh – but she was foreign to this isle as I was. 'There were sheep,' I said. 'Grazing. The other side of the barbed wire.'

'That was Provos,' said the wag, 'cleverly disguised as sheep.'

'No politics,' whispered McMichael.

'There's a nice metaphor there,' said Ian or Liam, a student poet.

'Lovely,' said Mary.

'What's metaphoric about Provos?'

'Sheep, I mean,' said Liam. 'And barbed wire.'

'No poetry please, we're Irish.'

'Some of us.'

'No politics,' said McMichael, this time darkly.

The man with the Massachusetts driver's license was telling about '66 when he was burnt out in Belfast – and was himself burnt out as a poet – he fled to Dedham where they executed those anarchist fellows and he had a wee nervous breakdown at Massachusetts General – and was himself electrocuted. The Americans offered thirty-six shock treatments all in a row and asked not a penny's recompense. For he was indigent and a poet.

'Dunn writes confessional verse,' explained the lawyer-poet Bannister.

'Could have had your thirty-six at Purdysburg, and no charge either.'

'Och there's always a charge to shock treatment.'

'An electrical one.'

'But the Americans,' chirped Dunn. 'Oh, the Americans.' He was all sentiment and nostalgia for the States. 'In America they do it up brown. And there there's no National Health.'

I did not know if I was being put down or set up, but the drinks had come.

'Let up, let up,' said Bannister the barrister, his beer mug a gavel. 'Man hasn't yet tasted the water of life.'

My drink was a handsome shot of amber (no ice) in a stemmed glass, then a half-pint of lager beside it, to quench the fire of the first.

Dr McDonald said something unintelligible and Arts Council translated, his pint aloft: 'To our right honorable guest.'

'Hear, hear.'

Glasses went up and I wondered if I was being put down.

'Our Poet in Residence, long may he reside.'

'*Distinguished* Poet in Residence,' Bannister amended.

The humor here was deceptive, if I was being put down. Impossible to assess the mockery of their remarks, all was said in dead earnest and never a smile as a giveaway.

'Hear, hear.'

'*Sláinte*.'

'*Sláinte*.'

'Health.'

'Cheers,' said Dr Singh, tilting her glass in my direction but not close enough to meet the Bush I tilted towards her.

Arts Council had wet the tips of his mustaches in Guinness, and continued his citation.

'Here's a man comes to us in pristine innocence. Not knowing one side from the other, Catholic from Protestant –'

'Sheep from Provos.'

'– think of the great good fortune *not to know*.'

Nor to know, they in their pristine innocence, a fabricated poet from the real thing.

'Hear, hear.'

'Nobody to ask the man "who are you?" or to bloody well care.'

'– a man, a poet – a *distinguished* poet comes to our province –'

'Country!'

'– under no cloud, no cloud such as we've known.'

'And squat beneath in squalor.'

'Let up, let up,' cried the lawyer-poet calling the company to order.

Although Arts Council had more to say on the subject of my innocence and good fortune, it was evident to all that he was incautiously stoned and might say damaging things – or rile O'Reilly the wag into saying them. To cover, the conversation broke into separate clusters of discussion, small talk about bicycle thefts and the cost of coffee and crew racing on the Lagan:

nothing more controversial than a comparison of the freshness of kidneys at two competing butchers on the Stranmillis Road. October had turned warm, Mary observed, and a hot time, O'Reilly added, at the Divis Flats – but McMichael shushed him . . .

Dr Singh was singularly attentive to the clock above the fireplace with *Guinness Is Good for You* written across its face. She was out of touch, the other side of a curtain, cut off. With nothing more to teach me, she was lost to me. Her concentration on the clock set me to winding my wristwatch.

I was still winding, and staring into the emptiness of the Old Poet's memorial chair, when the oddly smiling Liam came between me and my ghosts and said, 'I'm away, sir.' The he headed unsteadily for the gentlemen's.

When he had gone, a lecturer in English categorized Liam for me: 'First Year Honors.'

'Only nineteen,' sighed Dr Singh. 'He'll want to talk with you.'

'And talk,' said O'Reilly, 'and talk.'

Dr Singh gave the wag a look. But I was prepared to listen, and listen.

'Writes poetry,' the lecturer with a hyphenated name warned me. He was English.

(The Irish were mostly English in the King's English Department.)

'Shake a tree in Belfast and six poets will fall out.'

'Or a policeman,' said the wag.

'It's a disease here,' said someone, not a poet.

'Only nineteen,' said Mary, back to Liam. 'And drinks.'

'Like a poet, like a sponge.'

'Och he is a poet, and a sponge.'

Dr Singh came sharply to Liam's defense with, 'Enough of that.' It occurred to me that anyone who left a gathering, however convivial, was subject to trenchant review.

'And where,' asked Arts Council abruptly, 'might your wife be?'

All wrist movement ceased. I stopped winding my watch. I experienced a destabilising flutter of pulse.

'Some time ago.' I hesitated over whose wife I should refer to. 'My wife and I.' Then, in the interest of truth, and for Dr Singh's benefit, I offered the Americanism: 'My wife and I split.'

Deirdre tilted her head to one side in sympathy and Mary to the other side in surprise. The students were commenting among themselves in the soft shushing sounds, all consonants, I took to be Irish. Dr Singh was apparently unmoved.

It was not the politic time to excuse myself, but I asked directions from McMichael and learned the word loo from Dunn. Now of course I would be discussed and the gathering could decide my fate.

Music had started up in an adjoining lounge as I passed through. A rhythmic air, both plaintive and gay, reminded me of the square-dance tapes Miss Ryan used to play in Recreational Therapy. A woman fiddler was playing it while her partner was assembling parts of a flute out of an attaché case, like a plumber putting together sections of pipe. Above the music I could hear my name, the Poet's, bandied about, handed round for comment.

Arts Council was saying to Bannister, 'I thought you said your man would be black.'

COLIN GRAHAM

A Glimpse of America

'Ireland's a dreadful country! I heartily wish it was in the middle
of the Atlantic . . .'

ALFRED, LORD TENNYSON TO WILLIAM ALLINGHAM[1]

PHANTASM AND EXCESS

Launching Ireland into a mid-Atlantic abyss was one solution Tennyson
came up with as a salve to his irritation with the place. He also asked
Allingham: 'Couldn't they blow up that horrible island with dynamite and
carry it off in pieces – a long way off?'[2] The frustration which leads Tennyson
to imagine a violent terminality for Ireland is not just the typical fulmination
of an English, Victorian conservative, who saw the Irish as 'charming and
sweet and poetic' but 'utterly unreasonable'.[3] Tennyson's vision of Ireland
in the 'middle of the Atlantic' is more prescient than the dullness his
dismissive prejudice suggests. The phantasmic,[4] disappearing Ireland which
Tennyson can barely bring himself to articulate pre-exists and pre-empts
him. It is an Ireland which has anticipated its attempted destruction and
which finds one strategy for survival in moving off into an impossible

159

cultural geography at the very moment when it seems ready to submit to scrutiny.

Michael Allen, in his discussion of Seamus Heaney's relationship to America, notes the to-and-fro pull of America's gift of cosmopolitanism and Irish-American affiliation, an attraction–repulsion aesthetic which exists in opposition to the loss of a 'parish' aesthetic.[5] Heaney's America, Allen suggests, is always potentially undercut by the spectre of a 'properly' rooted home, and Allen uses the example of Paul Muldoon's 'eel-skin' briefcase which, Muldoon fears, will 'strike out' for the sea, ironically homing along the path of Heaney's Lough Neagh eels. Thus what Allen calls the 'hegemonic possibility' of 'transatlantic presences'[6] in Irish writing can be treated with caution, welcome or self-consciousness, and America as a place of possibilities can function as an analogy, an alternative, a refuge, a vacation. Following Allen's example, this essay discusses a variety of ways in which 'transatlantic presences' are figured obliquely as mid-Atlantic presences. The forces between 'The Parish and the Dream' can create an intense mirage hovering enticingly in the elsewhere of the lost possibility of an Atlantis, a Hy Brasil, a Tir na nOg – an imaginary place which is neither Ireland nor America, an unreality born of the necessity of that 'neither'.

As if calling his bluff, Tennyson's sea-faring, moveable Ireland had already been symbolically met with earlier in the century by the transported Young Ireland rebel John Mitchel who, in 1848, on his way to Van Diemen's Land via Bermuda, found himself the victim of a peculiarly meaningless form of national simulation: 'At last we arrived at the anchorage in front of the government island, where the dock-yard is established. This island is at the extreme northwest of the whole group, and its name is nothing less than *Ireland.*'[7] While this second 'Ireland' is 'nothing less' than its almost cruelly resonant name, its irony does fit Mitchel's narrative. Ireland meets a cross-Atlantic mirror image of itself as sign and, at this stage in the story of Mitchel's exile, 'Ireland' is on the point of setting out on a journey which parallels Mitchel's own – exiled from its grounded self, it will start to appear everywhere, in an 'overabundance of signs',[8] so that it soon becomes much more than its name, while being less certainly a definable, unitary site. Sailing towards Bermuda, Mitchel attempts to fix the Caribbean island in his mind by calling up its associations; in succession he remembers connections through Bishop Berkeley, Prospero and Ariel, and Thomas Moore, a curiously apt amalgam of the religious, the colonial and an Irish sentimentality. Docked in the bay of Ireland Island, Mitchel finds that the ship next to his has on board Lord Dundonald, whose Irish name and revolutionary tendencies cannot dissuade Mitchel that the admiral 'regards Irish revolutionists as [anything other than] highly immoral characters'.[9]

Mitchel's transportation initiates what Engels, describing the out of control 'gallop' of capitalist over-production, calls a 'crise pléthorique' (a term Engels borrows from Fourier).[10] This crisis begins to infect the semantics of the very word 'Ireland' itself, so that Mitchel stumbles in his attempts to keep these two Irelands apart, as when he writes: 'There is no such naval establishment as this in Ireland – I mean the other Ireland.'[11] Caught between an Ireland of desired return and an imprisoning Ireland which mocks that return, Mitchel's ability to define what is 'other' to his Ireland becomes more teasingly difficult to control. His dilemma is compounded by the 'Irishness' he cannot help but see around him and the Ireland he must construct from second-hand rumour and out-of-date newspaper reports. Mitchel is an early victim of a process which Fintan O'Toole identifies as a late twentieth-century phenomenon, in which Ireland dissipates into 'disappeared Irelands', so that: 'While the place itself persists, the map, the visual and ideological convention that allows us to call that place "Ireland" has been slipping away. Its co-ordinates, its longitudes and latitudes, refuse to hold their shape.'[12]

Ireland becomes a plenitude of images, replicating itself for continual consumption and at times achieving an over-satiation. It is here that the 'Ireland' which is excessive topples into an Ireland of ceaseless reproduction and commodification. David Harvey, describing such a 'crise pléthorique' in terms more fatalistically postmodern than Engels', sees this as a time 'when other paths to relieve over-accumulation seem blocked. Ephemerality and instantaneous communicability over space then become virtues to be explored and appropriated.'[13] Sure enough, Mitchel's solution to this promiscuity of Irelands, in which images and signs of Ireland circulate while attachment to the object itself wans, is a phantasmagoric form of 'instantaneous communicability' which oddly parallels Tennyson's. Mitchel writes: 'often while I sit by the sea, facing that north-eastern *arc*, my eyes, and ears, and heart are all far, far':

> and by intense gazing I can behold, in vision, the misty peaks of a far-off land – yea, round the gibbous shoulder of the great oblate spheroid, my wistful eyes can see, looming, floating in the sapphire empyrean, that green Hy Brasil of my dreams and memories.[14]

Under the intensity of the condition of exile, and pulling on the resources of the past ('memories') and the future ('dreams'), Mitchel's Ireland becomes more 'other' than it has ever been, as it leaves it moorings and enters the realm of mythology, defying the curve of the earth through the power of his imagination. Tennyson was inevitably quicker to turn Ireland similarly into a 'floating sign', but Mitchel's pained and pressurised imagination replays the same process. And while for Tennyson the goal is to find an end to having to talk of Ireland, Mitchel's desire is to perpetuate 'Ireland', to hold it in his mind as a place beyond the materiality of a world which is untrustworthy. For Mitchel, at once politically visionary and practical, the process involves and *uses* the very instruments of over-determined signification which are also symptomatic of the crisis he faces;[15] so as he fixes Ireland in his mind he does it through Keatsian, autumnal and bucolic images which verge on the kitsch ('rivers ... go brawling over their pebbly beds ... and chide the echoes with a hoarse murmur', for example[16]) – the memory of Moore, and the model of his sentimental backward look, become all the more important now. The clichés of unspoilt rurality, like 'that green Hy Brasil', are given significance and justification by their existence inside 'dreams and memories'. Mitchel's vision ends with the words: 'I see it, I hear it all – for by the wondrous power of imagination, informed by strong love, I do indeed live more truly in Ireland than on these unblessed rocks.'[17] This visionary liberation is followed by the recognition that the 'Queen of England' has 'banished me from the land where my mother bore me', and the moment ends. The next day's entry starts: 'Asthma! Asthma! The enemy is upon me'[18] – the panic of meaninglessness becomes physical and psychosomatic, turning the difficulty of establishing uncompromised intellectual contact with 'Ireland' into a corporeal effect.

The Ireland which Mitchel can hear and see temporarily, coming to meet him over the Atlantic horizon, is a conjuration in the sense which Derrida describes: 'A conjuration, then, is first of all an alliance, to be sure, sometimes a matter of political allegiance, more or less secret, if not tacit, a plot or a conspiracy. It is a matter of neutralizing a hegemony or overturning some power.'[19] Mitchel's floating, Atlantic Ireland is more than an act of desperate, exilic imagination. Detaching Ireland from its real place, he can re-place himself there, in an Ireland in keeping with the Ireland which circulates around him on Ireland Island – his summoning of Hy Brasil retains, as Derrida's comments would suggest, a sense of the political, and inwardly he 'plots' an overturning of the laws of nature, conspiring against the imperical in its conspiracy with the imperial. Mitchel conspires to do to

Ireland exactly what Tennyson wishes for Ireland's fate. Faced with a repletion of signs, Mitchel's radicalism becomes truly revolutionary in that it turns signifier and signified loose from each other, awaiting the time when they can be properly re-united. Harmony can only be restored to the sign 'Ireland' when the individual is there to accommodate the duality of this 'two sided psychological entity'.[20]

An Ireland can then begin to be traced in Mitchel which evades totality by turning 'Ireland' into a place which, just as it is about to be placed, moves; as it is about to be destroyed, as with Tennyson's dynamite, it seems to explode itself, only to reappear reformed elsewhere. Mitchel, wondering what Bermuda will be like, constructs it beforehand on the basis of Irish associations − when he gets there he finds that it is already 'Ireland', that it has anticipated his associative yearning and that it offers him a near-mystical path back to its origin, which is in turn only accessible as a 'conjuration'. Ireland's dissipation into a plethora of images and its formation of itself as a fantasy island are both aspects of a continually projected utopianism which acts as a bait and as a promise. Ireland is continually in the course of 'delay, delegation, sending back, detour, holding up, or putting in reserve',[21] a sign on the cusp of lost control, in danger of 'becoming the property of everyone'.[22] Saussure describes a language trying to fix itself for posterity as always doomed to failure because it will be 'borne along, willy-nilly, by the current that engulfs all languages'.[23] Whether the causes are identified as inherent in the strict teleology of nationalism, in the call to past and future which colonialism demands of the anti-colonial, or in the conditions of production inescapable in modern and postmodern capitalism, Ireland finds itself, in Mitchel, in Tennyson, and, I would argue, elsewhere in Irish culture, a concept trapped in, and trying to free itself by deploying, a complex utopianism; accepting, for now, the current of unfixability, 'Ireland' sails symbolically on the Gulf Stream, awaiting a docking with itself at some future (always future) moment.

'THE IRISH COLONIES FROM ATLANTIS'

At http://www.stanford.edu/~meehan/donnelly/ Richard L. Meehan puts together an examination of apocalypse which covers everything from

Gilgamesh to present day 'diseases such as AIDS, instability of global markets, floods and other signs of climate deterioration, geophysical chaos'. You can also visit Jennifer Lee's Honor thesis analysis of the site which suggests that its non-linear structure reflects the nature of reading the web as media event (and presumably the deterioration of certainty which Meehan is obsessed with). Meehan's site is called 'Ignatius Donnelly and the End of the World', and its relation to Irish utopias is twisted, strange and fascinating.

Ignatius Donnelly was a second generation Irish-American lawyer, politician and writer, born in Philadelphia in 1831. At various points in his life he was governor of Minnesota and a Senator. Donnelly is sometimes remembered as a populariser of the theory that Bacon wrote Shakespeare's plays; his *The Great Cryptogram* (1887) showed in a painstaking way how Bacon encrypted his name throughout Shakespeare's *oeuvre* – Donnelly's later *The Cipher in the Plays and on the Tombstone* (1899) 'proved' Bacon to be author of the plays of Marlowe, Jonson and *The Pilgrim's Progress*.[24] Donnelly also wrote *Caesar's Column*, a futuristic novel set in late twentieth-century New York, but his relevance for present purposes lies in his 1882 book, *Atlantis: The Antediluvian World*.

Atlantis is in one sense the world of antiquarian research in the nineteenth century gone into freefall, described by its most recent editor as an 'unwitting act of fiction … a prolonged poetic trope'.[25] Donnelly's argument is disarmingly simple, and begins with Plato's dialogue in which Atlantis is described – Donnelly takes Plato at his word, and Atlantis as fact. Using archaeological and anthropological evidence as his basis, he sets out to prove that the sinking of an entire civilisation is geophysically possible and that the culture of the Western world (and beyond) points to the plain fact that 'all the converging lines of civilization lead back to Atlantis'.[26] *Atlantis* has maps of the lost civilisation and its current position in (that is, under) the Atlantic Ocean; it reconstructs this lost paradise and fount of all culture. Donnelly's method is typified by his incredulity that any sane person could look at the Egyptian pyramids and the Peruvian pyramids and not deduce that somewhere between these two must be a place from which the idea sprang and from which it was exported. In this, Donnelly's imagination can be seen to use evidence in a very particular way; he says at one point that, before evolutionary theories, science tended to think of fossils as 'simply a way nature had of working out extraordinary coincidences in a kind of joke'.[27] Donnelly takes every living and dead piece of evidence seriously, so that all signs are real signs, and all signs point back to some unitary origin –

Donnelly's method is to then find a singular coherence which can be traced back through a process of migration and dispersal, and this is crucial to seeing the significance of his bizarre book in terms of an Irish utopian imagination.

Ireland figures in *Atlantis* in a variety of ways, and as Donnelly says: 'We would naturally expect, in view of the geographical position of the country, to find Ireland colonized at an early day by the overflowing population of Atlantis.'[28] Ireland's geographical place returns at the end of this chapter ('The Irish Colonies from Atlantis') in Donnelly's *Atlantis*. Preceding that, and throughout the book, Donnelly suggests that Irish material culture is replete with signs which connect with the common Atlantean root and its parallel signs throughout the world. Ireland has its own pyramids, for example, 'flattened on the top',[29] while the debate about Irish round towers is resurrected in a newly comparative form ('We find similar structures in America, Sardinia, and India'[30]). Other evidence is linguistic, geological (including evidence of recent volcanic eruption), fossilised (the great Irish elk), and cultural (down to Irish customs of playing jacks and saying 'God bless you!' when someone sneezes).

Donnelly's thesis is very obviously, in scientific terms, that of a crank, but it is also explicable through the same tropes which haunt Mitchel's exile. At the end of his analysis of how Ireland was 'drawn from the storehouse of Atlantis',[31] Donnelly turns to the voyage of the sixth-century Saint Brendan and his mythologised attempts to find, according to one's preference, the mystical land of Tir na nOg, or the Americas. Naturally, in Donnelly's scheme, Brendan was in fact 'guided' by 'the traditions of Atlantis among a people whose ancestors had been derived directly or at second-hand from that country'.[32] Brendan's voyaging was symbolically that of an Irishman in search of his lost Atlantean origins. Ireland is not now the land of origin itself, but a placed colonised by its inhabitants, and a place which must accept that those living on it have migration as their chief cultural and racial characteristic. Brendan is then almost a psychic preparation for Donnelly's last word on Ireland, which he hands over to his daughter, Miss Eleanor C. Donnelly and her poem 'The Sleeper's Sail'. In the poem, a 'starving boy dreams of the pleasant and plentiful land', uncannily echoing John Mitchel's Atlantic vision of Ireland. In this section of the poem, the boy tells his mother what he saw in his dream:

> 'And then I saw, the fairy city,
>   Far away o'er the waters deep;

Towers and castles and chapels glowing,
　　Like blessèd dreams that we see in sleep.'

'What is its name?' 'Be still, *acushla*
　　(Thy hair is wet with the mists, my boy);
Thou hast looked perchance on the Tir-no-n'oge,
　　Land of eternal youth and joy!'[33]

Donnelly's comment is rapturous and predictable:

> This is the Greek story of Elysion; these are the Elysian Fields of the
> Egyptians; these are the Gardens of the Hesperides; this is the region in
> the West to which the peasant of Brittany looks from the shores of Cape
> Raz; this is Atlantis.[34]

From inside her genetic folk memory, Ignatius Donnelly sees Eleanor
Donnelly summon a dream vision of the Irish dream country, poeticised
through a third generation Irish emigrant's voice. And Donnelly's response
is to universalise this 'evidence' like all else in his book. This Mitchel-like
view back across the Atlantic brings Ireland into sight through its own
myths, but Donnelly's impulse and interpretation moves a stage further than
Mitchel's, and, for all its eccentricity, it is a process intended to normalise the
position of Eleanor Donnelly and Ignatius Donnelly himself. Because
Donnelly's Ireland has ceased to be special and ceased to be the only possible,
genealogical point of solid return. Instead, in the middle of the Atlantic, there
is a now an invisible place from which America and Ireland have a common
root; by 'proving' the existence of Atlantis, Donnelly has turned the
experience of emigration from one of isolated disjunction from a 'settled'
place, to the only and universal global experience, including the Irish
experience in no special way. So Tir na nOg is not exclusive, it is simply one
among many metaphoric declensions of Atlantis. Ignatius Donnelly has a
utopian drive which is complicated because the emptiness at the heart of his
evidence is not the absent island of Atlantis but the unfulfillable desire to make
the past converge on the present just as the present converges in the Atlantean
past. Not surprisingly, his solution is to look forward to the future, to
science,[35] and to the museumification of Atlantis itself:

> We are on the threshold. Scientific invesitigation is advancing with giant
> strides. Who shall say that one hundred years from now the great

museums of the world may not be adorned with gems, statues, arms, and implements from Atlantis.[36]

For all its strangeness, *Atlantis* is in tune with, and to some extent running ahead of, the 'Ireland' discussed throughout this essay. Atlantis ultimately escapes Donnelly's capacity to describe the sign systems which it enables (hence the need for a future museum). Global material culture is everywhere Atlantean, yet Atlantis is nowhere, no place. 'Ireland' floats (again) as part of this sign system, but is only a 'second order' sign, a mythology, signifying the absent transcendent which all culture signifies, 'that is Atlantis'. So 'Ireland' progresses from Mitchel's transcendent vision of it, which detaches the concept from the land but which retains a future hope by keeping in view, in Derrida's evocatively geographical phrase, 'the horizons of potential presence'.[37] Donnelly's Ireland is not even able to retain the future promise of an Irish presence, since it is 'deconstructed' 'in its totality', by '*making* it *insecure* in its most assured evidences'[38] and by calling attention to the very temporality of the sign. Donnelly's 'Ireland' draws attention to the 'linearist concept of time [which] is ... one of the deepest adherences of the modern concept of the sign' and which leads to the inevitable evocation of a *res*, 'an entity created or at any rate first thought and spoken, thinkable and speakable, in the eternal present of the divine logos'.[39] Donnelly's madness is to name the logos and call it Atlantis – but in doing so he finds the faultlines in the idea of 'Ireland', in its past and future linearities, and in its equivocal synchronicity.

To put it simply, Donnelly's Irish-American view of Ireland makes emigration normal, makes 'Ireland' a migrating entity, and disallows the possibility that Irish culture helps the idea of Ireland secure itself to itself. It may be at the edges of logic, and at the margins of the logocentrism of nationalism, but Donnelly's Atlantis is an overblown exemplification of the dislocations of Irishness throughout its history. In its 'excess' of logic, its 'phantasms' of 'scientific' evidence, and its vision of an Ireland which is not Ireland but a remnant of Atlantis, Donnelly's Ireland is the apotheosis of Irish(-American) utopianism – Ireland is everywhere and nowhere, 'broken in pieces',[40] enveloped in a story in which its particularity, and therefore its definition, will never be resolved. And if you go to Richard L. Meehan's website you will find that, despite the media, he cannot replicate Donnelly's Ireland. Chapter III of his web-book, '*Geraldis Cambrensis*: The Nature of the Westerly Regions' is narrated by 'Donnelly', who has returned to visit the late twentieth century. 'Donnelly' suggests that the Ireland of Gerald's days, with all its unlikely wonders, is like the California of today. And while Meehan is able to allow Donnelly to point out that 'The Irish[,] like the Jews and the Armenians and certain Asiatic peoples, consider themselves as exiles', Meehan's comparativism can never recapture the complex radicalism of what Donnelly's Ireland meant to his Atlantean scheme, or, more importantly, the way in which Donnelly's Atlantean scheme sits as a final dispersal of the signs of 'Ireland', deconstructing their linearity, dispersing the space they seem to signify.[41]

IRELANTIS

Following Althusserian thought, Fredric Jameson says of the postmodern that its utopianism 'can be seen . . . not so much as the production of some form of Utopian space but rather as the production of the *concept* of such space'.[42] The introduction of such meta-space into a meta-narrative in Irish culture, means that 'Ireland' becomes emptied of Ireland, and Irish signs have a multiple 'valency' which effects an unsettling form of liberation from the object or *res*. Donnelly's Atlantis is a Utopian space which cannot be produced, except through continually conceptualising its own meta-space, and so his 'Ireland' is a Tir na nOg which is fated never to return and never to be arrived at. Baudrillard describes this theoretical position thus: 'Only affiliation to the model makes sense, and nothing flows any longer according to its end, but proceeds from the model, the "signifier of reference", which is a kind of anterior finality and the only resemblance there is.'[43] Donnelly's Ireland, I would suggest, is exemplary of the culminatory effects of all these possibilities, in which 'anterior finality', taken as a reverse utopianism, means that Ireland becomes subtended to the more powerful need for 'affiliation to the model' when all signifiers are 'of reference'. Donnelly's Ireland, like everything else in his book, is in danger of sinking into the sea in pursuit of Atlantis.

An alternative to this falling, mythical, empirical fantasy vision of 'Ireland' from America, can be found in a nearly contemporaneous text which fantasises 'America' as rising in the world because it is technologically (and socially) utopian, and which, in doing so, erases 'Ireland'. Bram Stoker's *A Glimpse of America*, delivered as lecture to the London Institution on 28 December 1885, eulogises the American Dream in a way that entirely undercuts any irony which might be read into the character of Quincey

Morris in *Dracula*. But in doing so it seems necessary for its own author to empty himself of his own Irishness, however qualified that might be. Stoker's praise of America is figured in terms of a heightened Englishness in which America is 'like ourselves', that is 'we English', and where that identification can be understood in terms of '*blood*, religion and social ideas' (emphasis added).[44] Stoker, as elsewhere in his writings, praises the newly energised 'chivalry' of American society, particularly 'the high regard in which woman is held'.[45] In this frenetic vision of American perfection Stoker's need to be English is a curious form of over-identification, and for a writer who could elsewhere confess his own Irishness, there seems little other than a deadpan pseudo-anthropological register when he notes that America is currently short on servants, a job usually undertaken 'by Irish and Negroes'.[46] Whatever fantasy America fulfills for Stoker in its heightened mixture of 'blood' and futurism, its representation of what Allen calls the 'desire for upward mobility'[47] means that the place of 'Ireland' is written out of Stoker's own voice as embarrassment and anachronism. Donnelly's American Ireland creates a shimmering mirage; Stoker's 'English' America erases Ireland's Atlantic presence entirely.

In 1999 the artist Seán Hillen published a book of 'paper collages' entitled *Irelantis*.[48] The first image in the book is 'The Great Pyramids of Carlingford Lough', in which a John Hinde postcard landscape is surveyed by a man in a typically garish red jumper. The vista of 'Carlingford', which Hillen points out in his commentary 'neatly marks the border between the North and the Republic of Ireland',[49] is interrupted by three pyramids from Giza and on the horizon the world rises up (or continues to set) over the sea. This landscape is a new, conglomerated version of Donnelly's Atlantean Ireland, with the anteriority of the sign abandoned and anachronism celebrated; 'a kind of a joke'. Each of Hillen's images undoes space and time so that 'Irelantis' exists outside synchronicity and diachronicity, but remembers both. Whether 'Irelantis' is future or past is unclear, since it is sometimes archaically Edenic ('The Colosseum of Cork') and at others apocalyptic (as with 'The Great Cliffs of Collage Green' and the two images which envisage the 'Great Eruption' in the Dublin mountains).

Hillen's work in *Irelantis* is described by Fintan O'Toole:

> Irelantis is, of course, contemporary, globalised Ireland, a society that became post-modern before it ever quite managed to be modern, a cultural space that has gone, in the blink of an eye, from being defiantly

closed to being completely porous to whatever dream is floating out there in the media ether. But this Ireland is also everywhere and nowhere. Hillen is dealing with displacement in a world where all borders − political, cultural and psychological − are permeable.[50]

This reading of *Irelantis* is indisputable in its identification of the 'everywhere and nowhere' nature of the work and its open permeability. But *Irelantis* is not necessarily proof of the course of Ireland's late entry to the race for postmodernisation. Given the texts examined above, we might wish to be less surprised by *Irelantis* and see it instead as a manifestation, in contemporary and ironic nuance, of the 'dreams' which have been 'floating out there' since and well before John Mitchel or Ignatius Donnelly. *Irelantis* has a knowing irony and an artistic agency that might separate it from the 'hyperreal'[51] world of John Hinde's postcards. But even Hinde's work, sometimes seen as the static equivalent of *Man of Aran* in its vain construction of an Ireland that never existed, gives us, as Luke Gibbons suggests, 'an uneasy feeling that we are getting a last glimpse of a world that is lost'.[52] The hint of the end-of-the-world in Hinde becomes a recorded scream in Hillen, but again anteriority and its alternate futurology are the taut edges of the images, and we should be wary of explaining the differences between the two only in terms of the progress of Western modernity − that progress, after all, is what they both set themselves at a not entirely oppositional angle to. If Ireland can be a 'lost world' and an Atlantis, its status is not simply in the past but in a startlingly radical sense 'everywhere and nowhere'.

What appears as ironic pastiche in Hillen, as melancholic, visionary exile in Mitchel, and the perversion of scholarliness in Donnelly is then an interaction of nostalgia and future visions in a 'crise pléthorique'; it is not necessarily just another a symptom of an Irish obsession with history. More likely it is evidence that, as Declan Kiberd argues, 'the Irish are futurologists of necessity'.[53] But even more so than Kiberd means; 'Ireland' as a sign and concept has its own mythology, in the sense that Roland Barthes rather than W.B. Yeats uses the term. And that mythology is constructed out of an interrogation of its own necessity and its own future. Not only does 'Ireland' cast itself into the future in order to be realised; it also turns inside-out the underlying need for the future, disarming the crisis of what the future might be by forcing it to exist in a 'plethora' of cultural images.

THE ATLANTIC FLYOVER

At the beginning of *Riverdance: The Homecoming*, the Irish emerge from the sea in a temptingly Atlantean way to populate the land. By the second half of the performance they have begun to emigrate to the United States, mix with Afro-American culture, and begin to return to Ireland. The message is similar to Ignatius Donnelly's – movement is the fate of the world, culture is an origin that moves too.

In 1991 the comic book *2000AD* ran a six-part 'Judge Dredd' story set in a future, post-apocalypse Ireland in which the entire island had been set aside as a holiday resort. Judge Dredd is sent to deal with the 'Sons of Erin', a terrorist group, hiding in the Charles Haughey Memorial Village, who want to stage a 'spectacular' to kill off the tourist industry ('No more leprechaun suits . . . No more top o' the mornin' to ye . . . No more patronising our entire nation for the stereotyped garbage in a tourist brochure by some jerk who thinks this country's just one big joke'[54]). Having eliminated the Sons of Erin in his usual way Judge Dredd leaves 'Emerald Isle' by the Atlantic Flyover and through the Black Atlantic Tunnel. The Flyover has directions to Mega-City (America), Brit-Cit (Britain) and, of course, . . . to Atlantis.

NICHOLAS ROE

Bringing it all Back Home

Pantisocracy, *Madoc*, and the Poet's Myth

literary Characters make *money* there

SAMUEL TAYLOR COLERIDGE[1]

What could be more apposite
than that into this vale

a young ass or hinny
bear Samuel Taylor Coleridge?

PAUL MULDOON[2]

Nearly everybody was over the rainbow. 'It is an age of revolutions, in which everything may be looked for'; 'It is time to effect a revolution in female manners ... to reform the world'; 'That blest future rushes on my view!'; 'The woods cast a more refreshing shade, and the lawns wear a brighter verdure, while the carols of freedom burst from the cottage of the peasant, and the voice of joy resounded on the hill and in the valley'.[3]

In his undergraduate rooms next to the lavatories at the back of Balliol College, Robert Southey joined those voices in welcoming the French Revolution: 'If France ... enjoys tranquillity who knows but Europe may become one great republic?'[4] If. One year later, the tumbrils were clattering through the streets of Paris: 'The murder of Brissot has compleatly harrowed up my faculties & I begin to believe that virtue can only aspire to content in obscurity'.[5] In calmer mood, Southey announced that he intended to emigrate, assuring his friend: 'Tis not ... a momentary frenzy that says this. Either in six months I fix myself in some honest means of living or I quit my country.'[6]

Southey never did 'quit [his] country' entirely, and by 1813 he had fixed-up a thoroughly dishonest 'means of living' as Poet Laureate. But we can appreciate, perhaps, how for Southey in 1794 nothing might seem more attractive than an emigrant adventure: his cash problems would be solved, and he would escape a reactionary Terror in England. Or so Southey himself believed when, on meeting Samuel Taylor Coleridge at Oxford in June 1794, they put together their scheme for an emigrant community in Kentucky, to be located somewhere between Pantle and Pantiple and named 'Pantisocracy'. The destination soon changed to Pennsylvania,[7] at the confluence of the East and West branches of the Susquehanna River, near the township of Milton and just a little upstream from Liverpool, Seven Stars and the Susquehanna haven of Independence. Their settlement would be close to the house of Joseph Priestley, the Unitarian scientist forced out of England by Church and King mobs, who had now reconstructed his laboratory with its phials and retorts in the New World. Southey and Coleridge, both of them broke and with nothing to their names, saw some advantage in setting up a community in which property would be held in common. With 'communism' and 'codamine' then asleep in the word hoard, Coleridge, who was not yet an opium addict, invented the term 'aspheterism' to describe their system: 'we really *wanted* such a word', Coleridge blithely informed Southey.[8] So, vocabulary primed, all was now set. 'My resolution with regard to America is taken', Southey announced in August 1794: 'Calmly and firmly – after long deliberation I pronounce – I am going to America. It is my duty to depart';[9] 'No prospect in life gives me half the pleasure this visionary one affords.'[10]

What exactly was the 'vision' Southey had in view? I imagine Southey had taken a pleasure-filled bowl of punch, or something stronger from STC's sea-green vial, when he wrote out this prospect:

> fancy me in America. Imagine my ground uncultivated since the creation
> & see me wielding the axe now to cut down the tree & now the snakes that

nestled in it. Then see me grubbing up the roots & building a nice snug little dairy with them. Three rooms in my cottage, & my only companion some poor negro whom I have bought on purpose to emancipate. After a hard days toil see me sleep upon rushes, & in very bad weather take out my cassette & write to you ... do not imagine I shall leave rhyming or philosophising[11]

A root-dairy? Bob Southey asleep on rushes? All of this explains why the 'Pantisocratic system' has been regarded as a preposterous cod amalgamated in the fug of tobacco smoke and libations of spiced wine in Southey's college rooms. How on earth could it become actuality? How would they have crossed the Atlantic to the Susquehanna? – Navigating by starlight? – with Coleridge at the helm, and Southey on the mast head squinting at the horizon from what Captain Scoresby (senior), a quarter century in the future, would invent as the 'crow's nest'?

Think of the equipment and supplies down in the hold: the great auger, the plow sock, the sacks of flour and sugar, the rip saw, axes, boxes of sea-salt, the cast-iron skillet, the meal ark, the ropes and barrel-hoops, salted herrings and salted pork, helves and handles, tallow candles, pewter candle-sticks, the keg of powder, the griddle, the dozen bags of seed, the cradle, the mahogany desk, the casks of rum, and the bath with claw feet. This catalogue of pantisocratic bric-a-brac comes, of course, from Paul Muldoon's Esteeseeophilic romance, *Madoc: a Mystery*, and a poem appropriately associated with the materialist philosopher Democritus, so-called 'laughing philosopher' of ancient Greece. 'Democritus' amasses the astonishing clutter necessary had Pantisocracy 'actually' got underway. Smuggled aboard, too, is 'the cast-iron skillet'. Not any old cast-iron skillet, notice, and apparently the same one that Coleridge wrote to Southey about, from the tedium of his 'lime-tree bower': 'dear Sara accidently emptied a skillet of boiling milk on my foot, which confined me'[12] – a detail which reveals that, rather than grubbing up roots or setting bird snares, STC would have been back at home, hogging the fire, warming his slippers on the fender, and pouring another tipple of the Baltimore Black Drop.

As a prospective Pantisocrat dear Sara Fricker had married Coleridge on 4 October 1795, making Southey, who had married her sister Edith, Coleridge's brother-in-law. Here is the catalogue of domestic items drawn up by Coleridge as he began married life, 'quite domesticated at Clevedon' in a 'comfortable Cot': 'A riddle slice; a candle box; two ventilators; two glasses for the wash-hand stand; one tin dust pan; one small tin tea kettle; one pair of candlesticks; one carpet brush; one flower dredge; three tin extinguishers; two mats; a pair of slippers; a cheese toaster; two large tin spoons; a bible; a keg of porter; coffee; raisins; currants; catsup; nutmegs; allspice; cinnamon; rice, ginger; and mace'.[13] What I want to do in this essay is to explore some equivalent 'tin tea kettle' practicalities – the arrangements necessary to make the Pantisocracy scheme work (or not) like the many other emigrant settlements in America since William Penn founded Philadelphia, Quaker 'City of Brotherly Love'. Next, I want to look at how the experiment in pantisocratising would bring together the visionary and the homely ('Coleridge leaps out of the tub. Imagine that'[14]) and how, in so doing, it would domesticate the millenarianism of earlier years. The scheme set the agenda of Southey's *Poems* of 1797, a collection which expresses the feelings of one sharply at odds with reactionary, repressive England. And in the concluding poem of Southey's collection we shall see Pantisocracy absorbed into a myth of the poet's development and, ultimately, some 'High Romantic' accounts of the imagination.

Southey had thought of emigrating to America before meeting Coleridge. He'd read in *The Rights of Man* and Adam Smith's *Wealth of Nations* political and economic arguments which favoured settling in America: 'As America was the only spot in the political world where the principles of universal reformation could begin', Paine wrote,

> so also was it the best in the natural world ... Its first settlers were emigrants from different European nations, and of diversified professions of religion, retiring from the governmental persecutions of the old world, and meeting in the new, not as enemies, but as brothers.[15]

It's worth mentioning that when Paine was writing 'emigrant' was a comparatively new word, dating from 1754 and referring originally to German emigrants to Pennsylvania. An earlier usage, which as we'll see was also relevant to Pantisocracy, was the seventeenth-century sense of 'emigration' as the migration or departure of the soul at death or through an ecstatic rapture. The two senses of emigration – physical removal and spiritual elation – overlapped for dissenters like William Hazlitt (father of the 'brow-hanging, shoe-contemplative' critic[16]), Richard Price, Joseph Priestley, Thomas Cooper and Coleridge, for all of whom religious liberty in America was an inspiring motive to emigrate across the Atlantic.

Much more down-to-earth, if not yet in the rush bed, Southey was impressed by Adam Smith's analysis of the costs of settling:

> fifty or sixty pounds is . . . a sufficient stock to begin a plantation with. The purchase and improvement of uncultivated land, is there the most profitable employment of the smallest as well as . . . greatest capitals . . . Such land, indeed, is in North America to be had almost for nothing, or at a price much below the price of the natural produce; a thing impossible in Europe, or, indeed, in any country where all lands have long been private property.[17]

Smith's calculations were attractive. 'According to the computation of Adam Smith', Southey announced in August 1794, 'the comforts of life may be procured by the daily toil of half an hour!'. His letter continues:

> would that state of society be happy where every man laboured two hours a day . . . where all were equally educated, where the common ground was cultivated by common toil, and its produce laid in common granaries, where none were rich because none should be poor, where every motive for vice should be annihilated and every motive for virtue strengthened? Such a system we go to establish in America.[18]

Southey had recognised that Smith sought to increase output by dividing labour, but upended Smith's capitalist endeavour so as to justify a minimal amount of 'daily toil': there would be leisure for rhyming and philosophising after all! This mixture of pragmatism and optimism is typical of Southey, and later reappeared in his projections for the sale of his bulky poem, *Madoc*, as a volume to be read and also (more realistically?) as an article of furniture which the 'gentry' would buy to fill up their empty bookshelves.

Theoretical backgrounds for Pantisocracy came from Paine and Smith, and the necessary 'motive to virtue' from Godwin's *Political Justice*. And there were practical handbooks about transatlantic emigration too, 'rough guides' written by the French Revolutionary Brissot, by Mary Wollstonecraft's lover Gilbert Imlay, and by the Manchester Radical Thomas Cooper. First-hand acquaintance brought valuable advice, as reported by Coleridge to Southey from what was evidently the snug bar of the 'Salutation and Cat' Ale-House in Newgate Street, London. 'We have a comfortable Room to ourselves − & drink Porter & *Punch* round a good Fire', Coleridge writes, adding with a surge of Pantisocratic rigour:

My motive for all this is that every night I meet a most intelligent young Man who has spent the last 5 years of his Life in America – and is lately come from thence as An Agent to sell Land ... He says, two thousand pounds will do – that he doubts not we can contract for our Passage under 400£. – that we shall buy the Land a great deal cheaper when we arrive at America – than we could do in England ... That 12 men may *easily* clear *three hundred* Acres in 4 or 5 months – and that for 600 hundred dollars a Thousand Acres may be cleared, and houses built upon them – He recommends the Susquehannah from it's excessive Beauty, & it's security from hostile Indians – Every possible assistance will be given us – we may get credit for the land for 10 years or more as we settle upon it – That literary Characters make *money* there ... He never saw a *Byson* in his Life[19]

What we overhear from the 'Salutation and Cat' is an account of colonising in which 'literary Characters' are as involved as everyone else in the scramble for gain. Pantisocracy, idealistic scheme, coined word, was a colonial foothold in the land of the 'hostile Indians'. 'That literary Characters make *money* there' suggests Coleridge's pantisocratic ideals were dwindling. The Pantisocrats would take out a contract for the voyage; they would deal with a land agent, seek credit for purchasing and clearing land, and then build houses for the community that would be established, Coleridge said, 'on the principles of an abolition of individual property'.[20] Taken altogether, the economic infrastructure that would make Pantisocracy viable was in place, and Southey was actively raising funds with subscriptions for his epic poem *Joan of Arc*.[21] All that was missing, in this account of the business, was a literary agent. 'We go at least twelve men with women and children', Southey announced, confident that 'by this day twelve months the Pantisocratic society of Aspheterists will be settled on the banks of the Susquehannah'.[22]

So who was to join the Pantisocratic society? Twelve men with women and children was the count in August 1794. Included were Southey's mother; his fiancé Edith Fricker, with her four sisters Elizabeth, Martha, Mary and Sara, and their mother Martha Fricker; George Burnett, an Oxford friend and early convert to the scheme, who proposed unsuccessfully to Martha Fricker; Robert Allen (one of Michael Allen's ancestors? which would make Michael a Pantisocrat too), acquainted from school and university with Coleridge and Southey; Robert Lovell, a Bristol friend and poetic collaborator of Southey's, who married Mary Fricker; and Coleridge who married Sara Fricker. This made up the core of twelve emigrants, but recruiting went on in Bristol, London and Cambridge and a month later the group was described by Southey as:

> Lovell, his wife, and two of his sisters: all the Frickers – my mother, Miss Peggy, and brothers; Heath, apothecary and man and wife; G. Burnett – S.T.Coleridge – Robt Allen and Robert Southey. Of so many we are certain, and expect more.[23]

That is, four Lovells; seven Frickers; five Southeys plus cousin Margaret (Peggy) Hill; three Heaths (apothecary plus man and woman servant); and the four others. A total of twenty-four, which rose to twenty-seven and beyond in the month following. It's possible to draw up a roll-call of prospective Pantisocrats from Southey's and Coleridge's letters in 1794-5, and it's likely that the community would have amounted to some thirty-eight individuals (there were probably more that I haven't been able to identify).

In the planning of Pantisocracy the Fricker factor was a considerable one. For all Southey's and Coleridge's theorising about equality and aspheterism, Pantisocracy was to be at heart a family settlement establishing the homes that neither Southey nor Coleridge had known since early childhood.[24] In one sense a visionary prospect in keeping with the revolutionary 1790s, Pantisocracy was also a practical scheme for domesticating the millenarian impulse, 'in the Dell / Of high-soul'd Pantisocracy to dwell'. That line comes from Coleridge's splendid poem which commiserates with 'a Young Jack Ass':

> Poor little Foal of an oppress'd Race,
> I love the languid Patience of thy Face!
> And oft with friendly hand I give thee Bread,
> And clap thy ragged Coat & pat thy Head ...
> How *askingly* it's steps toward me bend –
> It seems to say – 'And have I then *one* Friend?'[25]

The Young Ass and Southey's dog Rover were included as Pantisocrats too, and hailed as 'brother' along with the servant Shadrach Weeks who had been persuaded to come along too (doubtless hoping for reduced working hours). With them was the poet Thomas Chatterton, albeit not in person. Dead since 1770, Chatterton had already emigrated and so would be aboard as a kind of spiritual guide, as we find from Coleridge's 'Monody on the Death of

Chatterton' which included the following lines:

> O, CHATTERTON! that thou wert yet alive!
> Sure thou would'st spread the canvass to the gale,
> And love, with us, the tinkling team to drive
> O'er peaceful Freedom's UNDIVIDED dale;
> And we, at sober eve, would round thee throng,
> Hanging, enraptur'd, on thy stately song!
> And greet with smiles the young-eyed POESY
> All deftly mask'd, as hoar ANTIQUITY.
>
> Alas vain Phantasies! the fleeting brood
> Of Woe self-solac'd in her dreamy mood!
> Yet will I love to follow the sweet dream,
> Where Susquehannah pours his untam'd stream;
> And on some hill, whose forest-frowning side
> Waves o'er the murmurs of his calmer tide,
> Will raise a solemn CENOTAPH to thee,
> Sweet Harper of time-shrouded MINSTRELSY!
> And there, sooth'd sadly by the dirgeful wind,
> Muse on the sore ills I had left behind.[26]

Chatterton, poet of the 'antique' Rowley poems and (perhaps) a suicide in 1770 at the age of 17, was the self-destructive genius of Romantic myth – one of the 'mighty poets in their misery dead'. Here he is glimpsed in a context that identifies Pantisocracy as a release from oppression and untimely death – hence the Cenotaph overlooking the Susquehanna, not just a memorial but, cannily, an empty tomb from which Chatterton, Christ-like, has made a further emigration.

Chatterton as a Pantisocrat is vigorous and commanding, a powerful poet whose 'stately song' invigorates the community at 'sober eve' (unlike evenings at the Salutation and Cat). This is the alternative Chatterton of Romantic tradition – Chatterton as a liberal hero, the champion of liberty who had ambitions, like Southey and Coleridge, as a political journalist and poet of social critique.[27] Together the Cenotaph and Joseph Priestley's house and laboratory represented the complex endeavour of the Pantisocracy scheme, reminders of the old world and of the quest for 'new life new hope new energy'.[28]

As one might suspect, Coleridge had elaborated a theory to explain how 'new life' might be gathered to and diffused from Pantisocracy:

> The ardour of private Attachments makes Philanthropy a necessary *habit* of the Soul. I love my *Friend* – such as *he* is, all mankind are or *might be*! The deduction is evident –. Philanthropy (and indeed every other Virtue) is a thing of *Concretion* – Some home-born Feeling is the *center* of the Ball, that, rolling on thro' Life collects and assimilates every congenial Affection.[29]

This comes from a letter to Southey, 13 July 1794, in which Coleridge (who was on a walking tour of Wales) announces promisingly that he has 'positively done nothing but dream of the System of no Property every step of the Way'.[30] It suggests that 'home-born Feeling' was the emotional centre of Pantisocracy, which through a process of assimilation and *concretion* – and a little help from STC's friends – would bind the community together and attract new 'congenial' participants. Taking Coleridge's theory literally we might sketch out a plan of how Pantisocracy would embody physically, in its layout, the ideals and practicalities of the scheme that I've been exploring so far. The community is located at the confluence of the west and east branches of the Susquehanna River, close to Joseph Priestley's house, and rather above the most recent levels of flooding. Instead of forming a dispersed strip settlement along the riverbank, Pantisocracy has a circular layout with at its centre a Unitarian meeting house in which the Pantisocratic council meets. Up on the hills behind the settlement is the Chatterton Cenotaph, and carved upon it, in antique writing, are these words:

> Now doeth Englonde weare a bloudie dresse
> And wyth her champyonnes gore her face depeyncte;
> Peace fledde, disorder sheweth her dark rode,
> And thorow ayre doth flie, yn garments steyned with bloude.[31]

Pantisocracy was an attempt to get out of that 'dark rode', escape the violence of England, and, by moving to a new transatlantic community, to keep alive something of the hopes of former years as well as the private and domestic attachments threatened in a state whose 'garments [were] steyned with bloude'. When the Pantisocratic impulse faltered we can see how emigration would grow increasingly remote, leaving disengagement and retirement as alternatives. The practical scheme for Pantisocracy was short-lived, brought back from America and briefly relocated in Wales[32] – and then abandoned altogether when Southey and Coleridge quarrelled. But the idea of 'dwelling in the dell' persisted, relocating Pantisocracy in the personal, the private, and the homely – in poems such as Coleridge's 'Frost at Midnight', and Wordsworth's 'Home at Grasmere' which, as part of the *Recluse*, was intended to address the fall-out of failed revolution. Indeed 'dwelling in the dell' serves as a catch-all description of the Romantic retreats of Southey and Edith Fricker, Coleridge and Sara Fricker, and the Wordsworths at Nether Stowey, Alfoxden, Dove Cottage and Keswick. Glancing through some later generations we find Leigh Hunt and Marianne Kent, released from gaol and at the Vale of Health, taking

> A long, deep draught of silent freshfulness,
> Ample, and gushing

– and Seamus and Marie Heaney, inner émigrés, 'landed in the hedge-school of Glanmore', where

> . . . a rustling and twig-combing breeze
> Refreshes and relents

– and, finally, for this is what it amounts to now, in England, the numberless bolt-holes of John Betjeman's 'Metroland', that suburban Pantisocracy –

> Out into the outskirt's edges,
> Where a few surviving hedges
> Keep alive our lost Elysium . . .

– to which city commuters return to recuperate, with 'sandwich supper and the television screen', relieved that a hedge, or a fence, or a plasterboard wall is keeping the neighbours at bay.[33] Coleridge, at least, was aware that such retreats might be a temptation to throw-up the cause altogether, 'sinking into an almost epicurean selfishness, disguising the same under the soft titles of domestic attachment'.[34]

The 'titles of domestic attachment' are foregrounded in Southey's 1797 *Poems*. This is a collection which has been more-or-less overlooked by studies which focus on the Wordsworth-Coleridge axis of English Romanticism, studies which announce that one 'looks in vain in Southey for the imagination, the power of mind, the sense of the numinous, that distinguish the greater Romantics'.[35] I want to suggest that to look for these 'High Romantic' qualities in Southey's 1797 book is wrong from the start, and that some of the book's significance appears in themes close to the Pantisocracy episode, themes which were explored as well by some women poets of the time.

Southey's *Poems* avoids the egotism and self-assertiveness of Wordsworth–Coleridge Romanticism – the Romanticism, that is, of *Tintern Abbey* and *Dejection*. What we find in Southey's book, instead, is a strikingly miscellaneous gathering of poems (the miscellaneousness resembles his mastery of different genres, in later life, as a professional 'man of letters'). The collection opens with a sonnet 'To Mary Wollstonecraft' in praise of 'Woman triumph[ant]' in past and present generations; the next poem, 'The Triumph of Woman', takes a biblical parable to illustrate this theme. Then follow poems on the slave trade; a clutch of odes; eight inscriptions; the 'Botany Bay Eclogues' (a different kind of emigration, but, like Pantisocracy, the result of oppression); ten sonnets; and a monologue by Sappho just before her suicide, introducing a female counterpart to Chatterton, in a poem competing with Mary Robinson's 1796 sonnet sequence 'Sappho and Laon'. Next are some melodramatic lyrics; and the concluding blank verse meditation, the 'Hymn to the Penates' – that is, a 'Hymn' to the sustaining deities of the Roman household, the 'Gods dwelling in the store-cupboard' alongside the *Lares* who protected the house.

On reading through the whole collection, however, 'home' seems to be mentioned only because it has been left behind, lost, or is out of reach. Southey's world is populated by outcasts, beggars, slaves, strangers, wanderers, travellers, paupers, exiled prisoners, widows, wronged women, discharged soldiers and sailors, and murderers. And then there is the poet figure himself, introduced in the prefatory sonnet as 'a Pilgrim woe-begone', 'roving' on 'Life's sad journey', a 'solitary' and, in another poem 'On the Death of a Favourite old Spaniel', a melancholy school boy 'with the thought of distant home' (here is the seed of 'Frost at Midnight'). These are all figures of 'forlorn humanity', all 'from their poor and peaceful homes [expelled], / Unfriended, desolate, and shelterless'.

In the background is the unaccommodated 'thing itself' on the heath in Act 3 of *King Lear*, but I believe that Southey's immediate influence (which was also indebted to *Lear*) was Charlotte Smith's 1793 poem *The Emigrants*. Smith gives an account of royalists from revolutionary France, 'whose dejected looks'

> proclaim them Men
> Banish'd forever and for conscience sake
> From their distracted Country[36]

Set against home foresaken is the 'sighed for' prospect of a 'lone Cottage, deep embower'd', which you'll recall was one of the motifs of the Pantisocracy idyll. I suspect that Southey's idea of emigrating owed as much to Charlotte Smith's poem as to Paine, Smith and the American travellers, and that he was indebted to her for the more radical vision of humanity in his collection of poems. Smith's *The Emigrants* juxtaposes the plight of the French with this (*Lear*esque) image of alienated humankind:

> Poor wand'ring wretches! whosoe'er ye are,
> That hopeless, houseless, friendless, travel wide
> O'er these bleak russet downs; where, dimly seen,
> The solitary Shepherd shiv'ring tends
> His dun discolour'd flock ...
> Poor vagrant wretches! outcasts of the world!
> Whom no abode receives, no parish owns;
> Roving, like Nature's commoners, the land
> That boasts such general plenty [37]

This passage from *The Emigrants* supplies the keynote for Southey's 1797 volume, which develops the idea of houseless, friendless humanity in poems we might think of as individual studies of 'nature's commoners' (and this, remember, before Wordsworth's *Ruined Cottage* and 'Lyrical Ballads'). Some of the poems such as the 'Botany Bay Eclogues', 'The Soldier's Wife' and 'The Widow' articulate 'jacobin' social protest directed against the legal and penal systems, against war, poverty, and irresponsible aristocracy. The 'Botany Bay Eclogues', written in 1794, are a kind of antipodean Pantisocracy, a series of exile monologues which are set at different times of the day – as Smith's two-part emigrant narrative, published in 1793, had also been.

The poems may protest but there is no call for revolutionary action, nor is there anything resembling Coleridge's climactic, visionary poem *Religious Musings*, which was carefully placed at the close of his 1796 volume, *Poems on*

Various Subjects. Anticipating that a 'blest future' is about to 'rush upon [his] view', Coleridge echoes the excited, millenarian responses to Revolution in the hope that, even after war and terror, the visionary future is still imminent.[38] Meanwhile, in responding to contemporary women's poetry, Southey was ahead of the field and moving into a different tomorrow. If we read his 1797 collection alongside Coleridge's *Poems on Various Subjects* from the preceding year, we can see that where Coleridge looks forward to a spiritual revolution at the millennium, Southey chooses as the final statement of his own collection a poem which brings everything back home. The 'Hymn to the Penates' finds the domestic 'hallowed hearth' better fitted for 'visionary joys' and for 'pondering loftiest themes' (as Coleridge discovers in 'Frost at Midnight', when with the 'inmates of [his] cottage, all at rest', he is left to the solitude 'which suits / Abstruser musings'). In the same passage, Southey reintroduces his figure of the poet 'driven / Amid the jarring crowd', and he does so not by way of affirming the attractions of the 'hallowed hearth' and home attained, but to introduce a brief retrospect of the Pantisocratic settlement which has now been abandoned:

> I have strayed
> Where o'er the sea-beach chilly howl'd the blast,
> And gaz'd upon the world of waves, and wished
> That I were far beyond the Atlantic deep,
> In woodland haunts – a sojourner with PEACE.[39]

Elsewhere in the poem Southey gazes 'From some high eminence on goodly vales /And cots and villages embower'd below', and remarks,

> The thought would rise that all to me was strange
> Amid the scene so fair, nor one small spot
> Where my tir'd mind might rest and call it *home*.
> There is a magic in that little word;
> It is a mystic circle that surrounds
> Comforts and Virtues never known beyond
> The hallowed limit.[40]

Poems by Robert Southey replaces Coleridge's ever more belated millenarianism with a domesticated sociable endeavour – even if that 'hallowed limit' is, for the moment, a prospect rather than an actuality attained. In continuing the idea of settlement, Southey's *Poems* might be thought of as 'The Book of Pantisocracy' – a book which, incidentally, Coleridge had projected,[41] but never completed: perhaps the manuscript was eaten by Rover.

As we read through the 'Hymn to the Penates', however, we find a significant reformulation of Pantisocracy, located now within a myth of the poet's development as an ideal destination which is compelling yet forever out of reach (much as Charlotte Smith had found that no 'cot sequestered', no 'substantial farm' would 'terminate [her] walk'). The 'Hymn' concludes with Southey looking to a time when humanity 'shall' feel the 'sacred power' of domestic peace, living (as in Pantisocracy) 'in the equal brotherhood of Love'. Southey's 'Hymn' and the book as a whole close with the affirmation 'meantime, all hoping'.

Here Southey is setting the human scene (as Coleridge's 'blest future' of the elect does not) for one of the Romantic myths supposedly beyond his genius. I'm thinking of the recognition that came to Wordsworth when, in recalling his arduous and perplexed crossing of the Alps for *The Prelude*, he experienced an overpowering sense of alienation – 'lost as in a cloud'. His recovery from this mood brings an elated recognition: 'our home / Is with infinitude – and only there; / With hope it is ... / Effort, and expectation, and desire, / And something evermore about to be'.[42] Charlotte Smith and Robert Southey had pointed the 'woe-begone', refugee route leading up to that High Romantic home. Such ecstatic, Wordsworthian emigrations disclose neither the American coast, nor the Susquehanna, but the ever more elusive shores of an 'invisible world'.

'No prospect in life gives me half the pleasure this visionary one affords', Southey had written. The visionary pleasure and prospect of a 'home ... with infinitude' alike began, it seems, with Pantisocracy, with the idea of an emigrant community, and a list of what had to be lugged across the Atlantic,

> Old kettles, old bottles, and a broken can,

– a cast-iron skillet and that keg of porter, and a tub with curiously clawed feet, for Coleridge to leap out of.

PETER STONELEY

Dickinson and Cosmopolitanism

In *Emily Dickinson as an American Provincial Poet* (1985), Michael Allen explores the ways in which Dickinson transformed the apparent stigma of the 'provincial'. Even as she adopted the 'Boston literatus', Thomas Wentworth Higginson, as her 'preceptor', he served as a 'strategic construct' that allowed her to prove the superiority of her own 'unregenerate condition'. In being 'Orchard sprung' and seeing 'New Englandly', Dickinson asserted a poetic originality that, in Allen's words, 'stemmed from fidelity to the local terrain and community tradition'. For Allen, Dickinson is an example of 'the alienated creative individual' who has embraced an 'anti-role', a persona 'which the discourse of the cultural mainstream ha[d] invented as a focus of scorn, derision or disapproval'. Dickinson used a strategy that is familiar to us in other guises (embracing 'blackness', embracing 'queerness'), and her goal was to subvert and transcend the 'dominant and central values and patterns of social interaction'.[1] In what follows, I offer a supplement to Allen's discussion, in that I too look at the provincial-cosmopolitan tensions in Dickinson's life and work. My focus differs in that I pay particular attention to the twinned factors of gender and commerce. The tension between the province and the metropolis was also a tension between old and new modes of womanhood, and over woman's relation to the economic.

To frame the discussion with a legal anecdote, the case between the Todds and Lavinia Dickinson came to trial on 1 March 1898. It was ostensibly a contest over the rightful ownership of a strip of meadow. Vinnie Dickinson was trying to reclaim land that had been given up at the instigation of her brother, who had been Mrs Todd's lover. But as a spectacle, it offered the people of Amherst a great deal more. It dramatised, in particularly stark form, issues which had preoccupied this community and others for some time. Accounts of the litigants' styles of appearance, and of the lawyers' arguments, make it clear that this became a struggle between different types of womanhood. Vinnie presented herself in court in strikingly poor clothes: she wore an old blue flannel dress, yellow shoes, and a long black veil. She was accompanied by her long-standing servant, Maggie Maher, and a friend, Miss Buffum. Her female opposition was the much younger Mabel Loomis Todd. Mrs Todd had always displayed a subtle sense of style, exceptional in the relatively provincial milieu of Amherst. Of this occasion she was later pleased to remember that she had worn a black hat with white wings.

It may be that Vinnie did not have other, smarter clothes. But her ignorance of the imperatives of fashion also conveyed meanings to do with the entitlements of class. Whether calculatedly or not, Vinnie signified herself as a gentlewoman of the old school, unconcerned about making a showy appearance. As one contemporary observed, Vinnie was dressed in such a way as to suggest her 'unworldliness'. Her lawyer exploited this notion of her as a woman out of time. He portrayed her as the relic of a more venerable social order, who had been tricked out of her inheritance by an acquisitive and morally dubious modern woman. He emphasised that Vinnie 'live[d] alone with her maid in Amherst, in the house built by her grandfather, and the house in which her father lived, the old Dickinson Homestead'. Vinnie, he asserted, was 'very quiet, and according to the testimony of Mrs Todd, of "retiring" disposition.' Whereas Vinnie's old-style gentility was affirmed by the fact that she stayed at home and 'knew little of the world and nothing of business', Mabel Todd was 'very much a woman of the world'. Not only had she 'not spent her life in the seclusion of the little village of Amherst', but she had 'been somewhat extensively upon the lecture platform', and was therefore 'conversant with business affairs'. Vinnie's lawyer was suggesting that the case should be decided by considering these women's respective characters and experiences. He insinuated that a modern, public woman such as Mrs Todd might well defraud a woman such as Lavinia Dickinson. Of course the opposite was true. Vinnie perjured herself repeatedly in order to regain property that had been passed to the Todds with all due legal course.[2]

When Vinnie won the case, the public sentiment seems to have been one of approval, even though it was generally understood that she had not acted honestly. It never came up in court that the land had come to the Todds as a result of Mabel's adulterous liaison with Austin Dickinson, but this may have had a bearing. The community's happy acquiescence in the miscarriage of justice may also have reflected a yankee respect for Vinnie's cunning, as she played the unworldly and absent-minded old spinster. But there is also a hint of general dislike for Mrs Todd, who had always had a little too much style for the wife of a minor professor. She had affronted Amherst with everything from her long drives with Austin to her ideas for window-shades. In her time there, she had developed into a widely-travelled, published author and a sought-after lecturer, who had an attractive air of cosmopolitanism. From the outset she had aroused disapproval and envy. Vinnie's victory was Mabel's come-uppance. But these same traits of style and contemporaneity were also very attractive to many members of the comparatively staid middle class. Vinnie herself had long made use of Mabel's acquisitive skills. Before their disagreement, she frequently asked Mrs Todd's advice with regard to all sorts of purchases, and even asked Mrs Todd to shop for her in the Boston stores. She went so far as to copy the younger woman, asking to be bought a cloak like the one Mrs Todd herself wore. It is no accident that Vinnie lacked shopping expertise. Her life had been passed in the Homestead, privileged, virtuous, but without much in the way of disposable income. The elevated womanliness that consisted in isolation from the material world, could seem rather pinched. As, much later, Miss Buffum was to tell Mrs Todd's daughter Vinnie had 'never had control of a single cent, even to pay for a postage stamp except what came to her from the poems your mother edited'.[3]

Why should such biographical anecdotes interest us now? What the court case indicates, beyond the endlessly-debated personal conflicts, is a contest over the modes and meanings of middle- and upper-class womanhood. The lives of the Dickinson sisters present us with an older model of female gentility, which depended on a notionally invisible financial pedestal. Such women were supposed to transcend the public worldliness which governed the lives of men, even if the reality of their existence suggests something rather different. Mrs Todd represented the newly-prevalent, increasingly professionalised woman. She may have lost the court case, but her type of commodified and savvy womanliness was in the ascendent. She is one example of a more general shift, from class as behavior, to class as display. In what follows, I explore Emily Dickinson's own understanding of these shifts, in her life and especially in her work. It seems to me that she was keenly aware of them. She writes repeatedly, and in a variety of registers, about how the growth of commercial power had a bearing on notions of gentility and female self-presentation.[4] She demonstrates a sharp perception of economically-driven divergences that would become a feature of the court case between her sister and her friend. This discussion, then, is intended to supplement analyses of Dickinson and money, and Dickinson and gender. Although both areas have been thoroughly explored, this essay presupposes that there has been something of a failure when it comes to integrating them. Others have shown how nineteenth-century economics had a coercive structuring effect on the female psyche. Joan Burbick, for instance, has related notions of expenditure and frugality with 'the cultural language of desire for the Victorian woman in an age that attempted to "rob" the female body of delight'.[5] This deep, psychological reading is persuasive, and enables Burbick to offer compelling insights into Dickinson's poetry. But I would add that moralised notions of frugality were starting to lose ground. I pay more attention to the consumerised surfaces of the period. This wilfully superficial approach is more than justified by the fact that the moral and economic status of middle-class women was increasingly being reduced to – or rather, debated in the terms of – questions of style. With Dickinson, we move towards Veblen's age of 'conspicuous consumption', and James's age of 'unmitigated publicity'. The meanings of a woman's self-presentation, or indeed of her self-effacement, were in flux. I present a Dickinson who was sensitive to precisely this issue, of changes in the material and symbolic conditions of middle-class femininity.[6]

We may as well begin with the founding spectacle: the 'Myth of Amherst'. From among several possible versions, here is an account from Mabel Loomis Todd:

> [Austin's] sister Emily is called in Amherst 'the myth'. She has not been out of her house for fifteen years. One inevitably thinks of Miss Havisham in speaking of her. She writes the strangest poems, & very remarkable ones. She is in many respects a genius. She wears always

white, & has her hair arranged as was the fashion fifteen years ago when she went into retirement. She wanted me to come & sing to her, but she would not see me. She has frequently sent me flowers & poems, & we have a very pleasant friendship in that way.[7]

This early account contains all the recognised features, especially the suggestion of romantic injury and subsequent self-enclosure. An obvious, though easily missed point here is that this is the Amherst myth as much as the Dickinson myth: the town seems to have hungered for peculiarity, and Dickinson provided it. In Todd's excitement there lies a longing for mystery and the hidden in an otherwise fairly mundane and transparent community. This is confirmed by the fact that, for all Dickinson's perceived oddness, the elements of her myth are conventional. She has retreated from the world, as her social privilege allowed her to, and she has signified this withdrawal and self-purgation in the conventional way, in the wearing of white. She continues to do conventional ladylike things, such as sending flowers and writing poetry. However odd certain elements of her behaviour, she is in many ways typical. Vivian Pollak has noted this, arguing that Dickinson 'emerges as the spokeswoman for a whole generation of nineteenth-century women'. Pollak locates this typicality in Dickinson's 'recoil from the world, her attempt to live in a separate sphere, and her obsessive fascination with the sexual and social power she could never attain'.[8] Women were supposed to deny themselves at the behest of a patriarchal sexual economy: as Burbick argues, desire was 'managed' as much as other resources. This self-denial – a remaining private and non-productive, a restraint of vulgar appetite – signified gentility. However, in gestures which abound in subversive ironies, Dickinson took the conventions of proper womanhood – self-effacing modesty, purity of body and spirit – and exaggerated them to the point at which their significance was reversed. She confined herself, but to such an extent as to remove herself from the sexual market altogether. Taking the conventions of female gentility so much in earnest, she had effectively perpetrated a double bluff, and one which allowed her to sidestep the marital and procreative binds of Victorian womanhood. She becomes a more truly private woman, rather than a woman who affects privacy as a symbol of status.

There is, though, another significant factor here. Dickinson was conforming to a model of feminine behaviour which was already coming to seem dated when she undertook her reclusion. This contributes to the thrill, or to the uncanny 'storybook' quality of the myth. Dickinson represents an older, somewhat immured female virtue to a younger generation. She is the buried but undead femininity that the bright and upwardly-mobile Mrs Todd had superseded. This time-warped otherness was equally remarked upon by Thomas Wentworth Higginson, who felt so famously 'drained' of his 'nerve power' by his encounter with the poet.[9] The eerily parasitic figure of the undead lady would of course walk again, and much to Mrs Todd's cost, in the near-farcical form of Vinnie at the trial.

To simplify what was often fraught and ambiguous, the point of contrast is between class values as modest gentility, and class values as wealth displayed. The difficulty lies between a prized unworldliness, and an equally prized worldliness. The underlying awkwardness of American self-enrichment – within which both the Dickinsons and Mrs Todd were caught – is certainly not new. There is a longstanding fear that the value of the commodity displaces the intrinsic value of character. Authentic social intercourse gives way to reciprocal exhibitionism. To quote from a page that is turned down in Dickinson's copy of Emerson's 'Self Reliance': 'My life is for itself and not for spectacle. I much prefer that it should be at a lower strain, so it be genuine and equal, than that it should be glittering and unsteady.'[10] Tension over material culture is especially evident in Dickinson's own period, an age of great commercial expansion. There was a move ever further away from the 'homespun' values of worthy, if parochial, independence. The 'globalizing' tendency of commerce detracted from older forms of affiliation: place, and family. Dickinson's awareness of such developments is well documented. She writes in a series of letters about the excitement over the foundation of the Amherst and Belchertown railroad, in which her father played a significant part. Even as she participated in the excitement, she also offered a more sardonic version of events. As she wrote to her brother:

> The men begin working next week, only think of it, Austin; why I verily believe we shall fall down and worship the first 'Son of Erin' that comes, and the first sod he turns will be preserved as an emblem of the struggles and victory of our heroic fathers.[11]

Although she admitted that it all seemed 'like a fairy tale', she also implied that the enthusiasm was excessive and slightly misplaced. She grew tired of the rule of the 'almighty dollar', and became increasingly convinced of 'the hollowness and awfulness of the *world*'.[12] This indicates disenchantment with a progress which is mere ease. Although there has been a tendency to view

Dickinson as a delicate and overly precious creature, she had much of the old-fashioned woman's 'faculty', or ability to make and to do. She was a good cook, specialising in bread and puddings. She won seventy-five cents (the second prize) for her rye and Indian bread at the Amherst Cattle Show for 1856, and was elevated to the committee for rye and Indian bread for the following year.[13] The Dickinsons had numerous servants, and this might easily be taken to signify luxury and fierce hierarchies. However, this would be to underestimate the amount of household work that fell to Emily and Lavinia.[14] More generally the social borders are often surprising to the modern eye. Dickinson wrote sociable letters to her servants, and cried on a manservant's shoulder when her lover was ill. Other not altogether ephemeral details include the fact that servant Maggie Maher had visiting cards, and that the social leader of Amherst, Susan Gilbert Dickinson, helped to lay the poet out for burial. In some ways Dickinson and her female relations were approximate to the 'Soft – Cherubic Creatures' she made fun of in her writing, but she, and they, also bore the marks of a sterner tradition.

How does this carry through into Dickinson's attitudes to cosmopolitan display, and especially to the feminine display of clothes? Certainly she was not immune to their charms. Part of her admiration for her sister-in-law seems to have been based on Sue's sure touch when it came to fashion. In one of the very few detailed descriptions of clothing in her letters, she writes that Sue 'wore her new things … and looked beautifully in them – a white straw hat, trimmed with Rouches mantilla of fawn colored silk, very handsomely finished, and white Dress'.[15] Dickinson herself, of course, took to wearing white – at once a spectacular and a self-denying gesture. It was a sign of her 'election', of the attainment of a supreme grandeur that transcended the worldliness of such as Sue. Indeed, Judith Farr reads poem 325 as a comment on her own style in comparison to that of Sue:

> Of Tribulation, these are They,
> Denoted by the White.
> The Spangled Gowns, a lesser Rank
> Of Victors – designate –[16]

Dickinson's identification with white was at once a prideful assertion, and a symbol of retreat and humility. It signified an affiliation with the tribulation and the purity of Christ, which was also a claim to have achieved a meek sense of resignation. But she engaged with the symbolism of cloth in other ways. Half-jokingly, she confessed to Louise Norcross that her 'sphere is doubtless calicoes'.[17] Although calico was often printed with bright colors and strong patterns, it was a cheap cloth, and strongly associated with servants. But this playful humility is matched by ambition. Dickinson wrote that she sought a truth that, 'like Ancestors' Brocades', could 'stand alone'.[18] She links her truth to an antecedent grandeur. She enters into the metaphors of clothing and display with mixed motives, seeking to show resignation and modesty, but also a quasi-aristocratic independence.

Generally, Dickinson liked to see herself as out of, beneath, or above the fashions, belonging to a timeless realm that has been preserved for having been sealed off. Years before her actual reclusion, she wrote to Austin comparing herself to Hepzibah Pynchon, Hawthorne's elderly recluse in *The House of the Seven Gables* (1851), and Austin to Clifford, Hepzibah's mysterious brother. She makes the comparison, and then half-withdraws it: 'I dont mean that you are *him*, or Hepzibah *me* except in a relative sense, only I was reminded.'[19] She is thinking of the madly disorienting railroad journey that Clifford and Hepzibah undertake towards the end of the novel. But the reference is more specifically appropriate to Emily when we remember that *The House of the Seven Gables* opens with Hepzibah's timorous emergence from the grim haven of her ancient house. Faced with loss of caste and fortune in a changed world, Hepzibah tries to enter the new world of trade by selling sweets to boys. Even as a teenager, then, Dickinson could imagine herself as a figure whose womanly gentility was dated and uncertain in a more commercial environment. She seems to be exploring, here and elsewhere, the various guises that expressed her attraction to and aversion from the modern world. The fact that she explored both positive and negative possibilities reveals that she was perhaps more of her time than many are willing to allow. Her engagement was not always reluctant, timid, or ironical. She captured the tawdry insignificance of the pecuniary in her poem on the Civil War, which laments that 'lives – like Dollars – must be piled/ Before we may obtain' (# 444). But there is also an unguarded fascination with the operations of business and technology, as in her playful poem on the railroad, which begins: 'I like to see it lap the Miles –/ And lick the Valleys up –' (# 585). Even trading in stocks and shares could be construed as a sign of universal resilience, outweighing and compensating for individual annihilation:

'Tis sweet to know that stocks will stand
When we with Daisies lie –

> That Commerce will continue –
> And Trades as briskly fly – (# 54)[20]

This suggests a pleasurable interest in comic subversion more than terror over the loss of her old-style feudalised status.

Dickinson occupied an ambivalent position in relation to the commercialising and aggrandising culture around her. She was excited and impressed by the cool, monied displays of her favourites, but remained diffident in herself. In an era in which class distinction was increasingly based on wealth and display, and therefore prone to the fluctuations of the market, she withdrew to the apparent stability of the Homestead. Many critics have followed her in that journey, seeking to explain her work in terms of an interiorised, imaginative universe, a psychic estate governed by its own rules and vocabulary. There has long been a sense that Dickinson is 'above economics', that she 'seems peculiarly ahistorical'.[21] Whether of a belletristic, formalist, psychoanalytic or post-structuralist orientation, criticism has tended to ignore the socio-economic, often preferring yet once more to sift through the possible recipients of the 'Master letters', the poet's lost lovers, and so on. The relatively few 'cultural material' studies of Dickinson provide a useful alternative, elucidating the poet's worldly unworldliness. I want to move on from my generalised discussion of Dickinson's attitudes to commerce and self-display, to the related but more specific topic of the woman-shopper. I preface this with a brief survey of the studies which seem most nearly to anticipate my interest.

Robert Merideth, placing Dickinson's work within the context of an age of enterprise and of the rise of finance capitalism, argues that Dickinson was criticising 'a society which had no sense of the intrinsically valuable, and no idea that the intrinsically valuable was not for sale'.[22] In a similar vein, Vivian Pollak centres on the theme so powerfully suggested by poem 395:

> Reverse cannot befall
> That fine Prosperity
> Whose Sources are interior –

According to Pollak, Dickinson uses 'concepts of want and wealth and price and labor to work out a notion of subjective valuation and to delineate an intangible estate'. Her ultimate contention is one that again perceives an evasion of the economic order, in that 'the main emphasis is not in rejecting the commercial yardstick, but in using it to make [the] inner world visible, audible, and tangible'.[23] More recently, Betsy Erkkila has produced one of the most striking and important studies of Dickinson, exploring similarly socio-economical considerations. She looks at what she perceives to be Dickinson's fears of downward mobility in the age of Jacksonian democracy. There are echoes of Merideth and Pollak here, as Erkkila argues:

> [As Dickinson's father] sought to secure his social position through the acquisition of more money and more land, Dickinson sought to secure the declining status of both her gender and her class through the accumulation of cultural and spiritual capital, what she called 'My Soul's entire income' (# 270).[24]

Erkkila's readings sometimes seem forced and reductive, but she does give a powerful demonstration of the interpretive potential of a cultural materialist reading, making effective links between the Whiggish élitism of Dickinson's background and the 'order of rank, exclusion, and difference in which the "Door" of one's "own Society" is closed to all but a select few' (8).[25] The reason Erkkila occasionally produces rather flattened or one-sided readings, I would argue, is because she wishes to identify the poet too strongly and unambiguously with the class interests of her father. In doing so, she fails to acknowledge the extent to which Dickinson's very womanhood caused her to look askance at – to be both loyal to and treacherous of – the social order to which she belonged.[26] Erkkila tends to skew the relationship between Dickinson the woman, and Dickinson the socio-economic subject. As my mention of dress and cloth has suggested, the feminine display of hierarchy is symptomatic of the way in which gender and commodified class values had to be negotiated simultaneously. I want to expand upon this argument by looking more closely at some of the many poems to do with dress, shopping, and the ambiguously powerful figure of the 'consuming angel'.[27]

I begin with a poem, possibly unfinished, which places the speaker very obviously at odds with the systems of value that operate in her society:

> I – pay – in Satin Cash –
> You did not state – your price –
> A Petal, for a Paragraph
> Is near as I can guess – (# 402)

There is an incommensurability here, whereby the speaker's attempted engagement with the market fails to comprehend the current forms of exchange. She does not pay in 'hard cash', but in 'Satin Cash'. This cash is made up of petals, so the emphatically feminine 'language of flowers' is being tried out as a 'currency of flowers'. But the unlikely conjunction is rough and approximated: 'A Petal, for a Paragraph / Is near as I can guess.' Elsewhere, Dickinson writes of breezes as paragraphs (# 1175), and this is the sense here also. With each gust, the wind makes visible its force with the removal of another petal. In writerly terms, the speaker is unsure of how her own delicate forms of verse relate to the consonantally terse units of black and white – the paragraphs – to be found in the printed, public world. The world of publication is akin to the world of cash. The damage of being 'set' and 'justified' is equivalent to the satin bloom of the petal being lost with the constant handling and pocketing of trade. The implied exclusion or awkwardness of femininity with regard to the marketplace is equally suggested by satin as a cloth – a luxury commodity that is too good for everyday use. Of course, luxury goods are bought and sold like any other, but the luxury item appears to transcend the grubby world of trade. Satin is akin to the 'proper lady', in that she too was available in the marriage market, even though her gentility consisted in being unmindful of worldly activity. The use of satin here indicates the way in which Dickinson's language of cloth tends to be feminine, archaic, and privileged. She refers herself to brocade, satin, and velvet as opposed to broadcloth or linsey-woolsey. Typical of Dickinson's pleasure in approaching the same topic from contrary directions, she ironises this tendency to dress the self in aspirational clothing in the more famous poem 401, which begins:

> What Soft – Cherubic Creatures –
> These Gentlewomen are –
> One would as soon assault a Plush –
> Or violate a Star –
>
> Such Dimity Convictions –
> A Horror so refined
>
> Of freckled Human Nature –
> Of Deity – ashamed –

A stout but usually highly-figured cloth, dimity strives to excel its cotton base. It has gentle pretensions, but it can be bought, fairly cheaply, by the yard. Womanly refinement, the poet suggests, is very much in the marketplace that it seeks to transcend (even if each momentarily disorients the other). Dickinson also places such wishful fastidiousness in a sexual context, as a kind of false virginity: white dimity was often used to decorate bed-frames. 'Dimity Convictions' are fanciful, obfuscatory, and upwardly-mobile. The soft cherubic creatures are led astray by the possibility of dressing up in a gentility that lacks the resource of character. This is Dickinson in a Thoreauvian moment, as she celebrates the 'freckled' heterogeneity of the world. In the suppressed violence of her suggestion that one would as soon assault these ladies as one would a plush, she reminds one of the misogynist polemic of *Walden*, in which America is being smothered under velvet cushions (plush is a long-napped velvet).[28] Dickinson questions this overwhelming and conformist gentility of aspirational display, whereby 'Convictions' are worn with an air of fond self-regard. She herself, in poem 492, prefers the 'Satin' of the leopard's pelt because it is also spotted. She does not reject it because of its mixed or 'Tawny' quality, as might the softer, cherubic creatures:

> Civilization – spurns – the Leopard!
> Was the Leopard – bold?
> Deserts – never rebuked her Satin –
> Ethiop – her Gold –
> Tawny – her Customs –
> She was Conscious –
> Spotted – her Dun Gown –
> This was the Leopard's nature – Signor –
> Need – a keeper – frown?

The leopard is inimical to the orderliness desired by her keeper: her behaviour or 'Custom' is as 'Tawny' as her pelt. Dickinson relishes the smudged, dirty implications of the 'Dun Gown' as much as she does the splendor of coloring ('Gold') and texture ('Satin'). Her elevated preferences, then, are also inclusive. Her love of glory is not in the least conformist, and like another famous contemporary poet, it can embrace apparent contradictions. So although she strives for the uniformity of 'White Election' (# 528), and she sees 'Spangled Gowns' as of 'a lesser Rank' (# 325), she also recognises that, throughout her idealistic sorties, she can never entirely abandon her 'freckled' human nature.

Moving from 'Gentlewomen' who affect to have transcended commerce even as they participate in the democratisation of luxury, Dickinson often places the woman speaker in open and direct contradiction with the marketplace. At least, she often envisions an awkward relation to money and spending. Woman is cast in the notionally powerful role of buyer, but it transpires that this is closely circumscribed by masculine interests:

> I asked no other thing –
> No other – was denied –
> I offered Being – for it –
> The Mighty Merchant sneered –
>
> Brazil? He twirled a Button –
> Without a glance my way –
> 'But – Madam – is there nothing else –
> That We can show – Today?' (# 621)

The woman-buyer is ostensibly in a position of command: the 'Mighty Merchant' is nothing more than a retail clerk, at the service of 'Madam'. But 'Madam', caught up in the order of buying and selling, remains unfulfilled by it. She seeks to test its limitations. In asking for Brazil, she asks for something vast, spectacular, and exotic; recognisable but relatively uncharted. She seeks something of immense promise, something that could not possibly be contained in a shop.[29] The poem could be read narrowly as a desire for adventure, a wish to leave Amherst or the realm of 'Dimity Convictions'. But clearly it lends itself to the broader significance identified by Merideth and Pollak: that which is to be truly valued cannot be bought and sold. The woman-buyer in this poem may seem confused, but she is also confounding the commodified and gendered entrapments of her society. Dickinson anticipates the argument made by Ann Douglas, to the effect that women were 'bought off' by a masculine world that had little use for them. The reward for acquiescence in a male-ordered society was a material, aesthetic, and spiritual indulgence.[30] She also confounds that argument in that the Dickinson speaker's response to the bribes of consumerism is, in the words of another poem, to 'ask too large', to 'take – no less than skies –' (# 352). As with the exaggerated refinement of womanliness that allowed her to retreat from the world, the poet subverts the consumerist order by pretending to expect more from it than it can ever deliver. The 'Mighty Merchant' also leads us to assume that Dickinson uses the discourse of consumption to ironise the notion of God, the symbolic father of patriarchy. In this reading, too, the speaker is a discontented subject, who senses the vanity of the privileges accorded her, but who has not yet learnt an escape. The 'Mighty Merchant' can show his contempt, and try to fob her off with his own designs for her happiness. But in the end each is defeated, as no transaction takes place.

In so many of the poems which question the emergent order of purchase and display, Dickinson's critique is very much from a woman's point of view. The buyer is female, the shopkeeper male. Sometimes, as with 'I asked no other thing −', there seems to be a fairly direct questioning of the marketplace. At other moments, the buying-selling relation simply serves as a convenient metaphor for expressing the gendered imbalance of power. In 'I Came to buy a smile − today −' (# 223), the speaker is again a thwarted customer, implicitly female in that she wants to trade the diamond rings on her fingers. But here the emphasis is on the seller's power to withhold: 'I'm pleading at the "counter" − sir −.' Again there is the incommensurability of the different orders of exchange, emotional and pecuniary, which is seen to correspond to an equivalent incommensurability between the woman's desires and the man's, or between their separate registers of value:

> I've *Diamonds* − on my fingers −
> You know what *Diamonds* are?

Again, and in more desperate form, the woman's powerlessness is conveyed via this discourse of the purchase.

Another key feature of Dickinson's exploration of this theme is her recognition of the competitive nature of consumerist desire. The window-shopper is lured not so much by the object itself, as by a sense that the object is coveted by others. The need for the woman to wear diamonds is directly related to the hierarchy of display, whereby the value of a possession is determined in relation to the value of others' possessions:

> A Diamond on the Hand
> To Custom Common grown
> Subsides from its significance

> The Gem were best unknown –
> Within a Seller's Shrine
> How many sight and sigh
> And cannot, but are mad for fear
> That any other buy. (# 1108)

The shop becomes the 'Shrine' of a commodified culture, and the need to emulate others in this materialist order of merit produces a situation in which all are 'mad for fear'.

There are any number of Dickinson poems making use of the figure of buying and selling, and she explores a variety of possibilities in them. The final aspect that I wish to consider is the way in which Dickinson adopts a vocabulary which enables her to sidestep the 'hollowness & awfulness of the *world*'. This relates back to my sense of Dickinson as a woman out of her time. As Erkkila argues so powerfully, Dickinson uses a language of aristocratic hierarchy in order to perpetuate her sense of her own position in a democratising society, and I echo that argument here. Dickinson scorns to chase after wealth, but as with her father and brother, she is determined to have it in some form or other. Her desired luxury may take the form of a sunset, but a sunset that lends itself to a vision of imperial trade:

> Night after Night
> Her purple traffic
> Strews the landing with Opal Bales – (# 266)

In her reversion from a bourgeois shop-culture, she imagines a feudal or monarchical wealth which is stupendous and historical, not earned and exhausted. Via her 'purple traffic', she enjoys a largesse which is not prone to the fluctuations of the market. The 'wealth' of a Queen is always preferred to the 'cash' of the woman-shopper. Dickinson likes to move beyond 'bitter contested farthings' (# 125) to jewels, gems, and precious metals. Again there is the sense that mere money involves struggle among the masses, whereas royal riches enable one to leave all that behind. As with the paradox of the proper lady, the freedom to transcend material values is a material freedom, a liberty granted by immense wealth. This tendency is also evident in Dickinson's concern with ermine and escutcheons. She loves this more fixed decorum, and is again akin to Hawthorne, whose scarlet letter was rendered as an armorial bearing: 'ON A FIELD SABLE, THE LETTER A, GULES.'

Similarly affrighted by or disdainful of Hawthorne's 'damned mob of scribbling women', or indeed of any mob, Dickinson prefers the 'Antique Book' (# 371) to the modern mass product.

Ultimately, the securest wealth for Dickinson is death, that final and complete 'Escape from Circumstances' (# 382). She sought to requisition the 'Things that Death will buy', by entombing herself in advance of the event. This refusal to display herself further was not, though, an escape from material necessity (she had never been subject to immediate want anyway). It was an escape from her culture's insistence on the visibility, availability, promotion, commoditisation, of subjectivity. It was to seek another and more satisfactory idiom of womanhood and gender-relations, even if the poems foresee only too clearly that such a search would always prove futile.

In her diary for April, 1897, Mabel Loomis Todd made a note of an expedition:

> I went downtown in Boston for a look about and was appalled by the women shopping. Ten deep at the counters, and thronging the pavements, until I walked most of the time in the street among the cabs, as less dangerous. And in all the thousands not half a dozen *ladies*. All people who ought to have been over a washtub.[31]

By her middle age, Todd had clearly moved on from the young woman who had been so impressed by the wealth and style of Sue and Austin. Now she identified automatically with the socially superior, against the thronging masses who exercised their democratic right to spend money. She seems affronted by the hungry, shoving crowd, in which all are equal under the dollar. Even as she had used her career as Dickinson's editor to move beyond the restrictive society of Amherst, she also evinced a nostalgia for caste, and its attendant peacefulness. But the reception of Dickinson's work would have told her, if nothing else had, that the older hierarchies of social value were fast disappearing. For the critical response confirmed the idea with which I began, of Dickinson as a woman out of time, who felt herself to be immured within a hustling, commercial culture. Looking at how she was read by her early audiences, it is clear that her other-worldliness was a significant part of her attraction. Her first readers 'delighted in her "strangeness"'. Even those who were less appreciative framed their response in the same terms, seeing the poet as the 'enervated examplar of a waning New England school of letters'. Dickinson was, as *Book News* put it, 'the final flower which never quite fruits in anything worth having'. The brief but intense popularity of Dickinson's verse was part of a 'renewed vogue for New England "antiquities" of all kinds'.[32] It seems that, within five years of her death, Dickinson was being treasured as a relic of something much more distant in time.

Why might her supposed 'antiquity' and 'strangeness' have proved so attractive? It is telling that so many critics fell back on quoting whole poems, often several in the course of a brief review. This might indicate laziness on the part of the reviewers, but it also testifies to her oddness, to the fact that she seemed so hard to paraphrase. The difficulty of paraphrase, whereby only the original version is of value, does itself suggest the allure of writing which so obviously ran counter to the idea of ready manufacture. Still more 'Petal' than 'Paragraph', Dickinson was at odds with the endless reproduction which permitted the consumer boom of the late-nineteenth-century 'Chromo-Civilization'. Many commentaries, including Todd's own and that of the *Boston Evening Transcript*, place the interest of the poems in the context of 'this artificial generation', of 'our alleged modern artificiality'. Dickinson seemed a salutary reminder of individual authenticity in an age of commodified pretense. The irony is that the posthumous publication did put Dickinson in the marketplace, elegantly bound and boxed as a Christmas purchase for the cosmopolitan shopper. There was no escape, and never had been. But as this essay has attempted to show, Dickinson set out to testify to the circumscribed and false power of women in a culture of commodified display. Amid the insistent throng, she adopted the persona she considered most worthy – that of an awkward customer.

MEDBH McGUCKIAN

Poems

Photocall

I learned to sing 'The Shadow of his Smile',
swimming through the flooded rooms
of his childhood home. It was the sea
language of a mild, mild day; I discovered
a way of turning from the gold 'C'
on his sweater and eleven new faces
watching only me, listening to only me.

I borrowed his arrogance in the make-up
blood, so when I viewed the rushes
there was a single solid red frame
whose eyes belied the most bellicose
hymn to peace. We were dressed for yachting,
in Scotland doubling for China,
neither of us could feel any pain:

but through seven opening doors, the sun
set between our lips moving towards each other
the way the world might die – our requisite
screen kiss like a two-hour Latin Mass

where he matched lips only with the Italian,
pallbearer, boat-maker, ever acted upon,
flower of a dozen dancing lines.

The Change Worshipper

We came to anchor beyond memory,
standing on gradual reddish tiles
flaming back at a low red sun:
if this were indeed a room,
if the universe is paved with it,
all over into gold, the light-sprinkled
hall folded the sky up like a scroll.

Even the window-blind was not
a simple muslin blind, but a painted
fabric-roof that permitted twilight
though the sun furnished the day,
with a design of castles, and gateways,
and groves of trees and several peasants
taking a winter-bright walk.

To see his home put before me
was to hold a lighted match
inside my hand, a spray of red
berries in an opal pin in my coat.
My dusk was noonday and the day
without evening, for he was all
daylight and his own repose.

To find him truly at his leisure
within his today, his governing lifetime,
was some living-apart-together
like the boom of a warmed Atlantic

at the very tip of the Bosphorus.
My earth-imbalanced voice
posted a sentry before my lips

that snapped it like a spell
after he had found it,
a world to stretch the remotest
fibres of his senses in,
that could grow without changing,
its virtues wandering alone,
but extending their arms forever.

It was not to get the heavens
into his head I put my question
to the earth, that has at its heart
a collision. He no longer lays
his ear to the weapon of my lips,
(and he cannot lay his ear to my heart),
but with the lips of the spirit, sparkling, he drinks.

Melisma

His right hand cupped behind his ear
as he sits crouched, fingering a piece
of wood, is white as Circe's palace.
The film passes him by at a distance
like a mourner hiding from the end
of the light, as if its framework
wished to take prisoner the time
that had flowed freely, earlier on.

The piece is full of sunset, with traces
of the very oldest things, speechlessly nature,
in a three-quarters darkened hall.
Then with an interplay of diamonds,
the moon soothingly makes its entrance,

and self-contained as the entry of March,
it moves forward inexorably
without looking vertical or back.

A breathless breath amidst events,
image of something without images,
it goes to such heavenly lengths
in its unprecedented transparency
that a path leads up from the core
of his nature, even in this field scene,
or we just follow where his voice goes,
listening on crutches that are shy of sounds.

He offers the gold in his throat
for sale in the market place –
the inhuman beauty of his voice,
its musty inwardness like a clarinet
passage, as though its overleaf of music,
his for the asking, needed consoling,
or we could be comforted by open
sound which has not been imprisoned.

At every moment we have the togetherness
of a congregation, feeding on our belief
in sound itself, be it absent or damaged sound,
that is still brazen with his hired song.
When the temperature falls so dramatically,
all older music seems an ocean
of subcutaneous and iridiscent sounds,
keeping us chained to the city of his –

merest presence . . . .
which was the last thing the story wanted.

Oration

for Harper Daniel

You, command in the changing light,
are shedding your leaves, the oldest of them,
the oldest disciple: you know our martyrs.

As if one has just smashed something unearned,
everything takes place as if after your death,
the whole sea breaking up that comes each time,

its rhymes buried in folds of meaning
wrenched into a small space, the line engraved
around the mouth between the actor

and the crowd. You, ideal book
that contains the world, you question
born of unsatisfactory answers

and promise of a new question, not dreamt
upon but excavated, as dying,
the lilac drinks the watching world.

So its after-death is also a before-death
impossible to cross by will or grace.
You shattered, you surrounded by flowers,

that unheard-of number Shakespeare names,
fir unmoored the measure of the sky
not like that lifeless stone the moon,

prisoner of its calling and unflagging charm,
but the Boyne salmon prized in its bend
in water colour, never out of season,

its great eye redemptive in the weight
of its dry lustre. How it returns
hedging to its Virgilian setting

its motion heavy with rest, and
how I am forced by sound alone to learn
from that afflicting language

with its busy words, never to use
a word that has not first been won,
nor write your name till it becomes the man.

Black Raven on Cream-Coloured Background

I too was sorry that he was not shot,
really not thinking of it as quite possible
either, the rainbow lifted off the ground
and gathered into a turquoise ring –
I'll ground myself in its radiance.

Tired is not what I am, but I think
I really did know him, having seven
years to study him, still, he was different
every day. He was already a generation
old-a generation more, our paths would converge.

But he had to be given up for lost
so we would be a little scared all
the time by the unloved government,
its small excoriations, its semilunar
depresssions, its bells tied up and muffled.

And his heartsounds were not among us
for years, in any way the world
knows how to speak, his body and tang
abloom with tapers quenched,
his soft-collared, slightly uncomfortable smile.

Though it would take a ship
to hold all the messages, I only half-read
by hear-say all the other names
of the fields; how finishing his last field,
he then cut all the flowers in bloom

in the school garden. The allied fields
kept tryst with the grass being cut
from under my fingers by bullets.
He had invented a lamp with his last
look at the earth, to send the first leaf on,

walled in by himself, and fit for idling,
fit for restraint in handcuffs, waist belt,
muffs or jacket in splints. They said
the bonniest, most dashing of fighters,
his pistol in the ivy at the back of an old shed.

The Muse takes care of it, deeply recessed,
so primitively crushed: she holds
and freshens in this air of withering sweetness,
close-knit and somewhat stifling, the barest shadow
of its most stately, most mobile mouth.

'A sparrow hawk proud did hold in wicked jail
Music's sweet chorister, the nightingale ...'
      written for Thomas Weelkes, from Hesiod

Monody for Aghas

You won't be a voice to me any more,
the weather of my own creation
repeating the highest possible shared
symptoms of the day. You were born

in a leap year, just as one day
was ending and the next beginning,
in a new time zone where landscape
has become language ... blue bloom

of the faultless month of May,
with its heart set on conquering
every green glen ... springtime
in action, springtime unfolding

into words, a literature of spring,
spring in place, time and eternity,
she-bird in its velvet dress
of soft blackbird colour,

maroon seed dashed from the hand.
Let me taste the whole of it,
my favourite tomb, the barbarity
and vividness of the route,

my due feet standing all night
in the sea of your pale goldfish
skin without body, its glimmering
sponged out by a tall white storm:

the red flag could not have made you
less Irish, your once-red lips before
and after folded together and left down
quietly, never to be parted,

that were forced open, strapped open,
by a sort of meal of a fixed gag,
a three-foot tube previously
used on ten others,

dipped in hot water, and withdrawn
and inserted, clogged and withdrawn,
and cleansed ... your broad heart
became broader as you opened

to the Bridewell and the Curragh,
Mountjoy and Ship Street.
It was fifty hours without
plank bed or covering

while Max Green, Sir Arthur Chance,
Dr Lowe and the J.P.
almost wept, then attended
a banquet, before you smashed

the cell window for want of air,
and the Sisters of Charity
at the Mater Hospital
painted your mouth with brandy:

like a high-mettled horse,
soothing and coaxing him
with a sieve of provender in one hand
and a bridle in the other,

ready to slip it over his head
while he is snuffling at the food.
Today the fairest wreath is an inscape
mixed of strength and grace –

the ash tree trim above your grave.

BERNARD MACLAVERTY

Postscript

I worked at Queen's University Belfast as a Medical Laboratory Technician before becoming a student of English. So I had been around the university and had known Michael Allen through attending group meetings (new writing workshops) in Philip Hobsbaum's flat in the mid-sixties. Whatever piece of writing was being examined I found Michael's criticism of it always accurate and perceptive. When he was speaking, you always and inadvertently found yourself nodding. And if the criticism was adverse it was delivered in the gentlest, most diplomatic way. It could be done unconventionally, too. One time I showed him a short story and when he was giving it back to me in a tutorial room at the top of the English Department he discovered that he had no pen. Or pencil. And neither had I (I'm beginning to disbelieve my own stories now). So he picked a couple of dead matches out of an ash tray and began underlining the words he disliked with black scratches – he even tried to write words in the margin with the burnt point. We both ended up laughing. In this case I remember the man, but not the criticism.

The criticism I do remember to this day is what he taught in his American Literature course. And his approach to unseen poetry always revealed a brilliant mind. You'd be sitting there with a gestetnered sheet of unattributed poems positively looking forward to what Michael was going to say in the course of the tutorial. Another thing that I was impressed by was his method. I was with him one day at the front of the university fifteen minutes before he was to lecture us and he excused himself to walk around the Botanic Gardens. He said, 'I want to prepare what I am going to say.'

He had a way of encouraging students to contribute. You'd be verbally fumbling around for some time, having a stab at putting a thought into words and eventually Michael would step in to help. 'What I think you're saying here . . .' and out would come exactly what you wanted to say only it would be better the way Michael would say it. And the teacher in him knew that you'd be preening yourself so much that you'd believe, after a while, that you *did* say it. He made you see things. He was a joy to learn from.

Notes

FAITHS AND FIDELITIES
pp. 3–15

1 Louis MacNeice, 'To Hedli', *Collected Poems*, ed. E.R. Dodds (London: Faber, 1979), p. xvii.
2 Seamus Heaney, *Opened Ground: Poems 1966–1996* (London: Faber, 1998); Michael Longley, *Selected Poems* (London: Jonathan Cape, 1998).
3 Longley, *Selected Poems*, p. 22.
4 Ibid, p. 11.
5 Ibid, p. 35.
6 Heaney, *Opened Ground*, p. 15.
7 Ibid, p. 56.
8 Ibid, p. 251.
9 Ibid, p. 350.
10 Longley, *Selected Poems*, p. 123.

A TRULY UNINVITED SHADE
pp. 16–28

1 Marjorie Levinson, 'The New Historicism: Back to the Future', *Re-Thinking Historicism: Critical Readings in Romantic History* (Oxford: Blackwell, 1989), p. 54.
2 Cynthia Chase (ed.), *Romanticism* (London: Longman, 1993), p. 1.
3 Raymond Williams, *Culture and Society 1780–1950* (London: Chatto and Windus, 1958), p. xiii.
4 Seamus Heaney, 'The Makings of a Music: Reflections on Wordsworth and Yeats', *Preoccupations: Selected Prose 1968–1978* (London: Faber, 1984), pp. 61–2.
5 *Preoccupations*, p. 68.
6 Ibid, p. 65.
7 Ibid, p. 34.
8 Patricia Coughlan, '"Bog Queen's": The Representation of Women in the Poetry of John Montague and Seamus

Heaney', in Toni O'Brien Johnson and David Cairns (eds.), *Gender in Irish Writing* (Milton Keynes: Open University Press, 1991), p. 100.
9 Seamus Heaney, 'The Fully Exposed Poem', *The Government of the Tongue: The 1988 T.S. Eliot Memorial Lectures and Other Critical Writings* (London: Faber, 1988), p. 45.
10 Heaney, quoted in Neil Corcoran, *Seamus Heaney* (London: Faber, 1986), p. 153.
11 *The Government of the Tongue*, p. 124.
12 Seamus Heaney, *Place and Displacement: Recent Poetry of Northern Ireland* (Grasmere: Trustees of Dove Cottage, 1984), p. 3.
13 Seamus Heaney, 'The Place of Writing: W.B. Yeats and Thoor Ballylee', *The Place of Writing* (Atlanta: Scholars Press, 1990), p. 21.
14 Seamus Heaney (ed.), *The Essential Wordsworth* (New York: Ecco Press, 1991), p. 4.
15 *The Essential Wordsworth*, pp. 3–4, 6.
16 Ibid, p. 4.
17 See ibid, pp. 5–12.
18 See *Preoccupations*, p.17, and Seamus Heaney, interview with Clive Wilmer, *Poet of the Month*, Radio 3, (2 September 1990).
19 *The Essential Wordsworth*, pp. 7, 12.
20 Paul Muldoon (ed.), *The Essential Byron* (New York: Ecco Press, 1989), pp. 5–6.
21 Ibid, p. 6.
22 Kenneth Curry, *Robert Southey* (London: Routledge, Kegan and Paul, 1975), p. 142.
23 See Curry, pp. 160–1.
24 Marilyn Butler, 'Byron and the Empire in the East', in Andrew Rutherford (ed.), *Byron: Augustan and Romantic* (London: Macmillan in association with the British Council, 1990), pp. 71–2.
25 Marilyn Butler, quoted in Nigel Leask,

British Romantic Writers and the East: Anxieties of Empire (Cambridge: Cambridge University Press, 1992), pp. 25–6.

26 Paul Muldoon, 'Sweeney Peregrine', review of *Station Island, London Review of Books*, 1–14 November 1984, p. 20.

27 Muldoon, 'Sweeney Peregrine', p. 20.

28 Paul Muldoon, *Madoc: A Mystery* (London: Faber, 1991), p. 21. Subsequent references are given in the text as (*Madoc*, page number).

29 See, for example, 'Trout', in Seamus Heaney, *Death of a Naturalist* (London: Faber, 1966), p. 39.

30 Samuel Taylor Coleridge, 'The Devil's Thoughts', *The Complete Poetical Works of Samuel Taylor Coleridge*, ed. Ernest Hartley Coleridge (Oxford: Clarendon, 1912) vol. II, pp. 319–23. Also published as Robert Southey, 'The Devil's Drive', *The Poems of Robert Southey*, ed. Maurice Fitzgerald (London: Oxford University Press, 1909), pp. 421–5. Byron also wrote a parodic version of this under the title 'The Devil's Drive: An Unfinished Rhapsody', *The Poetical Works of Lord Byron*, ed. Henry Frowde (London: Oxford University Press, 1907), pp. 71–2, as did Shelley under the title 'The Devil's Walk', *Shelley Poetical Works*, ed. Thomas Hutchinson (London: Oxford University Press, 1971), pp. 878–80.

31 Katherine Cooke, *Coleridge* (London and Boston: Routledge & Kegan Paul, 1979), p. 118.

32 Richard Holmes, *Coleridge: Early Visions* (London: Hodder and Stoughton, 1989), p. 240.

33 Edna Longley, 'Introduction: Revising "Irish Literature"', *The Living Stream: Literature and Revisionism in Ireland* (Newcastle: Bloodaxe, 1994), p. 57.

34 Seamus Heaney, 'The Toome Road', *Field Work* (London: Faber, 1979), p. 15.

35 Tim Kendall, '"Parallel to the Parallel Realm": Paul Muldoon's *Madoc – A Mystery*' *Irish University Review*, vol. 25,

no. 2 (Autumn/Winter 1995), pp. 238–9.

36 For a thorough and sustained discussion of the shamanistic and trickster elements in Muldoon's work see Alan Lewis, 'Paul Muldoon's "Uncovering Deadly Depths": *Imrama*, the Shaman, and "a cure for glanders"', MA diss., Queen's University Belfast, 1993.

37 Linda Hutcheon, *A Poetics of Postmodernism: History, Theory, Fiction* (New York: Routledge, 1988), p. 5.

38 This conclusion is not so straightforward in Byron. As Jerome McGann points out, 'From his earliest to his latest work he cherished the idea (or the hope) that he could stand above or beyond the contradictions of his age . . . The grand and pitiful illusion reached its most extreme form in *Don Juan*, where Byron sought to establish his self-sufficiency and power through a comic panorama of the world's folly, evil, and self-deceptions. His last resort from his own illusion was to declare that the was the most disillusioned of mortals – the *être suprême* of human detachment who could at last take God's laughter over from Milton.' *The Romantic Ideology: A Critical Investigation* (Chicago: Chicago University Press, 1985), p. 138.

39 See Linda Hutcheon, *A Theory of Parody: The Teachings of Twentieth-Century Art Forms* (New York & London: Methuen, 1985), pp. 102, 11. My understanding and discussion of the workings of parody in this paper draw on Hutcheon's theories.

POPPYPETAL
pp. 36–53

1 Theocritus, *The Idylls*, trans. J.H. Hallard (London: Routledge, 1924), pp. 35, 26.

2 Maurice Maeterlinck, *Mary Magdalena*, trans. Alexander De Maltos (London: Methuen & Co., 1910), p. 41.

3 On repetition see especially Peter Sacks,

The English Elegy (Baltimore: The Johns Hopkins University Press, 1985) pp. 23–8.

4 *The English Elegy*, p. xii.

5 Ibid.

6 Ibid, p. 2.

7 See especially Jacques Derrida, *Memoires for Paul de Man*, 2nd edn., trans. Cecile Lindsay, Jonathan Culler, Eduardo Cadava, and Peggy Kamuf (New York: Columbia University Press, 1989); *Aporias*, trans. Thomas Dutoit (Stanford, CA: Stanford University Press, 1993); *The Gift of Death*, trans. David Wills (Chicago: Chicago University Press, 1995).

8 *The English Elegy*, p. 6.

9 Ellen Zetzel Lambert, *Placing Sorrow: A Study of the Pastoral Elegy Convention from Theocritus to Milton* (Chapel Hill: University of North Carolina Press, 1976), p. xiii.

10 *Placing Sorrow*, pp. xiv–xv.

11 Renato Poggioli, *The Oaten Flute: Essays on Pastoral Poetry and the Pastoral Ideal* (Cambridge, Mass.: Harvard University Press, 1975), p. 9.

12 See René Girard, *Violence and the Sacred* (Baltimore: Johns Hopkins Press, 1972) and *The Scapegoat*, trans. Yvonne Freccero (Baltimore: Johns Hopkins Press, 1986); Jacques Derrida, 'Plato's Pharmacy', in *Margins of Philosophy*, trans. Alan Bass (Hemel Hempstead: Harvester Wheatsheaf, 1982), pp. 307–33; Julia Kristeva, *Revolution in Poetic Language*, trans. Lean Roudiez (New York: Columbia University Press, 1984); Hélène Cixous, 'The Laugh of the Medusa', in Elaine Marks and Isabelle de Courtivon (eds.), *New French Feminisms* (Brighton: The Harvester Press, 1981), pp. 245–64, and 'Castration or Decapitation?', in Robert Con Davis and Ronald Schleifer (eds.), *Contemporary Literary Criticism: Literary and Cultural Studies* (London: Longman, 1989), pp. 479–91.

13 *Placing Sorrow*, p. xxvii.

14 *The Oaten Flute*, p. 14.

15 Walter Benjamin, *The Origin of German Tragic Drama*, trans. John Osborne (London: NLB, 1977), p. 166.

16 Paul de Man, *Allegories of Reading* (New Haven: Yale University Press, 1979).

17 *The English Elegy*, p. 7.

18 Alfred Lord Tennyson, *Selected Poems* (London: Penguin, 1991), pp. 144–5, 203.

19 W. David Shaw, *Elegy & Paradox* (Baltimore: The Johns Hopkins University Press, 1994), p. 221.

20 Tennyson, *Selected Poems*, p. 203.

21 This rejection of healthy mourning begins the period of modern elegy as Jahan Ramazani (*Poetry of Mourning: The Modern Elegy from Hardy to Heaney* (Chicago: University of Chicago Press, 1994)), and Shaw (*Elegy & Paradox*, p. 180) theorise it.

22 Eric Smith, *By Mourning Tongues: Studies on English Elegy* (Ipswich: Rowman and Littlefield, 1977), p. 2.

23 Ibid.

24 Ibid, p. 21.

25 It is a point most cogently made in Abbie Findlay Potts, *The Elegiac Mode: Poetic Form in Wordsworth and Other Elegies* (Ithaca, NY: Cornell University Press, 1967), p. 39.

26 *By Mourning Tongues*, pp. 5–6.

27 Julia Kristeva, *Black Sun: Depression and Melancholy*, trans. Leon S. Roudiez (New York: Columbia University Press, 1989), pp. 1–5.

28 Julia Kristeva, *Powers of Horror*, trans. Leon S. Roudiez (New York: Columbia University Press, 1982), pp. 3–4.

29 *The English Elegy*, p. 32.

30 *Poetry of Mourning*, p. 4.

31 Ibid.

32 *Elegy & Paradox*, p. 227.

MNEMOSYNE AND THE MISLAID PEN
pp. 54–68

1 See John Cooper (ed.), 'Theaetetus',

Plato: Complete Works (Cambridge: Hackett Publishing Company, 1997), pp. 212–14; Sigmund Freud, 'A Note upon the Mystic Writing Pad', *The Complete Psychological Works*, ed. and trans. James Strachey, vol. XIX (London: The Hogarth Press, 1961), pp. 227–35; W.F. Hegel, *Introduction to Aesthetics*, trans. T.M. Knox (Oxford: Clarendon Press, 1979).

2 See Henri Bergson, *Matter and Memory*, trans. Nancy Paul and W. Scott Palmer (London: Swan, Sonnenschein & Co., 1911).

3 Jean-Paul Sartre, *Being and Nothingness*, trans. Hazel Barnes (New York: Washington Square Press/Simon & Schuster, 1984), p. 174.

4 See Alan Baddeley, *Human Memory: Theory and practice* (Hove, East Sussex: Psychology Press, 1997).

5 Michael Longley, 'Remembering Carrickskeewaun', *Gorse Fires* (London: Martin Secker & Warburg, 1991), p. 12.

6 Friedrich Nietzsche, *On the Advantage and Disadvantage of History for Life*, trans. Peter Preuss (Cambridge: Hackett Publishing Company, Inc., 1980), p. 8.

7 Friedrich Nietzsche, *Thus Spake Zarathustra*, trans. Walter Kaufman (New York: Viking Press, 1966), p. 200.

8 Emily Oksenberg Rorty argues that rationality itself, 'patterns of inference, of calculation, of interpretation', are habit-based functions, functions that may or may not take precedence over other integrative strategies such as 'aesthetic disgust or delight, or certain intentional habits of style, ways of interpreting situations as (say) occasions for combat or for adventure'. See Rorty, 'Self-deception, Akrasia and Irrationality', in Jon Elster (ed.), *The Multiple Self: Studies in Rationality and Social Change* (Cambridge: Cambridge UP, 1985), p. 130. The fundamental problem for rationalists, and one that Rorty does not overly emphasise, is that habits, even habits of 'rational' thought, as they occur at a pre-reflective level,

most often resist rational self-reflection, and thus are not usually recognised as motivating habits unless disturbed by an outside force, or pointed out by others.

9 See Michael Allen, 'Rhythm and Development in Michael Longley's Earlier Poetry', in Elmer Andrews (ed.), *Contemporary Irish Poetry* (London: Macmillan, 1992), pp. 214–34.

10 Peter McDonald's description of the affective impact of Longley's nominative lists, as nouns that 'are meant to soothe, though they cannot pretend to console' (*Mistaken Identities: Poetry and Northern Ireland* [Oxford: Clarendon, 1997], p. 136), might be expanded upon in reference to Lyotard's description of deictics. Historical objects, notably absent from Longley's lists, according to Lyotard, stand in relation to a world, a stable complex of nominatives, whereas objects of perception stand in relation to a field of experience, an inconstant set of deictics which indicate something that needs to be said but cannot yet be in the currently available idiom. For Lyotard, this expressive lack nevertheless calls attention to the silent presence of an unspeakable wrong, one pointed to in literature that the institutional, or legal, language of society has yet to articulate. See Jean-François Lyotard, *Le différend: Phrases in dispute*, trans. Georges Van Den Abbeele (Minneapolis: University of Minnesota, 1988), p. 81.

11 Michael Longley, 'Wounds', *Poems 1963–1983* (London: Martin Secker & Warburg, 1991), p. 86.

12 Seamus Heaney, *Station Island* (London: Faber, 1984), pp. 72–3, 93. Subsequent references are given in the text as (*SI*, page number).

13 For a study of poetry as ritual language based upon parallel restrictions of linguistic choice, see Roman Jakobson, 'Grammatical Parallelism and its Russian Facet', *Language*, vol. 42 (1966), pp. 399–429.

14 *Matter and Memory*, p. 113.

15 Hans Ulrich Gumbrecht, 'Rhythm and Meaning', in Gumbrecht and Pfeiffer (eds.), *Materialities of Communication,* trans. William Whobrey (Stanford: Stanford University Press, 1994), pp. 170–82.

16 I would suggest that this proposition remains valid in relation to the processes produced in the act of silent reading. Studies of sub-vocalisation during silent reading suggest that physical response does occur, the overt sound vibrations produced during vocalisation transferred to other physical processes where they are covertly reproduced. See, for example, Hardyck and Petrinovic, 'Subvocal Speech and Comprehension Level', *Journal of Verbal Learning and Verbal Behaviour*, vol. 9 (1970), pp. 647–52.

17 Medbh McGuckian, 'Slips', *The Flower Master and Other Poems* (Oldcastle: Gallery Press, 1993), p. 21.

18 Pierre Nora, *Lieux de Mémoire/Realms of Memory*, ed. Lawrence Kritzman, trans. Arthur Goldhammer (New York: Columbia University Press, 1996), p. 12.

19 Jean-Luc Nancy, *The Muses*, trans. Peggy Kamuf (Stanford: Stanford UP, 1996), p. 22.

WAYS OF SAYING/WAYS OF READING
pp. 69–79

1 Paul de Man, *The Rhetoric of Romanticism* (New York: Columbia University Press, 1984), p. 122.

2 Gayatri Spivak, 'Reading the World: Literary Studies in the Eighties', *In Other Worlds: Essays in Cultural Politics* (London: Routledge, 1987), pp. 95–102, p. 95.

3 Paul de Man, *Aesthetic Ideology* (Minneapolis: University of Minnesota Press, 1996), p. 142.

4 Terry Eagleton, *The Illusions of Postmodernism* (Oxford: Blackwell, 1996), p. 75.

5 It is not hard to have sympathy with Eagleton's frustration but at the same time it is possible to argue that materiality's current amorphousness derives from the equally diffuse two-fold definition of materialism by Engels as 'the production of the means of existence' on one hand and 'the production of human beings themselves' on the other. See Annette Kuhn and Annemarie Wolpe (eds.), *Feminism and Materialism: Women and modes of Production* (Routledge: London, 1978), p. 7.

6 See J.Hillis Miller, 'Humanistic Discourse and the Others', ⟨http://pum12.pum.umontreal.ca/revues/surfaces/vol4/miller.html⟩

7 *Aesthetic Ideology*, p. 90.

8 Ibid, p. 89.

9 *The Rhetoric of Romanticism*, p. 290.

10 Ibid.

11 Paul de Man, 'Literature and Language: A Commentary', *Blindness and Insight: Essays in the Rhetoric of Contemporary Criticism* (London: Methuen, 1983), p. 282.

12 'Intentional Structure of the Romantic Image', *The Rhetoric of Romanticism*, p. 5.

13 Wlad Godzich, Introduction, *Blindness and Insight*, p. xix.

14 Ibid, p. xx.

15 Paul Muldoon, 'Something Else', *Meeting the British* (London: Faber, 1987), p. 33

16 It is impossible not to be reminded here of the title of de Man's essay on New Criticism ultimately collected in *Blindness and Insight*: 'The Dead-End of Formalist Criticism' (pp. 229–46).

17 See 'Control of Conscious Contents in Directed Forgetting and Thought Suppression' by Tony Whetstone and Mark D. Cross: 'In the thought suppression paradigm, some participants are asked not to think about a particular subject, but to report (e.g., by ringing a bell) if the forbidden thought does enter awareness. Suppression is difficult at best: participants in Wegner, Schneider,

Carter and Whites' (1987) Experiment 1 rang a bell indicating unsuccessful thought suppression an average of seven times during a five minute period' ⟨http://psyche.cs.monash.edu.au/v4/psyche-4-16-whetstone.html⟩.

18 Paul Muldoon, *The Last Thesaurus* (London: Faber, 1995).

19 Paul Muldoon, *The Annals of Chile* (London: Faber, 1994).

20 Paul Muldoon, *To Ireland, I* (Oxford: Oxford University Press, 2000).

21 That said, Muldoon's model of textual interdependence as I have outlined it does appear to support John Carey's hostile perception that 'if all previous literature vanished, Muldoon's poetry would instantly suffocate' ('The Stain of Words', *Sunday Times*, 21 June 1987, p. 56).

22 Clair Wills, *Reading Paul Muldoon* (Newcastle: Bloodaxe Books, 1998), p. 23.

23 See Edna Longley's influential *Poetry in the Wars* (Newcastle: Bloodaxe Books, 1986) and its insistence that 'Poetry and politics, like church and state, should be separated. And for the same reasons: mysteries distort the rational processes which ideally prevail in social relations; while ideologies confiscate the poet's special passport to *terra incognita*.' (p. 185).

24 Understood as such, *Meeting the British* prefigures the physical relocation to Princeton that Muldoon would make in 1987 after the collection's publication and in this context the collection's concluding poem '7, Middagh Street', a dramatisation of W.H Auden's move to New York in 1939, has an obvious significance. This, however, has to be encountered with some sensitivity as Muldoon has rejected a reading of his own emigration as constituting any form of political or artistic exile as 'not appropriate of me' (*The Prince of the Quotidian* (Dublin: Gallery Press, 1994), p. 36). Of course, it remains legitimate to wonder if Muldoon's recent appointment as Oxford Professor of Poetry will lead to another redirection in his poetry.

25 *Mules* (London: Faber, 1977), pp. 11–13.

26 *Reading Paul Muldoon*, p. 126.

27 An obvious comparative poem here is Elizabeth Bishop's 'One Art' with its focus on the activity of losing rather than the final state of 'having lost' (*Complete Poems*, London: Chatto and Windus, 1991):

It's evident
the art of losing's not too hard to master
though it might look like (*Write* it!) like disaster.

28 Introduction, *Blindness and Insight*, p. xx.

29 See Muldoon's earlier poems 'Quoof' and 'The More a Man Has the More a Man Wants' for variations on this technique (*Quoof*, London: Faber, 1983).

30 See 'Humanistic Discourse and the Others', ⟨http://pum12.pum.umontreal.ca/revues/surfaces/vol4/miller.html⟩.

31 General Accounting Office Thesaurus, ⟨http://www.gao.gov/thesaurus/materi.htm⟩.

32 Understood in these terms, the agonised circling of 'Something Else' is closely related to the rumination on slaughter that constitutes 'The Panther' from Muldoon's next collection after *Meeting the British*, *Madoc* (London: Faber, 1990), p. 9. In the same room as 'the last panther in Massachusetts' was hung up, Muldoon's wife, the poet Jean Hanff Korelitz, makes crab-apple jelly 'at once impenetrable and clear'. As she comments 'Something's missing. This simply won't take.' Like the jelly, the relationship between the death of the panther and the process of the poem is both clear (as it depends on the instinctive moment of aesthetic ideology) and yet entirely opaque (in that the materiality of the violence remains irreducible).

FREE STATEMENT
pp. 84–98

1 For a full account of the period see
R. Dunphy, *The Making of Fianna Fáil
Power in Ireland: 1923–1948* (Oxford:
Clarendon, 1995).

2 James Good, 'The Free State
Censorship', *New Statesman* (cited
subsequently as *NS*), vol. 31, no. 801 (1
September 1928), p. 132.

3 James Good, 'Free State Elections', *NS*,
vol. 29, no. 735 (28 May 1927),
pp. 206–7.

4 Good, 'The Free State Censorship',
p. 132.

5 See 'Notes of the Week', *Irish Homestead*
(cited subsequently as *IH*), 1 October
1921, pp. 668–70; and 'Democracy on
Trial', *IH*, 10 June 1922, pp, 361–2.

6 G.W. Russell, 'A Censorship over
Literature', *Irish Statesman* (cited
subsequently as *IS*), vol. 7, no. 23
(12 February 1927), p. 543.

7 See *IS*, vol. 11, no. 20 (19 January 1929),
p. 398.

8 G.W. Russell, 'Art and National Life',
IS, vol. 10, no. 12 (21 May 1928),
pp. 226–7.

9 See H. Summerfield, *That Myriad-
Minded Man: A Biography of George
William Russell 'A.E.' 1867–1935*
(Gerrards Cross: Colin Smythe, 1975),
p. 243.

10 See M. Adams, *Censorship: The Irish
Experience* (Dublin: Sceptre, 1968) for a
record of the Free State censorship's
legislative genesis.

11 'N&C', *IS*, vol. 10, no. 24 (18 August
1928), p. 464.

12 Russell wrote to Boyd in August 1925: 'I
thought of you long ago as an American
correspondent. I had suggested it to
Plunkett and between ourselves he was
alarmed lest your radicalism might upset
the Americans who contributed the
funds to start the Irish Statesman and
from whom he hopes to get more.' A.
Denson, *Letters from AE* (New York:
Abelard Schuman, 1961), p. 168.

13 G.W. Russell, 'The Censorship Bill', *IS*,
vol. 10, no. 25 (25 August 1928), p. 487.

14 Ibid.

15 'N&C', *IS*, vol. 10, no. 26 (1 September
1929), pp. 563–5.

16 G.W. Russell, 'Freedom and Coercion',
IS, vol. 11, no. 1 (8 September 1928),
p. 6.

17 'N&C', *IS*, vol. 11, no. 25 (23 February
1929), p. 487.

18 W.B. Yeats, 'The Censorship and St
Thomas Aquinas', *IS*, vol. 11, no. 3
(22 September 1928), pp. 47–8.

19 *Dáil Éireann. Parliamentary Debates:
Official Report. Vol. 26. Comprising the
Period from 10th October, 1928, to 9th
November, 1928, in the session beginning
11th October, 1927* (Dublin: Cahill, n.d.)
18 Oct. 1928, pp. 596–7. (Hereafter *Dáil
Debates* Vol. 26).

20 M. Lyster, 'Padraic Colum on the
Censorship', *IS*, vol. 11, no. 6
(13 October 1928), pp. 107–8.

21 'N&C', *IS*, vol. 11, no. 6 (13 October
1928), pp. 103–6.

22 *Dáil Debates* Vol. 26, 18 October 1928,
pp. 598, 602.

23 *Dáil Debates*, Vol. 26, 18 October 1928,
p. 594.

24 'The Debate on the Censorship', *IS*,
vol. 11, no. 8 (27 October 1928),
pp. 145–7.

25 Téry's friendship with Russell dated
from her experience as a journalist in the
Irish Civil War. She later wrote *The
Island of Poets* which contained a section
on Russell. Russell can be found writing
warmly of Téry in a letter to
L.R. Bernstein of February 1929. See
Denson, *Letters from AE*, p. 181.

26 S. Téry, 'As Others See Us IV: Interview
with Patrick Hogan and other
Ministers', *IS*, vol. 11, no. 8
(27 October 1928), pp. 147–9.

27 Horace Plunkett was proprietor of the
Irish Statesman and its predecessor, the
Irish Homestead. Russell edited this latter
journal from 1905 to 1923. Plunkett
founded the Irish Agricultural
Organisation Society in 1894. A pioneer

of co-operative business methods in rural Ireland, Plunkett evangelised for the combination of farmers to compete with foreign interests throughout his life. See Trevor West, *Horace Plunkett: Co-operation and Politics, an Irish Biography* (Gerrards Cross: Colin Smythe, 1986).

28 'N&C', *IS*, vol. 9, no. 8 (29 October), pp. 171–4.

29 It is speculation to suggest that the government picked Hogan to introduce the resumed second reading of the Censorship Bill to the Dáil to appease its literary critics. What is certain is that Hogan had before this date taken no previous part in Dáil debates on censorship.

30 *Dáil Debates* Vol. 26, 24 October 1928, p. 830.

31 Ibid, p. 829.

32 Ibid, p. 830.

33 'N&C', *IS*, vol. 11, no. 9 (3 November 1928), pp. 163–165, p. 163.

34 G.W. Russell, 'The Dominating Idea', *IS*, vol. 8, no. 5 (9 April 1927), pp. 106–108, p. 107.

35 G.B. Shaw, *Shaw on Censorship: Being an Extract from the Minutes of Evidence before the Joint Select Committee of the House of Lords and the House of Commons on the Stage Plays (Censorship), 1909* (London: Shavian Tract No. 3, 1955), p. 4.

36 H.A. Law, *Dáil Debates,* Vol. 26, 18 October 1928, pp. 621–2.

37 G.B. Shaw, 'The Censorship', *IS*, vol. 11, no. 11 (17 November 1928), pp. 206–8.

38 The banner headline 'Texaco is Coming' appears above a map of Ireland connected to an oncoming ship by bolts of lightning in the *IS*, vol. 11, no. 14 (8 December 1928) and *IS*, vol. 11, no. 15 (15 December 1928).

39 Under the subtitle 'Advance Cork' the *Irish Statesman* noted that the Ford factory was due to increase its production from forty to one hundred and fifty units a day, making it 'the biggest single industry in the Saorstat'. See 'N&C', *IS*, vol. 12, no. 22

(3 August 1929), p. 425.

40 Milton's *Areopagitica* is a classic anti-censorship text. In it Milton argues that 'he who is made judge to sit upon the birth or death of books, whether they may be wafted into the world or not, had need to be a man above the common measure, both studious, learned, and judicious; there may be else no mean mistakes in the censure of what is passible or not, which is also no mean injury. *Areopagitica and Of Education: With Autobiographical Passages from other Prose Works.* ed. G.H. Sabina (Illinois: Davidson, 1951), pp. 27–8. In the Free State, the Senate revised the Dáil's proposed membership of the Censorship Board from nine to five. The *Irish Statesman* responded to this in 'N&C', *IS*, vol. 12, no. 9 (4 May 1929), pp. 163–6.

41 J.W. Good, 'Comments', *NS*, vol. 32, no. 831 (30 March 1929), pp. 781–3.

42 Ulick O'Connor, *Oliver St. John Gogarty: A Poet and his Times* (London: Cape, 1964), p. 214.

43 For evidence of this mutual indulgence see Russell's 'To G.R. and O.G.', *IS*, vol. 8, no. 23 (13 August 1927), and Gogarty's 'To AE Going to America', *IS*, vol. 9, no. 20 (21 January 1928), p. 457. The 'G.R.' of Russell's poem is Graeme Roberts, the contributor of a poem entitled 'Mountain' to the same issue.

44 O. Gogarty, *Seanad Éireann Parliamentary Debates: Official Report. Vol. 12. Comprising the Period from 10th April 1929, to 25th July, 1929, in the Session beginning 11th October, 1927* (Dublin: Cahill, n.d.), 11 April 1929, p. 87. (Hereafter *Seanad Debates* Vol. 12).

45 G.W. Russell, 'Unrecognised Associations', *IS*, vol. 11, no. 26 (2 March 1929), pp. 509–10.

46 'N&C', *IS*, vol. 12, no. 4 (30 March 1929), pp. 63–6.

47 Russell, 'Unrecognised Associations', pp. 509–10.

48 For examples of Cooper's letters to the

Irish Statesman see *IS*, vol. 5, no. 14 (12 December 1925), and *IS*, vol. 6, no. 5 (10 April 1926). Lennox Robinson's affectionate *Bryan Cooper* (London: Constable, 1931) appeared after Cooper's premature death.

49 Keane felt that 'If ex-Senator Yeats, whom we miss so much, was here to-day he would put this case more forcibly than I could' (71). Keane saw the Censorship Bill as evidence of 'despair' (71) on behalf of a Catholic Church that did 'not have confidence in its power to control its members' (71), resorting to legal coercion rather than an appeal to faith. The Minister for Justice was 'sorry that questions of religion were pulled into this matter'. (128) *Seanad Debates* Vol. 12, 11 April 1929.

50 This subject is addressed in detail in my thesis, 'Political Visions: George Russell, 1913–1930', Unpub. Ph.D. Thesis, TCD, 2000. I argue there that Russell was subject to an intellectual formation common among late nineteenth-century British intellectuals. His interests, in theosophy, the epic, nationalism and co-operation, are typical in their variety of Victorian enthusiasms. From this, I trace Russell's political engagements from his early career to his mature involvement in the 1913 Dublin lock-out as editor of the *Irish Homestead* to the *Irish Statesman*'s final publication in 1930.

ULSTER PROTESTANTS AND THE
QUESTION OF 'CULTURE'
pp. 99–120

1 Stefan Collini, 'Culture Talk', review of Francis Mulhern, *Culture/Metaculture* (London: Routledge, 2000), *New Left Review* (January–February 2001), pp. 43–53; p. 50.

2 Amin Maalouf, *On Identity* (London: Harvill Press, 1998), p. 6.

3 *Irish Times*, 4 January 2000.

4 Maurna Crozier, (ed.), *Varieties of Irishness* (Belfast: Institute of Irish Studies, 1989), p. 19.

5 Aodán MacPóilin, 'Language, Identity and Politics in Northern Ireland', *Ulster Folklife* 45 (1999), pp. 108–32 (108).

6. Jim Smyth, 'Mise Disneyland', *Fortnight*, no. 392 (February 2001), pp. 26–7; 27.

7 Quoted *Irish Times*, 6 April 2001.

8 David Miller, (ed.), *Rethinking Northern Ireland: Culture, Ideology and Colonialism* (Harrow: Adddison Wesley Longman, 1998), pp. 9, xix.

9 Hastings Donnan and Graham McFarlane (eds.), *Culture and Policy in Northern Ireland* (Belfast: Institute of Irish Studies, 1997), pp. 103–4.

10 *Rethinking Northern Ireland*, p. xxiii.

11 *Culture and Policy in Northern Ireland*, p. 2.

12 Terry Eagleton, *Crazy John and the Bishop and other Essays on Irish Culture* (Cork: Cork University Press, 1998), p. 326.

13 Terry Eagleton, *The Idea of Culture* (Oxford: Blackwell, 2000), p. 77.

14 Bill Rolston, 'What's Wrong with Multiculturalism? Liberalism and the Irish Conflict', in *Rethinking Northern Ireland*, pp. 254, 272.

15 See, for instance, *Escape from the Anthill* (Mullingar: Lilliput Press, 1985), p. 1.

16 Quoted *Irish Times*, 22 February 2001.

17 Alan Finlayson, unpublished essay, 'Culture, Politics and Cultural Politics in Northern Ireland'. A revised version of this paper appears in *Mobilities*, no. 43 (Spring 2001), pp. 87–102.

18 Gillian McIntosh, *The Force of Culture: Unionist Identities in Twentieth-Century Ireland* (Cork: Cork University Press, 1999), p. 222.

19 Quoted in Colin Kidd, *British Identities before Nationalism* (Cambridge: Cambridge University Press, 1999), p. 251.

20 Ibid, p. 180.

21 Marianne Elliott, *The Catholics of Ulster* (London: Allen Lane, 2000), p. 160.

22 Patrick Grant, *Breaking Enmities: Religion, Literature and Culture in Northern Ireland,*

1967–97 (London: Macmillan, 1999), p. 43.

23 For example, Steve Bruce, *God Save Ulster: The Religion and Politics of Paisleyism* (Oxford: Oxford University Press, 1989); David Hempton and Myrtle Hill, *Evangelical Protestantism in Ulster Society 1740–1890* (London: Routledge, 1992).

24 Alan Megahey, *The Irish Protestant Churches in the Twentieth Century* (London: Macmillan, 2000), p. 1.

25 Ibid.

26 John Wilson Foster, *Colonial Consequences* (Dublin: Lilliput Press, 1991), pp. 114–32.

27 Barry Sloan, *Writers and Protestantism in the North of Ireland* (Dublin: Irish Academic Press, 2000), p. 3.

28 See *Church of Ireland General Synod: A Defining Moment* (Belfast: Catalyst, 1999).

29 Donald MacRaild, *Culture and Migration: The Irish in Victorian Cumbria* (Liverpool: Liverpool University Press, 1998), p. 203.

30 McIntosh, *The Force of Culture*, p. 103.

31 Colin Coulter, *Contemporary Northern Irish Society: An Introduction* (London: Pluto Press, 1999), pp. 51–9.

32 Declan Kiberd, *Irish Classics* (London: Granta, 2000), pp. 547, 543.

33 Graham Gudgin, *The Demonisation of the Protestant Community* (Belfast: Ulster Society, 1997).

34 Letter of invitation from the *Deutsch-Englische Gesellschaft*.

35 *Irish Times*, 11 February 1998.

36 Alan F. Parkinson, *Ulster Loyalism and the British Media* (Dublin: Four Courts Press, 1998), pp. 167, 103.

37 *Irish Times*, 22 July 1999.

38 John Dunlop, *A Precarious Belonging: Presbyterianism and the Conflict in Ireland* (Belfast: Blackstaff Press, 1995), p. 7.

39 *Observer*, 9 January 2000.

40 Susan McKay, *Northern Protestants: An Unsettled People* (Belfast: Blackstaff Press, 2000), p. 10.

41 Ibid, p. 369.

42 Ibid, p. 115.

43 Quoted by Finlayson. See note 17.

44 Linda Colley, *Britons: Forging the Nation 1707–1837* (London: Pimlico, 1992), p. 53.

45 McKay, *Northern Protestants*, p. 42.

46 See Ted Hughes, 'The Great Theme: Notes on Shakespeare', in William Scammell (ed.), *Winter Pollen: Occasional Prose* (London: Faber, 1994), pp. 102–20.

47 Tom Nairn, *After Britain: New Labour and the Return of Scotland* (London: Granta, 2000), p. 10.

48 Ian McBride, 'Ulster and the British Problem', in Richard English and Graham Walker (eds.), *Unionism in Modern Ireland: New Perspectives in Politics and Culture* (Dublin: Gill and Macmillan, 1996), p. 2.

49 Tom Nairn, 'Farewell Britannia: Break-Up or New Union?', *New Left Review* (January–February, 2001), pp. 62–3.

50 Graham Walker, 'The British-Irish Council', in Rick Wilford (ed.), *Aspects of the Belfast Agreement* (Oxford: Oxford University Press, 2001), p. 138.

51 On the language question see MacPóilin, 'Language, Identity and Politics in Northern Ireland'; John M. Kirk, 'Ulster Scots: Realities and Myths', *Ulster Folklife*, no. 48 (1998), pp. 69–93; M. Nic Craith, 'Politicised Linguistic Consciousness: The Case of Ulster Scots', *Nations and Nationalism*, vol. 7, no. 1 (2001), pp. 21–37; John M. Kirk and Dónall P. Baoill, (eds.), *Language and Politics: Northern Ireland, the Republic of Ireland and Scotland* (Belfast: Queen's University/ Cló Ollscoil na Banríona, 2000).

52 Graham Walker, *Intimate Strangers: Political and Cultural Interaction between Ulster and Scotland in Modern Times* (Edinburgh: John Donald, 1995), p. 159.

53 'Scotland and Ireland', *Irish Times* Special Report, 30 November 1999.

54 Foster, *Colonial Consequences*, p. 115.

55 Cairns Craig, *The Modern Scottish Novel: Narrative and the National Imagination* (Edinburgh: Edinburgh University

Press, 1999), pp. 16, 18.

56 Ibid, p. 35.

57 Tom Clyde, (ed.), *Ancestral Voices: The Selected Prose of John Hewitt* (Belfast: Blackstaff Press, 1987), pp. 108–9, 113.

58 Edwin Muir, *Scott and Scotland: The Predicament of the Scottish Writer* (London: Routledge, 1936), p. 179.

59 Steven Matthews, *Yeats as Precursor: Readings in Irish, British and American Poetry* (London: Macmillan, 2000), p. 15.

60 Christopher Prendergast, 'Casanova's Literary Cosmos', *New Left Review* (March–April 2001), pp. 110–11.

61 Peter McDonald, *Mistaken Identities: Poetry and Northern Ireland* (Oxford: Oxford University Press, 1997), p. 81.

62 Miller, *Rethinking Northern Ireland*, p. 209.

63, Grant, *Breaking Enmities*, p. 30.

64 Kiberd, *Irish Classics*, p. 542.

65 Tom Paulin, *The Day-Star of Liberty: William Hazlitt's Radical Style* (London: Faber, 1998), p. 291.

66 McDonald, *Mistaken Identities*, p. 107.

67 Sloan, *Writers and Protestantism in the North of Ireland*, p. 3.

68 Ibid, p. 200.

69 Edna Longley, 'Derek Mahon: Extreme Religion of Art', in Michael Kenneally (ed.), *Poetry in Contemporary Irish Literature* (Gerrards Cross: Colin Smythe, 1995), pp. 280–303.

70 Fran Brearton, *The Great War in Irish Poetry: W.B. Yeats to Michael Longley* (Oxford: Oxford University Press, 2000), p. 215.

71 Johnston McMaster, *Churches on the Edge: Responding Creatively to a Changing Time* (Belfast: Catalyst, 2000), p. 8.

72 Louis MacNeice, Preface to *Modern Poetry* (1938; Oxford: OUP, 1968).

73 Seamus Heaney, *The Place of Writing* (Atlanta: Scholars Press, 1989), p. 29.

74 Matthews, *Yeats as Precursor*, p. 85.

75 Kiberd, *Irish Classics*, p. 544.

76 Seamus Heaney, *The Redress of Poetry* (London: Faber, 1995), pp. 198–200.

ANTIC DISPOSITIONS IN SOME RECENT IRISH FICTION
pp. 121–41

1 Kenneth Gergen, 'The Healthy, Happy Human Being Wears Many Masks', in Walter Truett Anderson (ed.), *The Fontana Post-Modernism Reader* (London: Fontana, 1996), p. 138.

2 Robert Jay Lifton, 'Protean Man', *Partisan Review* (Winter 1968), pp. 13–27; p. 17.

3 Ibid, p. 13.

4 Ibid, pp. 22, 24, 25.

5 Ibid, p. 21.

6 Ibid, p. 27.

7 Seamus Deane, 'Introduction', Terry Eagleton, Frederic Jameson and Edward Said, *Nationalism, Colonialism and Literature* (Minneapolis: University of Minnesota Press, 1996).

8 Lifton, 'Protean Man', pp. 20–1.

9 See Hugh's warnings against the dangers of 'fossilization' in Brian Friel, *Translations*, in *Selected Plays*, ed. Seamus Deane (London: Faber, 1984), p. 445.

10 'Protean Man', p. 24.

11 Robert MacLiam Wilson, *Ripley Bogle* (London: Picador, 1989), p. 12. Subsequent page numbers are given in parentheses in the text.

12 Homi Bhabha, *The Location of Culture* (London: Routledge, 1993), p. 44.

13 Eve Patten, 'Fiction in Conflict: Northern Ireland's Prodigal Novelists', in I.A. Bell (ed.), *Peripheral Visions: Images of Nationhood in Contemporary British Fiction* (Cardiff: University of Wales Press, 1995), pp. 136–7.

14 Louis MacNeice, 'Snow', *Collected Poems* (London: Faber, 1966), p. 30.

15 Bhabha, *The Location of Culture*, p. 86.

16 Ibid, p. 91.

17 David Lloyd, *Anomalous States: Irish Writing and the Post-Colonial Moment* (Dublin: Lilliput Press, 1993), p. 110.

18 Luke Gibbons, *Transformations in Irish Culture* (Cork: Cork University Press, 1996), p. 145.

19 'Protean Man', p. 13.

20 Ibid, p. 16.
21 Patrick McCabe, *The Butcher Boy* (London: Picador, 1992), p. 158. Subsequent page numbers are given in parentheses in the text.
22 'Protean Man', p. 16.
23 Ibid, p. 19.
24 Declan Kiberd, *Inventing Ireland: The Literature of the Modern Nation* (London: Vintage, 1996), pp. 380–1.
25 Ibid, p. 389.
26 Eoin McNamee, *Resurrection Man* (London: Picador, 1994), pp. 7–8. Subsequent page numbers are given in parentheses in the text.
27 *Inventing Ireland*, p. 391.
28 Frederic Jameson, *Postmodernism, or The Cultural Logic of Late Capitalism* (London: Verso, 1991), p. 16.
29 Jean Baudrillard, 'The Evil Demon of Images and The Precession of Simulacra', in Thomas Docherty (ed.), *Postmodernism: A Reader* (Edinburgh: Harvester Wheatsheaf, 1993), p. 196.
30 Jean Baudrillard, extract from *Simulations*, in Patricia Waugh (ed.), *Postmodernism: A Reader* (London: Edward Arnold, 1992), p. 186.
31 Brian Friel, *Translations*, in *Selected Plays*, p. 419.
32 'Protean Man', pp. 25–6.
33 Gerry Smyth, *The Novel and the Nation: Studies in the New Irish Fiction* (London: Pluto Press, 1997), pp. 121–2.
34 Lionel Trilling, 'Introduction', *Isaac Babel: Collected Stories* (Harmondsworth: Penguin, 1961), p. 10.
35 See Picador, 1994 edition of *Resurrection Man*. No page number.

A GLIMPSE OF AMERICA
pp. 159–71

1 Quoted in William Allingham, *William Allingham's Diary*, intro. by Geoffrey Grigson (London: Centaur, 1967), p. 293.
2 Quoted ibid, p. 297.
3 Quoted ibid, p. 298.
4 See the discussion of 'Phantasmal France' and 'Unreal Ireland' in Seamus Deane, *Strange Country: Modernity and Nationhood in Irish Writing Since 1790* (Oxford: Clarendon, 1997), pp. 1–48.
5 Michael Allen, 'The Parish and the Dream: Heaney and America 1967–1987' in Eve Patten (ed.), *Returning to Ourselves: Second Volume of Papers from the John Hewitt International Summer School* (Belfast: Lagan Press, 1995), pp. 227–239.
6 Ibid, p. 232.
7 John Mitchel, *Jail Journal* (Dublin: M & H Gill, 1918), p. 34.
8 Jean Baudrillard, *Revenge of the Crystal: Selected Writings on the Modern Object and its Destiny, 1968–1983*, ed. and trans. Paul Foss and Julian Pefanis (London: Pluto, 1990), p. 75.
9 Mitchel, *Jail Journal*, p. 35.
10 Frederick Engels, *Socialism: Utopian and Scientific*, trans. Edward Aveling (London: George Allen & Unwin, 1936), p. 65.
11 Mitchel, *Jail Journal*, p. 36.
12 Fintan O'Toole, *The Lie of the Land: Irish Identities* (Dublin: New Island, 1998), p. 2.
13 David Harvey, *The Condition of Postmodernity: An Enquiry into the Origins of Cultural Change* (Oxford: Blackwell, 1991), p. 288.
14 Mitchel, *Jail Journal*, p. 65.
15 For a reading of the 'absurd' geometry which the *Jail Journal* is capable of see Christopher Morash, 'The Rhetoric of Right in Mitchel's *Jail Journal*', in Joep Leerssen, A.H. van der Weel and Bart Westerweld (eds.), *Forging in the Smithy: National Identity and Representation in Anglo-Irish Literary History* (Amsterdam: Rodopi, 1995), pp. 207–18.
16 Mitchel, *Jail Journal*, p. 65.
17 Ibid.
18 Ibid.
19 Jacques Derrida, *Spectres of Marx: The State of Debt, the Work of Mourning & the New International*, trans. Peggy Kamuf,

NOTES

intro. Bernd Magnus and Stephen Cullenberg (London: Routledge, 1994), p. 47.

20 Ferdinand de Saussure, *Course in General Linguistics*, intro. Jonathan Culler (London: Fontana/Collins, 1978), p. 66.

21 Derrida from *Positions*, quoted in and trans. by Chistopher Butler, *Interpretation, Deconstruction and Ideology* (Oxford: Clarendon, 1984), p. 62.

22 Saussure, *Course in General Linguistics*, p. 76.

23 Ibid.

24 See E.F. Bleiler, 'Ignatius Donnelly and Atlantis', in Ignatius Donnelly, *Atlantis: The Antediluvian World* (1882; New York: Dover, 1976), pp. v–xx.

25 Bleiler, 'Ignatius Donnelly and Atlantis', p. xi.

26 Donnelly, *Atlantis*, p. 133.

27 Ibid, p. 418.

28 Ibid, p. 408.

29 Ibid, p. 342. The reference here is to ancient burial mounds.

30 Ibid, p. 417.

31 Ibid, p. 414.

32 Ibid, p. 420.

33 Ibid, p. 421.

34 Ibid.

35 Donnelly's ideas were seen in exactly this way by Madame Blavatsky who, in *The Secret Doctrine*, used Donnelly extensively as a source for her own writings on Atlantis: 'Even the clever work of Donnelly . . . is put aside, notwithstanding that its statements are all confined within a frame of strictly scientific proofs. But we write of the future': H.P. Blavatsky, *The Secret Doctrine: The Synthesis of Science, Religion, and Philosophy: Volume II Anthropogenesis*, Third Point Loma Edition (Point Loma: Aryan Theosophical Press, 1925), p. 334. My thanks to Selina Guinness for pointing me to this use of Donnelly's work.

36 Donnelly, *Atlantis*, p. 480.

37 Derrida, *Of Grammatology* (Baltimore and London: John Hopkins UP, 1976), p. 67.

38 Ibid, p. 73.

39 Ibid, pp. 72–3.

40 Phrase taken from a description of Ireland in C.J. O'Donnell, *The Irish Future, with the Lordship of the World* (London: Cecil Palmer, 1931), p. 17.

41 http://www.stanford.edu/-meehan/donnellyr/gerald.html

42 Fredric Jameson, *Postmodernism, or, the Cultural Logic of Late Capitalism* (London: Verso, 1993), p. 165.

43 Jean Baudrillard, *Simulations*, trans. Paul Foss, Paul Patton and Philip Beitchman (New York: Semiotext(e), 1983), p. 101.

44 Bram Stoker, *A Glimpse of America: A Lecture Given at the London Institute 28 December 1885* (London: Sampson, Low, Marston, 1886), pp. 7, 10.

45 Ibid, p. 23.

46 Ibid, p. 13.

47 Allen, 'The Parish and the Dream', p. 238.

48 Seán Hillen, *Irelantis* (Dublin: Irelantis, 1999). On Hillen's art and its relationship to John Hinde's postcards see Mic Moroney, 'Postcards from the Edge', *Cara* (March/April 1998), pp. 20–28. On *Irelantis* see Rosita Boland, 'Hillen's Hinde-sight', *The Irish Times* (Weekend Section), 9 October 1999, p. 5. My thanks to Rosita Boland for supplying me with copies of these articles.

49 Hillen, *Irelantis*, p. 6.

50 Fintan O'Toole, 'Introducing Irelantis' in Seán Hillen, *Irelantis*, p. 5.

51 Moroney, 'Postcards from the Edge', p. 20.

52 Luke Gibbons, *Transformations in Irish Culture* (Cork: Cork University Press/Field Day, 1996), p. 40.

53 Declan Kiberd, 'Anglo-Irish Attitudes' in Field Day Theatre Company (ed.), *Ireland's Field Day* (London: Hutchinson, 1985), p. 95.

54 'Emerald Isle', Part 2, *2000AD*, 27 April 1991.

BRINGING IT ALL BACK HOME
pp. 172–85

1 *The Collected Letters of Samuel Taylor Coleridge*, ed. Earl Leslie Griggs (6 vols, Oxford: OUP, 1956–71), vol. I, p. 99, hereafter *Collected Letters*.

2 Paul Muldoon, 'Parmenides', *Madoc – A Mystery* (London: Faber, 1990), p. 21.

3 Responses to the French Revolution from Richard Price, Tom Paine, Mary Wollstonecraft and Helen Maria Williams.

4 For Southey's rooms see Richard Holmes, *Coleridge: Early Visions* (London: Hodder and Stoughton, 1989), p. 61; for France, see Robert Southey to Grosvenor Bedford, 21 October 1792, in *New Letters of Robert Southey*, ed. Kenneth Curry (2 vols., New York and London, 1965), vol. I, p. 10, hereafter *New Letters*.

5 This letter of October 1793 is in the collection of manuscript letters of Robert Southey at the Bodleian Library, Oxford.

6 *New Letters*, vol. I, p. 54.

7 The change of plan occurred some time between 1 August and 22 August 1794, see *New Letters*, vol. I, pp. 67, 71.

8 *Collected Letters*, vol. I, p. 84.

9 *New Letters*, vol. I, p. 70.

10 *The Life and Correspondence of Robert Southey*, ed. C.C. Southey (6 vols., London, 1849–50), vol. I. pp. 193–4.

11 Bodleian Southey Letters.

12 *Collected Letters*, vol. I, p. 334.

13 Ibid, p. 160.

14 Paul Muldoon, 'Archimedes', *Madoc*, p. 41.

15 See *The Rights of Man*, ed. H. Collins (Harmondsworth: Penguin, 1969), pp. 181–2.

16 Coleridge's description of Hazlitt.

17 See Adam Smith, *An Enquiry into the Causes of the Wealth of Nations* (2 vols., London, 1776), vol. 1, pp. 505–6.

18 *New Letters*, vol. I, p. 70.

19 *Collected Letters*, vol. I, p. 99.

20 Ibid, p. 96.

21 *New Letters*, vol. I, pp. 71–2.

22 Ibid, pp. 70–1.

23 Ibid, p. 75.

24 See in particular Holmes, *Coleridge: Early Visions*, esp.pp. 21–4, and Mark Storey, *Robert Southey: A Life* (Oxford: OUP, 1997), pp. 6–7.

25 *Collected Letters*, vol. I, pp. 142–3.

26 S.T. Coleridge, *Poems on Various Subjects* (London and Bristol, 1796), pp. 10–11.

27 See David Fairer, 'Chatterton's Poetic Afterlife, 1770–1794: A Context for Coleridge's Monody', in *Thomas Chatterton and Romantic Culture*, ed. Nick Groom (Basingstoke: Macmillan, 1999).

28 *New Letters*, vol. I, p. 81.

29 *Collected Letters*, vol. I, p. 86.

30 Ibid, p. 90.

31 From 'Eclogue the First' in Thomas Chatterton, *Poems, Supposed to have been Written at Bristol, by Thomas Rowley, and Others, in the Fifteenth Century* (Cambridge, 1794), p. 204.

32 'As to the Welsh scheme – pardon me – it is nonsense – We must go to America', *Collected Letters*, vol. I, p. 132, letter to Southey of 9 December 1794.

33 Leigh Hunt, 'Sonnet to Hampstead. VI' (1815), *The Poetical Works of Leigh Hunt*, ed. H.S. Milford (Oxford: OUP, 1923), p. 238; Seamus Heaney, 'Glanmore Sonnets, II and III', *Field Work* (London: Faber, 1979), pp. 34–5; John Betjeman, 'Middlesex', *A Few Late Chrysanthemums* (London: J.Murray, 1954).

34 *Collected Letters*, vol. I, p. 527.

35. See Jonathan Wordsworth's Introduction to Robert Southey, *Poems* (1797; Oxford, 1989).

36 *The Poems of Charlotte Smith*, ed. Stuart Curran (New York and Oxford: OUP, 1993); I, l. 95–8.

37 Ibid; I. l.296–300; 303–6.

38 *Poems on Various Subjects*, p. 163.

39 See Southey, *Poems*, p. 207.

40 Ibid., p. 218.

41 See *Collected Letters*, vol. I, p. 115.

42 William Wordsworth, *The Prelude* (1805) (New York & London: Norton Critical Edition, 1979); VI. l. 604–8.

DICKINSON AND COSMOPOLITANISM
pp. 186–202

1 Michael Allen, *Emily Dickinson as an American Provincial Poet* (Letchworth, Herts.: British Association of American Studies, 1985), pp. 7, 12–13, 15.

2 For accounts of the trial, see Millicent Todd Bingham, *Ancestors' Brocades: The Literary Début of Emily Dickinson* (New York: Harper, 1945), and Polly Longworth, *Austin and Mabel: The Amherst Affair and Love Letters of Austin Dickinson and Mabel Loomis Todd* (New York: Farrar, Straus, Giroux, 1984). The characterisations from Vinnie's lawyer, Mr Taft, are quoted by Longworth, pp. 421–2.

3 Bingham, *Ancestors' Brocades*, pp. 231–2, 369–70.

4 It is implicit here that I am interested in the nineteenth-century awareness of the ambiguities and deterioration of 'separate spheres'. In this I agree with the spirit of recent analyses which see gendered bifurcations as partial, contested, and dynamic, more usefully construed as a starting-point than as a conclusion. See the special issue of *American Literature*, 'No More Separate Spheres', ed. Cathy N. Davidson, vol. 70, no. 3 (September 1998), and also Lora Romero, *Home Fronts: Domesticity and its Critics in the Antebellum United States* (Durham: Duke Univ. Press, 1997).

5 Joan Burbick, 'Emily Dickinson and the Economics of Desire' in Judith Farr (ed.), *Emily Dickinson: A Collection of Critical Essays* (Englewood Cliffs, N.J.: Prentice-Hall, 1996), p. 88.

6 Notions of privacy as status, and display as the means of class definition, would indeed become the topic of more sustained and explicit debate at the turn of the century, in such texts as Thorstein Veblen's *Theory of the Leisure Class* (1899) and Henry James's *The American Scene* (1907).

7 Mabel Loomis Todd, Journal, 15 September 1882; quoted in Richard B. Sewall, *The Life of Emily Dickinson* (1974; Cambridge: Harvard Univ. Press, 1997), p. 217.

8 Vivian R. Pollak, 'Thirst and Starvation in Emily Dickinson's Poetry' in Farr (ed.), *Critical Essays*, pp. 74–5.

9 See Sewall, *Life of Emily Dickinson*, p. 563. Joanne Dobson makes a fascinating connection between Dickinson and Higginson's mention in *Women and the Alphabet* (1881) of the 'Invisible Lady', a carnival attraction who 'apparently had no human organs except a brain and a tongue'. See *Dickinson and the Strategies of Reticence* (Bloomington: Indiana Univ. Press, 1989), p. 56.

10 Judith Farr notes the marking of Emerson, in *The Passion of Emily Dickinson* (Cambridge: Harvard Univ. Press, 1992), p. 46. This recognisable and widespread attitude finds characteristic local expression in a moment of struggle within Amherst's First Church in 1857. A proportion of the congregation was reluctant to buy new chandeliers. In Austin's rather sneering account, these 'hunkers' were appalled by such modern innovation, which, they claimed, 'portended of the theatre'. Eventually Austin and his supporters got their way, and the chandeliers were bought (Sewall, *Life of Emily Dickinson*, p. 120).

11 Emily Dickinson to Austin Dickinson, 6 February 1852; in *The Letters of Emily Dickinson*, ed. Thomas H. Johnson (Cambridge: Harvard Univ. Press, 1986), p. 173.

12 Emily Dickinson to Austin Dickinson, 19 June 1853, in *Letters*, p. 257; and Austin Dickinson to Susan Gilbert Dickinson, quoted by Sewall, *Life of Emily Dickinson*, p. 435.

13 Sewall, *Life of Emily Dickinson*, p. 468.

14 In 1870, for instance, only one servant was living in the Edward Dickinson house, and two in the Austin Dickinson house. See Jay Leyda, *The Years and Hours of Emily Dickinson* (1960; reprint,

Hamden: Archon Books, 1970) II,
p. 149.

15 Emily Dickinson to Austin Dickinson,
19 June 1853, in *Letters*, p. 256. Her
beloved Austin was also something of a
dandy, presiding over town meetings in
lavender trousers and a Prince Albert
coat (Sewall, *Life of Emily Dickinson*,
p. 92).

16 All numbers, and all quotations, are
taken from *Emily Dickinson: The
Complete Poems*, ed. Thomas H. Johnson
(London: Faber and Faber, 1975).

17 *Life of Emily Dickinson*, p. 629.

18 Emily Dickinson to Thomas
Wentworth Higginson, November
1871, in *Letters*, p. 491. Johnson notes
that Dickinson is drawing on an image
from George Eliot here, whose Mrs
Glegg in *The Mill on the Floss* has
inherited from her grandmother 'a
brocaded gown that would stand up
empty, like a suit of armour'. See *Letters*,
p. 420.

19 Emily Dickinson to Austin Dickinson,
11 November 1851, in *Letters*, p. 155.

20 Dickinson is punning on stocks as
flowers, and stocks as rights in the
wealth of companies. She does the same
in # 247, in which she claims to have
'shares' in Primrose 'Banks' –/ Daffodil
Dowries – spicy "Stocks" –'.

21 The phrase 'above economics' is from
George Whicher's biography of the
poet; it is quoted by Robert Merideth in
'Emily Dickinson and the Acquisitive
Society', *New England Quarterly*, vol. 37,
no. 4 (December 1964), pp. 435–52; see
p. 435. Dobson, who does explore the
context of Dickinson's work, observes
that she 'seems peculiarly ahistorical'
(*Dickinson and the Strategies of Reticence*,
p. xi).

22 Merideth, 'Emily Dickinson and the
Acquisitive Society', p. 440.

23 Vivian R. Pollak, '"That fine
Prosperity": Economic Metaphors in
Emily Dickinson's Poetry', *Modern
Language Quarterly*, vol. 34, no. 2
(June 1973), pp. 161–79; 163, 171.

24 Betsy Erkkila, 'Emily Dickinson and
Class', *American Literary History*, vol. 4,
no. 1 (Spring 1992), pp. 1–27; 16–17.

25 To give one example of what seems to
me somewhat forced, in poem 452, 'The
Malay – took the Pearl –', the speaker
laments that a 'Swarthy fellow' dived
and took the 'Jewel'. For Erkkila, the
implication is that the 'Jewel' belongs, 'it
would seem, to the white and
aristocratic speaker' (12). While this is
true, it is also misleading. It ignores the
speaker's humorous self-deprecation, as
the Malay shows the courage to seize the
prize, while the supposedly superior
speaker 'feared the Sea – too much –'.
This is not a poem in favour of racialised
snobbism, in that the speaker's prideful
cowardice is not affirmed but mocked.
The poem seems more of a play on the
familiar Christian theme, as expressed in
Romans, that the chosen people are not
always those who hold themselves to
be so.

26 Erkkila's essay reappeared in a dispersed
form in her book, *The Wicked Sisters:
Women Poets, Literary History, and Discord*
(New York: Oxford Univ. Press, 1992).
Interestingly, in this much fuller
version, Erkkila presents Dickinson in a
positive as well as a negative light, and
explores the subversive intentions at
work in many of the poems.

27 I take the phrase 'consuming angel' from
Lori Anne Loeb's *Consuming Angels:
Advertising and Victorian Women* (New
York: Oxford Univ. Press, 1994).

28 'I think that in the railroad car we are
inclined to spend more on luxury than
on safety and convenience, and it
threatens without attaining these to
become no better than a modern
drawing room, with its divans, and
ottomans, and sunshades, and a hundred
other oriental things, which we are
taking west with us, invented for the
ladies of the harem and the effeminate
natives of the Celestial Empire, which
Jonathan should be ashamed to know
the names of. I would rather sit on a

pumpkin and have it all to myself, than be crowded on a velvet cushion.' Henry David Thoreau, *Walden* (1854; New York: Norton, 1992), p. 25.

29 As George Monteiro observes in 'Emily Dickinson's Merchant God', *Notes and Queries*, vol. 204, no. 11 [new series 6.11] (December 1959), pp. 455–6: 'Like *Potosi*, *Tunis*, *Eden* and *Apennine* of other poems, [*Brazil*] is one of the poet's proliferating terms. In her idiosyncratic usage it denotes the exotic, the distant, the timeless, the spiritually valuable, the eternal, the immortal' (456). Judith Farr explains the currency of South America as an image in the form of Frederic Church's massively influential paintings, especially *The Heart of the Andes* (1859); see Farr, *The Passion of Emily Dickinson*, pp. 231–6.

30 Ann Douglas, *The Feminization of American Culture* (1977; London: Macmillan, 1996).

31 Longworth, *Austin and Mabel*, p. 411.

32 Willis J. Buckingham, ed., *Emily Dickinson's Reception in the 1890s: A Documentary History* (Pittsburgh: Univ. of Pittsburgh Press, 1989), pp. xii, xiv, 488. Buckingham is also relying on earlier work by Barton Levi St. Armand here. See *Emily Dickinson and Her Culture* (Cambridge: Cambridge Univ. Press, 1984).

Notes on Contributors

NICHOLAS ALLEN is an editorial assistant to the Royal Irish Academy's Dictionary of Irish Biography. A graduate of Queen's University Belfast and the University of Dublin, he is author of a number of articles on Irish literature and is currently at work on a study of George Russell.

ELMER KENNEDY-ANDREWS is a Senior Lecturer in English at the University of Ulster at Coleraine. He received his PhD from Queen's University Belfast, where he studied under Michael Allen. He is the author of a number of books, including *The Poetry of Seamus Heaney: All the Realms of Whisper* (1988), *The Art of Brian Friel* (1995), and *Nathanial Hawthorne: 'The Scarlet Letter': A Reader's Guide to Essential Criticism* (1998).

CIARAN CARSON was born in Belfast and has been awarded the *Irish Times* Literature Prize, the T.S. Eliot Prize and the *Yorkshire Post* Prize. His collections include *The Irish for No*, and *Belfast Confetti*. He has recently turned to prose writing with *The Star Factory* and, most recently, *Shamrock Tea* (2001). He is currently preparing a translation of Dante's *Divine Comedy*.

COLIN GRAHAM is lecturer in English at Queen's University Belfast, and author of *Ideologies of Epic: Nation, Empire and Victorian Poetry*, and co-editor, with Richard Kirkland, of *Ireland and Cultural Theory: the Mechanics of Authenticity* (1999). His *Deconstructing Ireland* will be published in 2001.

SEAMUS HEANEY was born in County Derry, and educated at Queen's University Belfast. In 1995 he was awarded the Nobel Prize for Literature. *Electric Light*, his eleventh collection, appeared in 2001.

PATRICIA HORTON received her PhD from Queen's University Belfast, in 1997. She is the author of a number of articles on Scottish and Irish writing, and currently works as an editor at Blackstaff Press.

ADRIENNE JANUS received an MA in Irish writing from Queen's University Belfast. She is currently finishing a doctorate in comparative literature, specialising in French and Irish writing, at Stanford University.

RICHARD KIRKLAND is a lecturer in the Department of English and American Studies, University of Manchester. He received his PhD from Queen's University Belfast, where he studied under Michael Allen. Recent work includes *Literature and Culture in Northern Ireland since 1965: Moments of Danger* (1996) and the co-editing (with Colin Graham) of *Ireland and Cultural Theory: the Mechanics of Authenticity* (1999).

EDNA LONGLEY is Professor of English at Queen's University Belfast, and author of a number of books, including *The Living Stream: Literature and Revisionism in Ireland* (1994) and *Poetry and Posterity* (2000). She is also editor of *The Bloodaxe Book of 20th Century Poetry* (2000).

MICHAEL LONGLEY was born in Belfast and educated at Trinity College Dublin. In 1991 his fifth collection, *Gorse Fires* won the Whitbread Prize for Poetry. It was succeeded in 1995 by *The Ghost Orchid* and *Selected Poems* in 1998. His most recent collection, *The Weather in Japan* (2000), was awarded the Hawthornden Prize and the T.S. Eliot Prize.

PETER McDONALD has published two books of poetry, *Biting the Wax* (1989) and *Adam's Dream* (1996), and two critical books, *Louis MacNeice: The Poet in his Contexts* (1991) and *Mistaken Identities: Poetry and Northern Ireland* (1997). *Serious Poetry: Form and Authority from Yeats to Hill* is forthcoming in 2002. He is Christopher Tower Student and Tutor in Poetry in English at Christ Church, Oxford.

MEDBH McGUCKIAN was born in Belfast where she lives with her family. She studied English at Queen's where she was later writer-in-residence. She has won numerous awards, including the Rooney Prize, and the Bass Ireland Award for Literature. Her *Selected Poems* appeared in 1997. Her most recent collection is *Shelmalier* (1998).

BERNARD MacLAVERTY was born in Belfast, where he worked for ten years as a medical laboratory technician, before studying English at Queen's University Belfast. He now writes full time and lives in Glasgow. His novels *Lamb* and *Cal* have both been filmed, and he has published four volumes of short stories including *A Time to Dance* and *Walking the Dog*. His most recent novel, *Grace Notes*, was *The Scotsman* Scottish Book of the Year.

PAUL MULDOON, who was born in Northern Ireland in 1951, is the author of eight collections of poetry. His *Poems 1968–1998* was published in 2001. Paul Muldoon is Howard G.B. Clark '21 Professor in the Humanities at Princeton University and Professor of Poetry at the University of Oxford.

NICHOLAS ROE is Professor of English at the University of St Andrews, and formerly taught at Queen's University Belfast. He is the author of a number of books including *The Politics of Nature: Wordsworth and Some Contemporaries* (1992) and *John Keats and the Culture of Dissent* (1997).

PETER STONELEY is lecturer in English at Queen's University Belfast, and author of *Mark Twain and the Feminine Aesthetic* (1992). He has written extensively on American literature.

WILLIAM WATKIN is a lecturer in literature at Brunel University, London. He is the author of *In the Process of Poetry: The New York School and the Avant-Garde*. He has also published work on Mallarmé, James Schuyler, John Ashbery and Lyn Hejinian. He is currently writing his second book entitled *The Smear: Elegy, Absence, Otherness and Loss*.

WILLIAM WISER is a former writer-in-residence of Queen's University Belfast. He has published five volumes of fiction in the US, and three non-fiction books about expatriates in Paris. He has taught at several American universities, and is now Professor Emeritus at the University of Denver in Colerado. His most recent publication is *The Twilight Years* (Carroll & Graf).

•

FRAN BREARTON is a lecturer in English at Queen's University Belfast, and author of *The Great War in Irish Poetry: W.B. Yeats to Michael Longley* (2000).

EAMONN HUGHES is a lecturer in English at Queen's University Belfast and editor of *Culture in Politics in Northern Ireland* (1991).